OECD Business and Finance Outlook 2017

OECD
BETTER POLICIES FOR BETTER LIVES

This work is published under the responsibility of the Secretary-General of the OECD. The opinions expressed and arguments employed herein do not necessarily reflect the official views of OECD member countries.

This document and any map included herein are without prejudice to the status of or sovereignty over any territory, to the delimitation of international frontiers and boundaries and to the name of any territory, city or area.

Please cite this publication as:
OECD (2017), *OECD Business and Finance Outlook 2017*, OECD Publishing, Paris.
http://dx.doi.org/10.1787/9789264274891-en

ISBN 978-92-64-27488-4 (print)
ISBN 978-92-64-27489-1 (PDF)

The statistical data for Israel are supplied by and under the responsibility of the relevant Israeli authorities. The use of such data by the OECD is without prejudice to the status of the Golan Heights, East Jerusalem and Israeli settlements in the West Bank under the terms of international law.

Photo credits: Cover © iStockphoto.com/OttoKrause.

Corrigenda to OECD publications may be found on line at: *www.oecd.org/about/publishing/corrigenda.htm*.

Foreword

This is the third edition of the *OECD Business and Finance Outlook*, an annual publication that presents unique data and analysis that looks at what might affect and change, both favourably and unfavourably, tomorrow's world of business, finance and investment. Using analysis from a wide range of perspectives, this year's edition addresses some of the forces influencing economic developments that have contributed to recent surprises in elections and referendums. The common theme of these surprises has been voter discontent with globalisation and immigration that are perceived to be causes of unemployment and/or falling living standards for substantial parts of society. This *Outlook's* focus is on ways to enhance "fairness", in the sense of strengthening global governance to ensure a level playing field in trade, investment and corporate behaviour, through the setting and better enforcement of global standards. A brief review of important developments contributing to post-war globalisation is provided and a number of policy domains are covered. These include exchange rates and capital account management, financial regulation since the recent financial crisis, the rising weight of state-owned enterprises in the global economy, competition policy to deal with international cartels, the cost of raising capital, responsible business conduct and bribery and corruption.

The *Outlook* is complemented by a sister publication, the *OECD Business and Finance Scoreboard 2017*. The *Scoreboard* contains indicators and data that support analysis of developments in the financial markets and corporate sectors.

The *OECD Business and Finance Outlook 2017* is the joint work of staff of the OECD Directorate for Financial and Enterprise Affairs. It has benefited from comments by delegates of relevant committees and other parts of the OECD Secretariat.

Table of contents

Tables

Figures

Boxes

Follow OECD Publications on:

http://twitter.com/OECD_Pubs

http://www.facebook.com/OECDPublications

http://www.linkedin.com/groups/OECD-Publications-4645871

http://www.youtube.com/oecdilibrary

http://www.oecd.org/oecddirect/

This book has...

StatLinks
A service that delivers Excel® files from the printed page!

Look for the *StatLinks* at the bottom of the tables or graphs in this book. To download the matching Excel® spreadsheet, just type the link into your Internet browser, starting with the *http://dx.doi.org* prefix, or click on the link from the e-book edition.

Acronyms and abbreviations

3T minerals	tin, tantalum, tungsten
AQSIQ	General Administration of Quality Supervision, Inspection and Quarantine
BEPS	base erosion and profit shifting
BNEF	Bloomberg New Energy Finance
BRIICS	Brazil, Russia, India, Indonesia, China, and South Africa
CCCMC	Commerce of Metals, Minerals and Chemicals Importers & Exporters
CCP	centralised clearing counter-party
CEO	chief executive officer
CFSI	Conflict-Free Sourcing Initiative
COK	cost of capital
COP21	21st Conference of the Parties to the UNFCCC in December 2015 in Paris
CRR	capital requirements regulation
CSR	corporate social responsibility
DTD	distance-to-default
FDI	foreign direct investment
FSB	Financial Stability Board
G20	Group of 20 (Argentina, Australia, Brazil, Canada, China, France, Germany, India, Indonesia, Italy, Japan, Mexico, Russia, Saudi Arabia, South Africa, Korea, Turkey, the United Kingdom, United States and the European Union)
GATT	General Agreement on Tariffs and Trade
GDP	gross domestic product
GICS	Global Industry Classification Standard
G-SIB	globally systemically important bank
GW	gigawatt
IPO	initial public offering
ISCO	International Standard Classification of Occupations
ISCO	International Standard Classification of Occupations
ISDS	investor-state dispute settlement
iTSCi	ITRI Tin Supply Chain Initiative
M&A	mergers and acquisitions
MFN	most-favoured nation
MNE	multinational enterprise
NAFTA	North American Free Trade Agreement

NPL	non-performing loan
NSFR	net stable funding ratio
OECD	Organisation for Economic Co-operation and Development
OPEC	Organization of Petroleum Exporting Countries
PFI	Policy Framework for Investment (OECD)
PPP	public-private partnership
RBC	responsible business conduct
ROE	return on equity
SOE	state-owned enterprise
TA	total assets
UNDERVAL	undervaluation index
UNEP	United Nations Environment Programme
USCC	US-China Economic and Security Review Commission
WGB	OECD Working Group on Bribery in International Business Transactions
WTO	World Trade Organization

Editorial

The globalisation of the world economy has advanced dramatically in recent decades, even if the recent crisis slowed its pace for a while. Trade, cross-border investment and international migration have all increased strongly during the past 30 years as emerging market economies have become increasingly integrated with more advanced OECD countries. Productivity gains have been widely diffused, the variety of goods available to consumers at favourable prices has steadily risen and hundreds of millions of people have emerged from poverty.

There has been a backlash against globalisation, however, in segments of society in a number of OECD countries. This appears to be driven by the fact that parts of the populations of advanced countries do not consider that these benefits are being evenly shared. General well-being for many people in the middle and lower parts of the income distribution in some countries has suffered as incomes have been stagnant or falling while the relative cost of basics such as housing, education and healthcare has risen. Employment conditions and social mobility have too often deteriorated. At the same time, the top income groups have prospered, sometimes spectacularly.

Among the factors that have contributed to these developments, is the failure of international co-operation to match the pace of changes wrought not only by economic globalisation but by accompanying social, demographic and technological change. Governance of the world economy needs to catch up with these developments while at the same time ensuring national sovereignty and democratic legitimacy. Regulation of global financial markets and institutions is one important area where more needs to be done. Other domains that need attention at the international level include competition policy (especially global cartels), state-owned enterprises, business accountability, foreign bribery and corruption. Ways to make progress in these areas are the subject matter of this year's *OECD Business and Finance Outlook.*

Strengthening global governance involves establishing "rules of the game" which will create a level playing field for participants in the global economy which are both fair and perceived by all to be fair. International co-operation has successfully been applied over the years to achieve this in a number of domains, both economic and in other spheres such as climate change (c.f. the Paris Agreement). Such co-operation can range from legally binding instruments to voluntary codes of conduct, "best endeavour" measures or simply shared commitments. There is considerable scope for doing more in many of the domains considered in this *Outlook*.

International organisations like the OECD have an important role in developing these rules. Indeed, the OECD has been a leader in this regard, developing some 270 legal instruments since its creation in 1961. In many of the domains examined in this Outlook the OECD is already the leading standard-setter, with the G20/OECD Principles of Corporate Governance, the OECD Anti-Bribery Convention, the OECD Code of Liberalisation of Capital Movements and the OECD Guidelines for Multinational Enterprises providing cases in point. Many of these instruments reach beyond OECD's membership to include large emerging markets. More needs to be done to broaden adherence to these instruments. There is also considerable scope for improving the implementation of these standards and building on them to increase international co-operation to level the globalised playing field. Together with effective domestic policies, this can help ensure that the benefits of globalisation, open trade and open financial arrangements are better shared throughout all segments of society.

Angel Gurría
OECD Secretary-General

Executive summary

There is a growing perception that globalisation is not working for large sections of society, in both advanced and emerging economies, and that it is driving inequality and hurting less-skilled workers. While much needs to be done with domestic policy to improve outcomes, there is also a strong need for better alignment of domestic and international policies and a more level playing field in the cross-border activities of businesses. This requires countries participating in globalised markets to commit to a common set of transparent principles that are consistent with mutually-beneficial competition, trade and international investment. But the governance of trade, international investment and competition has not advanced enough at the global level to foster better outcomes. This *Outlook* provides empirical evidence on how an uneven playing field can block economies of scale, misallocate resources and undermine fair competition. It also discusses global governance issues (the "rules" and "norms") in a number of policy domains.

Exchange rate and capital account management

Whether undertaken by advanced or emerging economies, exchange rate targeting supported by capital account management, and/or the setting of traded goods prices for market share (with state support), distorts relative prices. These practices have the potential to prevent gains in foreign sales of firms from one country in favour of those of another, and therefore to block company paths to higher productivity via economies of scale. The OECD Codes of Liberalisation are designed to make capital account management policies more transparent and provide a framework for moving towards more openness in the longer run, while still allowing for different stages of economic development.

Financial regulation and risk

Inconsistent financial regulations are driving risks into new areas. There has been huge progress in regulatory reform concerning banks but two anomalies remain, counter to the goal of a level playing field. One derives from differences in the role of banks versus capital markets in different jurisdictions, which leads to competitiveness and considerations other than financial stability in writing regulatory rules in practice. The other relates to the Basel risk-weighting system which gives banks scope to have different leverage for the same capital rule in different banks and jurisdictions. Overall, efforts to deal with the effects of regulatory reform and bank business model changes may lead to a rise in contagion risk; this is being monitored by the Financial Stability Board and other international organisations.

State-owned enterprises and excess capacity

Distortions resulting from subsidies and other advantages accorded to state-owned enterprises (SOEs) tend to be greater than for private companies. SOEs have grown as a share of key world industrial sectors and most are domiciled in Asia. Importantly, they include very large financial companies which play a key role in funding other SOEs across most business sectors and sometimes on favourable terms. This and other forms of government support raise concerns about unfair practices and lead to excess capacity in some industries. Rules to ensure a level playing field for private versus SOE competition remain necessary. The OECD has published several guidelines for SOE governance and ownership best practices which are designed to deal directly with many of these issues.

Cross-border cartels

Collusion through cross-border cartels can deny consumers the benefits of competition between multinational enterprises and ultimately pass them instead to the owners of shares through higher prices to profits. The extent of this overcharging is significant. Two hundred and forty cross-border cartels were detected and fined between 1990 and 2015, affecting USD 7.5 trillion in sales. The need to address the issue of cross-border cartels and overcharging goes hand in hand with other considerations bearing on the level playing field. OECD instruments on bid rigging, dealing with hard-core cartels and the way to enhance co-operation between competition agencies are all designed to deal with these issues.

High costs in underwriting and the cost of capital

Equity finance is preferable to debt for a long-term focus on investment projects and yet, since the crisis, corporate debt issuance has been enormous (particularly from emerging markets) and equity initial public offerings (IPOs) have fallen off. While the one lead underwriter model has given way to consortiums of banks and more cross-border involvement in underwriting for corporate issuance, high levels of fees and parallel pricing appear to have increased. In the case of IPOs of less than USD 100 million, the average cost is 9 to 11% of the transaction. This means that for every 10 IPOs, the market value on an entire new company accrues to fees. This increases the cost of equity and works against long-term productive investment. Reinforcing competitive conditions in these markets could lead to better outcomes.

Cross-border barriers to trade in financial services

Direct barriers to trade in financial services (like other trade restrictions) work against a well-functioning global economy. This *Outlook* provides three examples: the benefits of international reinsurance, domestic rules and regulations for pension funds that encourage them towards a home-country bias, and Brexit. In regard to Brexit, commitments under the OECD Codes of Liberalisation provide ample room for a pragmatic approach to the United Kingdom's exit from the European Union.

Responsible business conduct in global supply chains

Responsible business conduct (RBC) is concerned with social and moral issues as well as global business outcomes in the context of supply chain management and its perceived impact on affected communities. Sustainable supply chains and better company financial performance can go hand in hand – a "win-win" outcome. Due-diligence strategies in supply chain management have strong potential to improve trust and reduce social and environmental disruptions to trade and international investment flows that block firm-level paths to better productivity and sustainable growth. OECD instruments relating to multinational enterprises and supply chain due diligence are well suited to this task.

Bribery and corruption

Bribery of foreign officials and corruption distort the allocation of resources and undermine the benefits of globalisation, causing economic rents to be diverted to private benefits (including to dictators and military leaders) rather than being invested in technology, education and training, and quality infrastructure in the host country. Greater adherence to, and enforcement of, the OECD Anti-Bribery Convention would help to increase the number of less corrupt foreign investment destinations, thereby helping to level the playing field and promote sustainable growth. Stricter enforcement would help to improve the face of globalisation in the world economy.

Chapter 1

Overview: Globalisation and the role of international governance

Globalisation has become associated with difficulties for less-skilled workers, inequality and a general sense that it is not benefitting large sections of society, in both advanced and emerging economies. While there is much to be done with domestic policy to improve outcomes, there is also a strong need for better alignment of domestic and international policies and a more level playing field in the cross-border activities of businesses. This requires a commitment by countries participating in globalised markets to a common set of transparent principles that are consistent with mutually-beneficial competition, trade and international investment. This would reduce the problems left to be dealt with by domestic policy by improving resource allocation (promoting productivity growth) and reducing the extraction of rents (that harm consumers). Major factors that make for an uneven global playing field are examined in this Outlook. Empirical evidence is provided on their importance and rules that could help to improve outcomes for trade, innovation, investment and competition are discussed.

Perhaps the single most important issue in the outlook for business and finance is heightened political uncertainty resulting from the rebuff to globalisation which has been gaining traction. Recent major surprises in elections and referendums seem to have a common theme: discontent with globalisation that is perceived to be the cause of unemployment and/or the stagnation in absolute living standards for significant sections of society.[1] This year's *OECD Business and Finance Outlook* discusses some of the more important global (cross-border) factors that influence such outcomes. It makes the case for policies that promote greater "fairness" (in the sense of a level playing field in trade, investment and corporate behaviour) through the setting and better enforcement of global standards. Improving outcomes in this way would reduce the burden on domestic policy from the outset.

Globalisation is being tested

Evidence presented in this *Outlook* shows that globalisation, in particular growing trade and investment flows and the increased involvement of emerging markets in the world economy, has brought benefits to all countries. This is quite different from saying that the gains are also shared evenly. The great surges in income inequality post-WWII seem to have occurred after two significant globalisation movements and, in recent years, there is strong evidence of a hollowing out of the middle classes in advanced countries related to trade and technology. This suggests the need for a debate on the issue of globalisation and fairness in the distribution of gains from trade and international investment. This very complex issue needs to move beyond generalisations about "openness" towards providing more detailed ("granular") evidence on the diverse factors at work.

The extraordinary success some large emerging economies have had in pulling millions of people out of poverty in the past couple of decades is one of the most positive aspects of globalisation. This has also had many benefits for advanced economies, such as cheaper imported consumer goods and increased exports to these newly-industrialising nations. Evidence is also presented to show that in recent years the sheer scale of these successes, in conjunction with other related developments such as digitalisation, technology and innovation, is adversely affecting some less-skilled and middle-class jobs in advanced countries.

In a sense, the whole process of globalisation is being put to the test and raises questions about the balance between traditional domestic policies and the need for stronger global level-playing-field rules for cross-border activities.

On the domestic policy side, advanced economies have not done enough with respect to infrastructure investment, structural reforms, safety nets, worker retraining, education, and kick-start adjustment support for trade-exposed workers. These aspects at least have the advantage that sovereign governments can take decisions to do more. There is no such authority for the international governance of all cross-border activities of private companies and state-owned enterprises. Advanced and emerging economies have not done enough to promote a level playing field.

This *Outlook* focuses mainly on these cross-border issues, the combined effects of which have neither been adequately researched nor addressed in effective policy action.

Better global governance is urgently required

To set the scene for this discussion, two issues are addressed at the beginning of this *Outlook*: the impact of the greater role of emerging markets on world trade; and the effects of this and technological advances on labour markets and the "hollowing out" of the middle class. Firstly, with respect to trade, evidence shows that post-2001 there is a 15% to 18% rise on average of all bilateral exports (not just those with emerging markets) due to the increased overall size of the world market. Secondly, as economic theory would predict, wage growth and employment for less-skilled workers in advanced economies were affected as emerging-economy workforces began to be integrated into global value chains.[2] Labour market mobility in advanced countries in particular has been limited – with impacted workers not moving to new locations and industries. Those suffering from the "downside" of more trade openness and related technological change have been unable to adjust adequately to the new environment. Conventional economic wisdom has always called for active labour market policies and retraining. While some of these measures have been employed, they have tended to be piecemeal and inadequate to the task, so more needs to be done.[3]

However, in addition to improved domestic labour market adjustment and macro policies, what is needed is globalisation that operates according to a common set of rules and principles. This has been the relatively neglected area where not enough progress has been made. Without this, countries and companies acting in their own self-interest may use tactics and policies to distort the outcomes of greater openness in their favour. In so doing, they risk retaliation and this interferes with market-based economic adjustments, blocks the path of firms to improved productivity growth and exacerbates effects on trade- and technology-exposed workers. Thus, the net gains from openness will be smaller than they might have been and may not be shared according to productivity-based economic merit. Left unaddressed, the burden on domestic policy is unnecessarily increased.

Company insights on globalisation

The ability of the world to grow with stable and rising living standards for all depends on productivity growth which makes it possible for all participants in the economy to be better rewarded over time. Enabling factors at the macro level such as well-developed infrastructure are available to all players, but not all firms succeed in taking advantage of them to drive innovation and growth. The business and finance aspects of the current economic situation demand a closer look at companies. Why some firms succeed and others fail, and whether there are enough of the former and an appropriate exit of the latter, is critical for understanding the impact of globalisation on those most exposed to greater integration with the rest of the world.

Based on a large global sample of companies, this *Outlook* presents empirical research results which are consistent with the new firm-based trade and productivity theories. This is a process whereby the most successful (cash-flow-generative) firms invest more in technology (via research and development), attract higher-skilled labour and expand through increased foreign sales. This, in turn, generates further economies of scale and innovations. The evidence shows that it is precisely the companies that succeed the most in raising productivity through entry to foreign markets and innovation that are associated with better returns, and rising value added and wages per worker. Companies that do not innovate and/or compete well globally see declining returns and falling average value added and wages for their workers. These pressures occur within industries, rather than between them. While all industries are affected in this way, evidence from the vast "Materials" and "Industrials" sectors is provided and shows them to be amongst the clearest examples of this phenomenon.

Openness promotes opportunities for business. But the governance of trade, international investment and competition has not advanced enough to foster better outcomes. The *Outlook* provides empirical evidence on how uneven elements of the playing field block economies of scale, misallocate resources and undermine fair competition. The global governance issues (the "rules" and "norms") that affect the "levelness" of the playing field are discussed in relation to eight contributing factors: *(i)* exchange rate and capital account management; *(ii)* financial regulation; *(iii)* subsidies for (and the governance of) state-owned enterprises; *(iv)* collusion in the form of cross-border cartels; *(v)* higher costs of underwriting new equity and bond financing resulting from the way fees are charged by global financial firms; *(vi)* barriers to trade in financial services that have unintended consequences preventing insurance and pension funds from doing an adequate job; *(vii)* responsible business conduct in global supply chains; and *(viii)* bribery and corruption in international investment.

The holistic discussion in Chapter 2 of the *Outlook* is followed by three more detailed chapters where further elaboration was felt to be necessary, particularly with respect to the OECD instruments that target better global governance.

Exchange rate and capital account management

The first set of issues concerns exchange rate targeting (whether by advanced or emerging economies) supported by capital account management, and/or the setting of traded goods prices for market share (with state support), that distort relative prices (discussed in section 2.3). These practices have the potential to block gains in foreign sales of firms from one country in favour of those of another, and therefore to block companies' paths to higher productivity via scale economies. Empirical evidence is presented on the extent of over- and under-valuation which suggests the issue is quite complex. Based on purchasing power parity, the real exchange rate is found to be overvalued for most advanced countries (above the level justified by real living standards) and more neutral for China following recent weakness (despite heavy intervention to resist appreciation in earlier years), while other emerging economies such as India appear undervalued. Given their level of development, countries may wish to resist moving into overvaluation territory (as advanced countries tried to do in early post-WWII years). The exchange rate effects in a gravity model of exports are found to be not that strong. Exchange rates may, however, be less important than a tradable-goods-pricing strategy focused on winning and maintaining market share. With government backing, profit margins of state-owned enterprises, for example, can be used to offset changes in costs and the exchange rate, and subsidies and other cost-reduction factors may also help in this regard.

The evidence from a gravity model of exports is much clearer for the capital account management policies that often accompany managed exchange rate regimes. Since 2001, when the vast Asian market became better integrated into expanding global value chains, openness with respect to investment and the capital account has become more important in supporting bilateral trade. This evidence relates both to foreign direct investment (FDI) and banking and portfolio flows. In terms of better level-playing-field rules in this area, the OECD Codes of Liberalisation are designed to make capital account management policies more transparent and provide a framework for moving towards more openness in the longer run, while still allowing for different stages of economic development.

The level playing field in financial regulation is rolling risks into new areas

The second set of issues concerns inconsistent financial regulations (between countries and sectors) that are driving risks into new areas (section 2.4). There has been huge progress in improving the quality and quantity of bank capital, and new Basel regulations have helped to deal with liquidity and funding problems that emerged in the crisis. But two anomalies remain. One derives from differences in the role of banks versus capital markets in different jurisdictions that leads to competitiveness and considerations other than financial stability in writing regulatory rules in practice. The other is more technical in nature, and stems from persisting with the Basel II idea that it is permissible to allow banks to use internal risk models to calculate capital weightings. It is shown that the Basel risk-weighting system gives banks scope to have different leverage for the same capital rule in different banks and jurisdictions, in contradiction to the goal of a level playing field. On average, the ratio of risk-weighted assets to which the capital rule applies for global systemically important banks was driven down (i.e. leverage up) from 50% in 2003 to 34% by 2008. The aftermath of the crisis has seen deleveraging and a sharp pulling back of capital from cross-border activities in most advanced countries as re-regulation proceeds.

The attempts (by "shadow banks" and countries previously dependent on cross-border banking flows) to deal with the effects of regulatory reform and bank business model changes in advanced countries may increase contagion risk between sectors. For advanced countries, empirical evidence shows improvement in this regard only in the United States, with contagion risk between banks and shadow banks largely unchanged post-2008 in Europe and the United Kingdom, and some mixed evidence in Japan and Australia. Increased contagion is most extreme in emerging markets, where the use of off-balance sheet special purpose vehicles (particularly so-called wealth management products managed by banks) has contributed to the emergence of two-way contagion risk between the riskiness of banks and shadow banks (significant even at the 1% level). This was not statistically identifiable prior to 2008. Broad principles that would serve to level the regulatory playing field are discussed.

State-owned enterprises and excess capacity

The third set of issues, discussed in section 2.5, concerns distortions resulting from subsidies and other advantages accorded to state-owned enterprises (SOEs) which tend to be greater than for private companies. Unlike exchange management, this support, where present, is pointed to particular industries and enterprises of strategic interest. SOEs have grown as a share of key world industrial sectors and most are domiciled in Asia. Importantly, they include very large financial companies which play a key role in funding other SOEs across most business sectors, sometimes on favourable terms.[4] This and other forms of government support have raised concerns about unfair practices that make for an un-level playing field and lead to excess capacity in some industries. This, in turn, exerts downward pressure on margins and the return on equity (ROE) versus the cost of capital (COK) more generally. In advanced countries, ROE versus the COK for a large selection of private and state-owned enterprises moves in line, but has declined from the 8% to 10% range in 2005 to 4% to 6% more recently. ROE minus the COK for emerging-economy companies on the same basis has fallen from 4% to 6% to -1% to 1%.

Where excess capacity has emerged, concerns also arise about the difficulty of reducing production potential and facilitating the exit of inefficient firms in the SOE sector. Company data show the high levels of debt of emerging economy SOEs. Since fixed costs are high, this indebtedness gives rise to incentives to produce and export more in order to reduce variable costs. Section 2.5 also provides evidence on the exporting of excess capacity. Industrial policies based on infant-industry protection and state aid need to be carefully calibrated if they aim to correct market failures; otherwise they will undermine competitive neutrality and weaken incentives for the entry of more productive firms and the exit of inefficient ones. Such policies result in trade and investment tensions, including barriers to cross-border FDI flows, when unfair support is suspected. Rules to ensure a level playing field for competition between private and state-owned enterprises remain necessary. The OECD has published several guidelines for SOE governance and ownership best practices which are designed to deal directly with many of these issues.

Cross-border cartels

The fourth set of issues relates to the treatment of consumers (section 2.6). Competition between multinational enterprises drives out inefficiencies and creates economies of scale. This helps to reduce prices and pass on the benefits of globalisation to consumers. However, collusion through cross-border cartels can deny consumers these benefits and pass them instead, through higher prices, to profits and ultimately to the owners of shares. This overcharging hurts consumers and hits low-income families hardest in what they pay for necessities (including banking, pharmaceuticals, retail services, transport, white goods, etc.). This is no small matter. Two hundred and forty cross-border cartels were detected and fined between 1990 and 2015, affecting USD 7.5 trillion in sales. Average overcharging amounted to 20% of sales, and was at times much higher in some key commodities, such as pharmaceuticals.

In a sense, the import competition-exposed worker is hit twice: via lower employment and wage remuneration while paying higher prices for essential goods and services. The need to address the issue of cross-border cartels and overcharging goes hand in hand with other considerations bearing on the level playing field – consumers as well as companies need to be treated fairly. The cross-border activities of SOEs also fall into the competition policy domain, intersecting with the corporate governance issues noted above, if competitive neutrality is to be maintained. OECD instruments on bid rigging, dealing with hard core cartels and the way to enhance co-operation between competition agencies are all designed to deal with these issues.

High costs in underwriting and the cost of capital

A fifth set of issues on the activities of some global firms that adversely affects the ability of others to grow illustrates that it is not only government support that undermines competitive outcomes (section 2.7). Equity finance is well-suited to long-term risk taking on investment projects (where a failure does not leave a firm with an unsupported debt burden), and yet, since the crisis, corporate debt issuance has been enormous (particularly from emerging markets) and equity initial public offerings (IPOs) have fallen off. This has been associated with US, UK and European banks losing market share in their investment banking activities to China and other parts of Asia. While the one lead underwriter model has given way to consortiums of banks and more cross-border involvement in underwriting for corporate issuance, high levels of fees and parallel pricing appear to have increased. The median underwriting fee for US IPOs is 7%, and this has risen to 8% in Japan and China (doubling in the case of the latter). These high fees, which constitute more than 60% of the total cost, are a neglected aspect of the explanation for falling IPO issuance. In the case of IPOs of less than USD 100 million, the average cost is 9% to 11% of the transaction. This means that for every 10 IPOs, the market value on an entire new company accrues to fees. This increases the cost of equity and works against long-term productive investment. Reinforcing competitive conditions in these markets could lead to better outcomes.

Cross-border barriers to trade in financial services

Direct barriers to trade in financial services will (like other trade restrictions) work against a well-functioning global economy. Three examples are provided in section 2.8. First, the benefits of international reinsurance in terms of being able to absorb the burden of large-scale catastrophe losses may not be realised where (unwarranted) regulatory impediments are placed on insurance companies' ability to transfer these risks within international markets. This is because global pooling is critical to reinsurance. Examples from the Great East Japan Earthquake and Superstorm Sandy are provided. Second, domestic rules and regulations for pension funds that encourage them towards a home-country bias increase the difficulty of achieving funding targets and reduce diversification benefits. Finally, with respect to Brexit, the City of London is an agglomeration that serves the global financial system from which economies of scale and scope (internal to the location) are derived. Commitments under the OECD Codes of Liberalisation provide room for a pragmatic approach to the United Kingdom's exit from the European Union.

Responsible business conduct and due diligence in global supply chains

Section 2.9 discusses issues relating to responsible business conduct (RBC). While most of the previous sections focus on distortions to pricing or inconsistent regulations that raise "fairness" issues, RBC pertains to global business outcomes in the context of sustainability of supply chains. Gains from trade and international investment apply to all points (upstream and downstream) in the supply chain, and sustainability of these cross-border linkages is important for long-term growth. Supply chains may be disrupted when human rights issues, damage to the local environment, and over-exploitation of resources result in disputes with local communities, strikes, government interventions and legal processes. It is important not to focus on short-term profits at the expense of supply-chain sustainability and longer-term financial performance for investors.

Sustainable supply chains and better company financial performance can go hand in hand – a "win-win" outcome. Evidence is presented which shows (after allowing for other control factors) that a rise in the social score component of the Thomson Reuters Economic, Social and Governance (ESG) index improves company financial outcomes. A rise of 0.5 in the ESG score (a normalised Z-score between 0 and 1.0 that is based on a survey of 6 000 global companies) increases, on average, the return on equity for companies in the sample by around 2.5 percentage points. Numerous academic studies also support the positive impact on company results. Thus, pursuing due-diligence strategies in supply chain management could have a strong potential to improve trust and reduce social and environmental disruptions to trade and international investment flows which block firm-level paths to better productivity and sustainable growth. OECD instruments relating to the behaviour of multinational enterprises and supply chain due diligence are well suited to this task.

Bribery and corruption

The final level playing field issue, discussed in section 2.10, concerns the bribery of foreign officials. These activities distort the allocation of resources and undermine the benefits of globalisation. Rent-seeking behaviour through bribery and corruption is estimated by the World Bank to be 2% to 3% of world GDP (equivalent to the size of the French economy). This wastes resources. Thus less dynamic firms can win contracts in countries with weak bribery laws and/or poor enforcement at the expense of more productive ones. Bribery and corruption cause economic rents to be diverted to private benefits (including to dictators and military leaders) rather than being invested in technology, education and training, and quality infrastructure in the host country. Such investment would enhance productivity growth and allow real incomes to support demand in emerging economies. An empirical study presented in that section shows that strong bribery laws consistent with the OECD Anti-Bribery Convention cause adherent countries to invest less in corrupt regimes and more in countries with sound property rights and accountability. A one point rise in the World Bank corruption index in the host country (within a 0-10 range) will see FDI from countries that have ratified the OECD Anti-Bribery Convention fall by between 4% and 9%. Corrupt countries therefore forego the benefits of more investment (and hence better productivity growth) from the OECD countries that are amongst the largest FDI investors.

This section also takes a first look at bribes paid by financial intermediaries that play a key role in the allocation of resources. The perception that high-level managers of financial firms from wealthy countries bribe officials from poor countries (most often inside SOEs) appears to be correct. This contributes to creating an investment climate whereby globalisation does not benefit large parts of the population. Greater adherence to, and enforcement of, the OECD Anti-Bribery Convention would help to increase the universe of less corrupt foreign investment destinations, thereby helping to level the playing field and promote sustainable growth. Stricter enforcement could help to improve the face of globalisation in the world economy.

Conclusions

The 2017 *OECD Business and Finance Outlook* provides detailed evidence that suggests the problems (such as inequality, the hollowing out of the middle class and employment of less-skilled workers in advanced countries) often associated with globalisation do not originate from economic "openness" as such. Instead, while recognising that not enough has been done with respect to domestic structural adjustment policy, the *Outlook* shows that the absence of a level playing field in a number of cross-border areas that affect trade, investment and competition outcomes is also playing an important role. This evidence warrants policy action. Levelling the playing field would help to reduce the extent of the problems to be dealt with by domestic policy. OECD standards can play a leading role in shaping this conversation, and promoting globalisation on a level playing field. This requires a commitment by countries participating in globalised markets to a common set of transparent principles that are consistent with mutually beneficial competition, trade and international investment.

Notes

1. For example, Pew research found in a survey of the US adult population that among the factors that hurt American workers most are outsourcing (80%) and imports (77%). Pew Research Center (2016), Social and Demographic Trends, 6 October, www.pewsocialtrends.org/2016/10/06/the-state-of-american-jobs/.

2. The generalised Stolper-Samuelson theorem predicts that for real factor returns increased trade will see the return to the scarce factor go down while that for the abundant factor go up. In advanced countries, capital is more abundant and unskilled labour relatively scarce and the reverse is true in emerging economies. Increased trade will reduce the return for unskilled labour in advanced countries and vice versa in emerging economies. Separately, if unskilled wages are sticky in advanced countries and cannot fall sharply enough to increase attractiveness relative to capital, then unemployment of unskilled workers would rise .

3. While not the focus of this study, it should be noted that other macro policy settings also affect labour market flexibility in unintended ways. For example, very low interest rates can stimulate house price inflation in more prosperous regions which may, in turn, influence the ability of workers to move from declining trade-affected areas (with low house prices) to more prosperous regions with more expensive housing. Macro prudential measures to dampen regional house-price bubbles could also be useful alongside traditional labour market policies.

4. The other SOEs are smaller than the banks as state industrial policy is often organised on a regional basis. Chapter 2.4 discusses some issues about the activities of these banks from a financial stability perspective.

Chapter 2

Globalisation and the level playing field

Evidence shows that the increased participation of emerging markets in the world economy has lifted trade for all countries (rather than diverting it). At the same time, the middle class is being hollowed out in advanced countries and living standards have been affected adversely by trends in trade and technology. Insights based on micro data suggest that these two latter factors are linked, as the most productive companies sell more to foreign markets (via trade or investment) to gain scale economies and take advantage of digitalisation and innovation. Productivity growth driven in this way benefits from open access to markets for successful firms and the exit of inefficient ones. Companies that do not innovate and compete well globally see declining returns, average value added and wages for their workers. These pressures occur within industries, rather than between them. The extent of these problems would be reduced if the gains from globalisation were distributed more equally on the basis of a level playing field.

Note by Turkey:

The information in this document with reference to "Cyprus" relates to the southern part of the Island. There is no single authority representing both Turkish and Greek Cypriot people on the Island. Turkey recognises the Turkish Republic of Northern Cyprus (TRNC). Until a lasting and equitable solution is found within the context of the United Nations, Turkey shall preserve its position concerning the "Cyprus issue".

Note by all the European Union Member States of the OECD and the European Union:

The Republic of Cyprus is recognised by all members of the United Nations with the exception of Turkey. The information in this document relates to the area under the effective control of the Government of the Republic of Cyprus.

2.1 Introduction

Globalisation refers to a process of economic integration via trade, investment, technology, migration and finance that is supranational in nature. Individuals and companies interact across national borders, but without a process of governance equivalent to that which prevails within any nation state. Indeed different cultures, political systems and concepts of self-interest complicate the very notion of global governance and attempts to impose rules on trade and investment are sometimes inconsistent with some policy preferences of sovereign governments. Economic theory has long argued that there are gains from trade and foreign investment, so the feeling in recent years that globalisation has led to greater inequality suggests that these gains are not being shared equally. This raises the question as to whether improved global standards (rules of the game) that promote a level playing field could do more to create a greater sense of fairness.

Historically there is no clear relationship between openness and inequality. Figure 2.1 shows the income share of the top 1% of the population in a number of advanced and emerging economies over all of the 20th century to the present. This long perspective is instructive as a starting point.

- Prior to World War II (WWII), with the exception of the German experience with hyper-inflation, income distribution was very unequal: the share of the top 1% of earners was around 20% of the total, in what was a fairly unregulated global system.
- WWII changed all that with the destruction of assets and wealth affecting income of the top 1% more than others. The share fell to around 10% of the total. The role of regulations following the Depression and wartime controls should also not be forgotten.
- After the war, the Bretton Woods conference set new forms of regulation to support fixed exchange rates. The 10% share was reasonably stable in the 1950s and 1960s (although in the United Kingdom, the share fell more due to redistributive policies, poor per-capita growth compared to other countries, and strong unions). Inflation and the oil shock in the 1970s saw another decline in the share of the high earners.
- Interestingly, income inequality does not seem to be affected by the opening of trade in this period. For example, a full customs union was established in Europe by 1968, with tariffs and quotas on internal trade being abolished and a common external tariff on third countries coming into effect. Figure 2.1 shows that German and French income distribution tended to become more, not less, equal. So, for countries with broadly similar structures and living standards, trade opening and inequality were not linked. This suggests that the issues here are not simple and that the more recent rebuff to globalisation cannot be put down to generalisations about trade openness.
- The remarkable reversal towards rising income inequality began around the start of the 1980s, coinciding with the globalisation of finance and investment: the dismantling of regulations on cross-border capital controls, interest rates ceilings and other measures. The upward trend paused for a while in the early 1990s (at an average 14% share), and then surged in a number of countries after about 1995.
- In Anglo-Saxon countries, there is a clear cyclical influence of the equity cycle on the share of the top 1%, particularly in the USA, but also in Canada and the UK.

Where there is a share ownership culture, the highest income earners benefit from dividends, share buybacks and the buying and selling of assets in tax-effective ways. These move up and down with the monetary policy and asset price cycle (the tech bust followed by easing and the same with the 2008 crisis). Employee stock ownership programs (including stock options) for the top echelons are also a factor in bonuses of the highly paid. The general upwards trend in all countries, however, suggests other common factors may be more important.

Figure 2.1. **Income shares of the top 1% over 100 years, 1913-2015**

(Per cent)

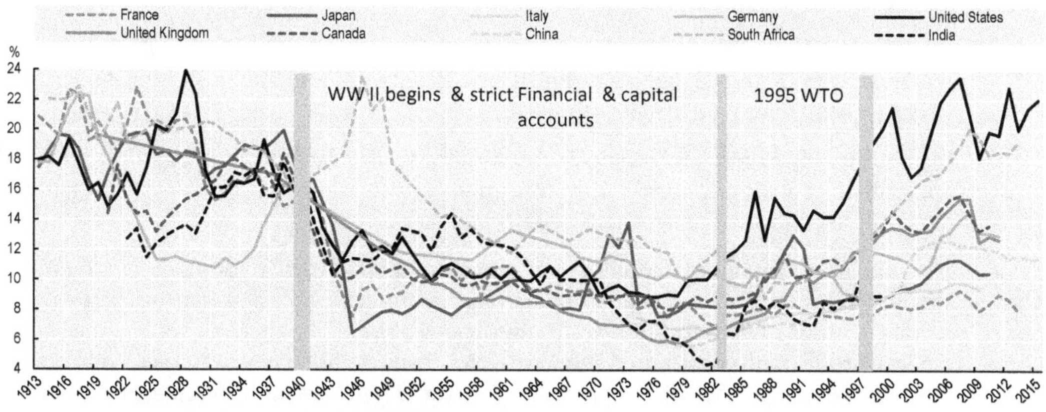

Source: World Wealth and Income Database, OECD calculations.

StatLink http://dx.doi.org/10.1787/888933476470

In recent decades, segments of the labour market have been adversely affected in advanced economies and signs of excess capacity are present in some global sectors (see below). Flexible markets should ameliorate such effects as trade is opened up – only transitional dislocation should occur. Most of the "opening up" of trade during the Bretton Woods era was between advanced economies – with Europe playing a leading role. Successive General Agreement on Tariffs and Trade (GATT) rounds furthered the goal of greater openness. In this period improved trade volumes between advanced countries did not lead to major income distributional shifts. Two subsequent rounds (Tokyo and Uruguay, culminating in the formation of the World Trade Organization (WTO) in 1995) doubled the number of participants in the GATT – more emerging economies joined. However, problems began to be encountered in the Doha Round (launched in 2001), which focused on areas more difficult to agree between advanced and emerging economies (agriculture, labour standards, non-tariff measures, patents, competition and investment). The Doha round was never completed and, instead, bilateral trade negotiations have become more common.[1]

The world economy had already successfully absorbed rapid Japanese growth in the post-WWII period. Subsequently this was repeated for the rapid gains in exports by the 'Asian Tigers' (see below). This was interrupted by the crisis in Asia in 1997, when earlier liberalisation of hot money flows in the good years reversed once the dollar started to rise against the yen, and the accumulated trade advantages versus Japan over ten years began to reverse. This crisis did not disrupt advanced economy labour markets in any significant way. In 2001 China joined the WTO, and this was associated with a surge in trade with advanced economies.

Box 2.1. **Economic theory and empirical wisdom to the early 2000s**

- As countries come into the open world trading system they will specialise in what they do best. A capital abundant country, like the United States, will specialise in capital intensive goods, and a labour abundant country in labour intensive goods.[1] Lower-skilled workers would become less valued in advanced economies, but labour mobility would see adjustments begin through regional and sector mobility.
- The main explanation of the presence of shifts in wage inequalities in advanced economies is skill-based supply and demand shifts. The impact of trade (other than a small component due to any outsourcing that induces skill demand shifts) and immigration is very small.[2] Immigration, while providing overall benefits to the economy, may have minor adverse effects on some segments of the native population (mainly "high school dropouts"). Competition would even-out skill differentials for workers in both traded and non-traded goods sectors, and not discriminate against traded goods sector workers as such.[3]
- Income maintenance and trade-exposed adjustment support packages would be appropriate policies to deal with transition effects, helping to avoid secular re-distributive effects within and across skill categories.[4]
- As emerging economies urbanise and generate savings for investment, productivity should rise in their traded goods sectors (e.g. manufacturing), and real wages in these sectors will also begin to improve. Rising real wages create demand for the output of the low-productivity non-traded services sector, causing prices there to rise – and hence the real exchange rate will appreciate over time. This, in turn, should encourage a substitution towards demand for foreign goods.[5] Technology transfer between rich and poor countries will see productivity continue to rise as the urbanisation process matures.
- These patterns can be repeated, pulling millions of people out of poverty without long-term dislocation – each country moving up the value added chain with all countries benefitting from globalisation.

1. See the Heckscher-Ohlin and Stolper-Samuelson models and subsequent developments and modification based on them.
2 See Katz and Murphy (1992), Freeman (1995), Borjas Freeman and Katz (1997), and Krugman (2000).
3. See a discussion in Acemoglu and Autor (2011).
4 See, for example, Box 1 of OECD, ILO, World Bank and WTO (2010).
5. The Harrod-Balassa-Samuelson effect: wages will also tend to rise in the non-traded sector in order to retain workers, and this is passed on in in higher non-traded prices. As this occurs over long periods of time the general price level will rise versus the price of goods overseas.

On the foreign investment side of things, a major catalyst to the opening up of capital accounts occurred as a result of the actions of the OPEC cartel and the first oil shock: exhaustible resource rents were diverted to oil producing countries and globalisation took a new route due to: the need to recycle OPEC surpluses; and inflation control issues that caused the breakdown of the fixed exchange rate system. Many capital controls were dismantled from advanced economies by the early 1980s. Within the European Union, this process was completed by the Single Market legislation in 1992, by which no country could restrict entry of goods or capital into each other's domestic markets. This "opening up" led to a greater role for foreign direct investment (FDI) in economic growth and development.

In principle, opening markets through globalisation should allow more people to be pulled out of poverty globally, as productivity advances and real wages rise, without any major disruption to living standards in advanced economies. Permanently affected industries would see workers shift to other industries and/or localities if some of the basic building blocks of market economics and accepted empirical findings continue to hold (see Box 2.1).

The take off in world trade due to Asia

From China's entry into world trade in 2001 to 2014, global merchandise exports exploded upwards by more than 190%. This in itself is very positive, giving rise to opportunities for all global companies.

In earlier decades, the Asian Tigers (Chinese Taipei; Hong Kong, China; Korea; and Singapore) chose development models focused on trade expansion combined with investment controls to support exchange rate management, though Hong Kong, China, chose a currency board and an "investment openness" approach. These approaches were in contrast to the more autarkic routes taken by India, Indonesia, Pakistan, Turkey and much of Latin America and Africa in these earlier years. The Asian Tigers benefited enormously from Asian trade regionalism, and the post-1960s success of Japan. Their strategic location allowed them to benefit from investment and trade trends following globalisation events of the early 1980s. In the 1980s these countries expanded their share of world merchandise exports rapidly, achieving an 8% share by the early 1990s (shown in Figure 2.2, alongside other countries, all measured in the same way). After China joined WTO in 2001, regional trade integration consistent with "gravity" theories of bilateral trade increased further, helping the Asian Tigers to maintain their share of world exports.

China's total merchandise exports as a share of the world total, shown in Figure 2.2, rose from 3.4% in 2000 (less than half that of the Asian Tigers) to 14% of the world total by 2015. This is larger than the United States, Germany, the four Asian Tigers (whose combined size is even exaggerated as intra-trade has not been netted out) and certainly Japan (whose share declined markedly from the mid-1980s). In the case of manufacturing exports (90% of the total) the rise for China is to 18% of world exports over the same 15 years. This impressive performance corresponds with their accession to the WTO in December 2001. WTO opened markets previously blocked by tariffs and other measures, and freed companies not to have to sell via state intermediaries (except for certain goods like cereals, tobacco, fuels and minerals and some services such as restrictions on transport and distribution logistics inside the country). It also gave access to cheaper imports of raw material and capital goods, improving competiveness. The United States had already given most-favoured nation (MFN) status to China in 1994 (subsequently renewed each year by Congress). Japan signed the Japan-China Trade Agreement in 1974, which mutually granted MFN status for trade. Japan also signed a bilateral investment treaty in 1988 through which it obtained National Treatment status within China (improving scope for local production abroad as opposed to exports). Both the United States and Japan saw a rise in Chinese import penetration prior to 2001, in contrast to Europe where this was largely delayed until WTO entry (see Figure 2.3). Import shares from China rose in all regions after 2001.

China's capacity to produce for export was facilitated by a boost of saving and investment. Figure 2.4 shows that from 6% of the world total in 2000, China's gross fixed capital formation rose to be over 26% of the world total by 2015.

Figure 2.2. **Share of world merchandise exports of selected countries, 1960-2015**

(Per cent of world total)

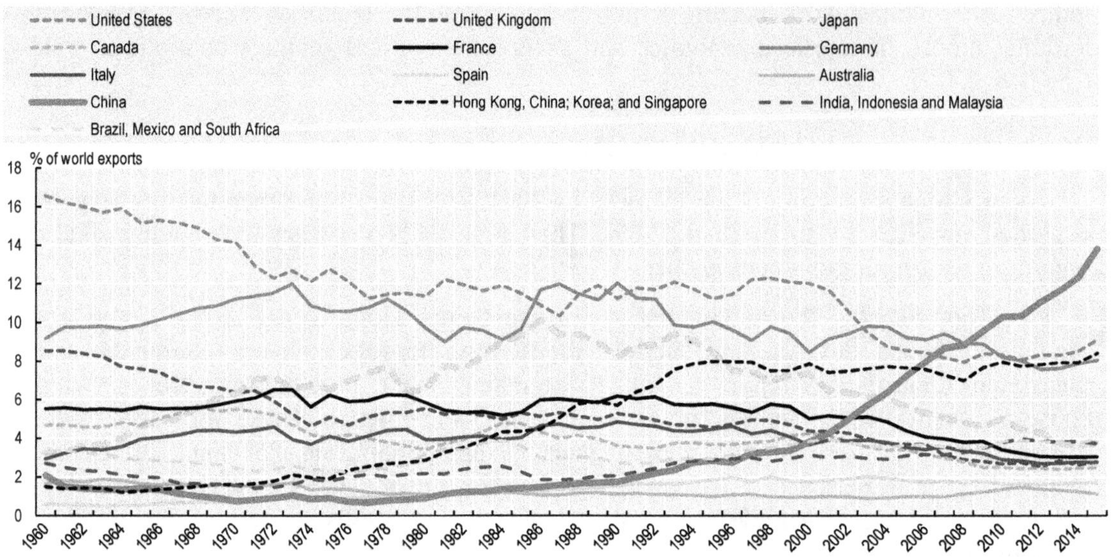

Source: International Monetary Fund, OECD calculations.

http://dx.doi.org/10.1787/888933476480

Figure 2.3. **China's share of imports for selected countries, 1980-2015**

(Per cent)

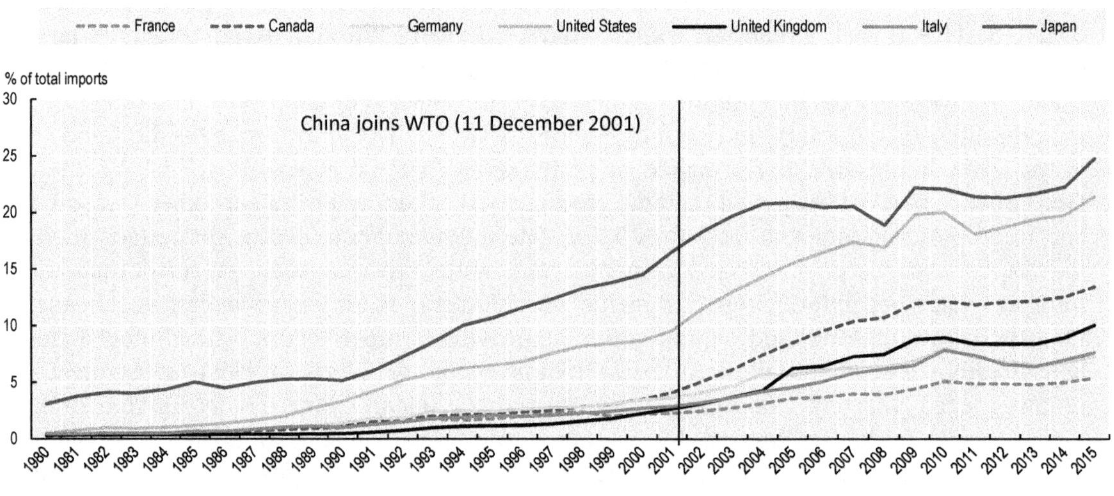

Source: International Monetary Fund, OECD calculations.

http://dx.doi.org/10.1787/888933476491

Figure 2.4. **Share of gross fixed capital formation of selected countries, 1960-2015**

(Per cent of world total)

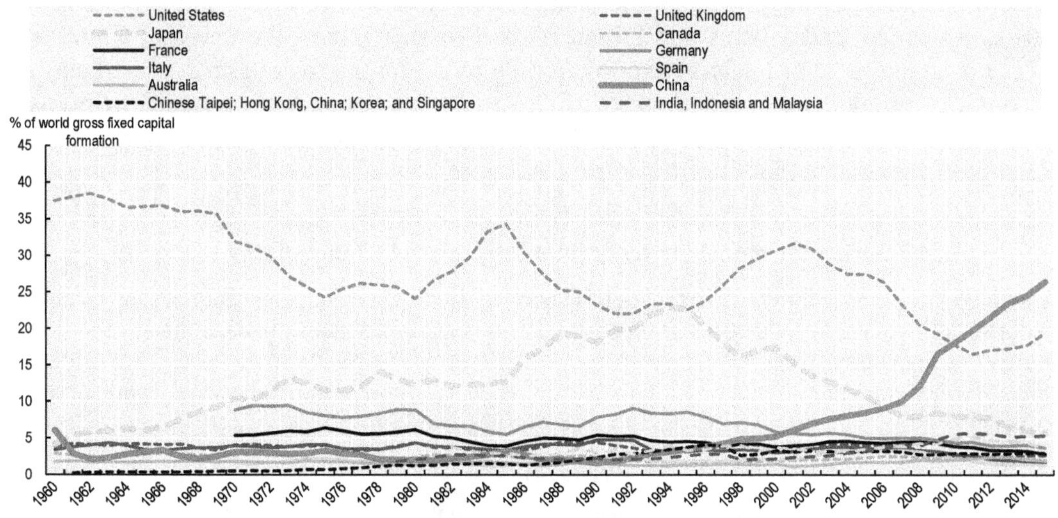

Source: The World Bank, OECD National Accounts, OECD calculations.

http://dx.doi.org/10.1787/888933476507

Investment and net export multipliers are key influences on growth. China managed to take advantage of these by pushing up saving via three primary factors. First, state-driven investment combined with selective capital controls, interest rate ceilings and credit rationing "bottles up" saving and increases the correlation between national savings and investment.[2] Second, to facilitate investment the state fully or partly privatised around two-thirds of its SOEs and state assets between 1995 and 2005. From 1998 to 2004, six in ten employees of SOEs, some tens of millions of workers, were laid off.[3] This boosted corporate profits in the state and private sectors and hence company saving. Third, pension reforms at the end of the 1990s reduced benefits, increased contributions and became partially funded, requiring increased household saving (Ma, G. and Y. Wang, 2010).

This spectacular success as a development strategy enabled China to pull millions out of poverty. Other emerging economies are also trying to enact their own developments strategies, but the above size aspects are the reason for a greater focus on China.

The effect on world trade

China's export surge could be trade diverting with little benefit for other countries (other than commodity suppliers) or, alternatively, positive spillovers could increase the "size of the cake" and improve outcomes for all players.

Some evidence concerning the impact of China's entry into WTO on world trade is set out in more detail in Box 2.2, which presents a gravity model based on just under 40 000 observations of destination-origin exports pairs over the period 1997-2014. The main factors driving exports are: the size of markets (captured by GDP) and the distance in kilometres between partners that affect the transport cost of trade. These gravity factors are conditioned by three 'directional' variables: the degree of FDI openness (FDI restrictions mean that setting up subsidiaries abroad to overcome distance costs are blocked and partners must export to that destination country instead); political instability (more instability in the destination country is bad for exports) and the bilateral exchange rate (domestic currency per unit of that of the foreign partner). A dummy variable is included for the post-2001 period. The directional variables are discussed further in section 2.3. At this point, the focus is on the dummy variable (DID_DUMMY) which is positive and strongly supported by the data. The coefficients of 0.157 and 0.179 suggest that regardless of trade shares and labour market impact issues, the entry of China into WTO raised the level of bilateral exports (via its effect on the overall size of markets) for all countries on average in the range of 15.7% to 17.9% depending on which of the two "openness variables" is used (FIOP or FDIRI). This large positive impact indicates that China has generated some benefits for trade partners.

Box 2.2. **Gravity model for trade, and the effect of China joining the WTO**

A relatively parsimonious gravity model is used to study the main determinants of bilateral exports. All explanatory variables are measured one year earlier than the dependent variable to mitigate endogeneity issues with the regressors. Difference-in-difference approach is considered to test for a significant impact of China's participation in globalisation following its adherences to WTO in 2001. The model takes the following form:

$$Ln\_X_{ijt} = \beta_0 + \beta_1 \, DID\_DUMMY_{,t} + \sum_{k=1}^{K} \beta_k Z_{j,t-1} + \alpha_{ij} + \varepsilon_{ijt}$$

Where the variables (including the explanatory set E/R, DIST etc. in Z) are:

- $Ln\_X_{ij,t}$ is the export indicator; measured as the natural logarithm of exports from origin country (i) to destination country (j) at time (t) in billions of US dollars.
- DID_DUMMY_t is a dummy variable equals 1 since 2002, and 0 otherwise.
- $Ln\_GDP\_Co_{i,t-1}$ and $Ln\_GDP\_Cd_{j,t-1}$ are natural logarithms of GDPs in billions of US dollars for the origin country (i) and the destination country (j) in time (t-1). Positive signs are expected.
- $Ln\_E/R_{j,t-1}$ is the natural logarithm of the real bilateral exchange rate of the exporting country. It is expressed as domestic currency per unit of the destination country currency. So, a rise is a depreciation. A positive sign is expected.
- $Ln\_DIST_{j,t-1}$ is the natural logarithm of distance between origin and destination countries. A negative sign is expected.
- $PI_{j,t-1}$ measures perceptions of the likelihood of political instability and/or politically-motivated violence, including terrorism (a negative sign).[1] A negative sign is expected.
- Ln_FIOP j,t-1 is an indicator of capital account openness in the destination country. The index was initially introduced in Chinn and Ito (2006). It is the natural logarithm of normalised Chinn-Ito index.[2] Ln_FDIRI j,t-1 is an indicator of statutory restrictions on foreign direct investment[3] in the destination country. It is the natural logarithm of the index. These openness indicators are introduced alternately in the regressions. Openness permits trade more easily and the sign is unambiguously positive.
- The bilateral export data are from the OECD Bilateral Trade in Goods Database. Data for GDP in millions of US dollars and the trade openness indicator are taken from the International Monetary Fund's (IMF) World Economic Outlook and Direction of Trade Statistics (DOTS) databases. The political instability variable is taken from the World Bank's Worldwide Governance Indicators database (www.govindicators.org). The exchange rate data are from the IMF database. The sample is based on an unbalanced panel dataset of annual data on 54 origin-destination countries over the period 1997 to 014. Therefore a dyadic model is used, including the one-year lagged dependent amongst the set of explanatory variables. This model is estimated using quasi fixed-effects OLS estimators. Random dyad countries effects are included alongside time-invariant indicator (i.e. such as the distance between origin and destination countries). Standard errors are clustered on dyads in order to be fully robust toward arbitrary autocorrelation and heteroscedasticity.

Box 2.2. **Gravity model for trade, and the effect of China joining the WTO** (cont.)

Table 2.1. **Gravity model for the determinants of bilateral exports, 1997-2014**

		[1]	[2]	[3]	[4]
Ln_GDP_Co	c(1)	0.593*** (32.66)	0.631*** (35.15)	0.623*** (36.48)	0.632*** (36.69)
Ln_GDP_Cd	c(2)	0.619*** (39.22)	0.638*** (39.70)	0.640*** (42.26)	0.655*** (42.86)
Ln_E/R	c(3)	0.010 (0.95)	0.019* (1.86)	0.013 (1.28)	0.009 (0.90)
Ln_FIOP	c(4)	–	–	0.095*** (4.59)	0.080*** (3.78)
Ln_FIOP*DID_DUM	c(5)	–	–	–	0.034*** (13.65)
Ln_FDIRI	c(6)	0.506*** (4.31)	0.529*** (4.72)	–	–
Ln_FDIRI*DID_DUM	c(7)	–	-0.616*** (-12.10)	–	–
Ln_DIST	c(8)	-0.870*** (-33.44)	-0.895*** (-35.36)	-0.903*** (-37.14)	-0.906*** (-37.57)
PI	c(9)	-0.146*** (-7.42)	-0.134*** (-6.78)	-0.092*** (-5.36)	-0.084*** (-4.89)
DID_DUM	c(10)	0.157*** (14.12)	–	0.179*** (17.39)	–
Constant	c(11)	-1.969*** (-7.22)	-2.433*** (-8.99)	-2.914*** (-10.55)	-3.101*** (-11.10)
R-squared	–	0.708	0.723	0.713	0.716
Observations	–	38922	38922	45781	45781
Fisher Test (Statistic and p-value)					
c(4)-c(5)=0					4.31 (0.038)
c(6)-c(7)=0		–	84.44 (0.000)	–	–

Notes:

This table shows the results of estimating dyadic quasi-fixed effects models for a cross sectional unbalanced panel data on bilateral FDI flows from 54 countries over the period 1997-2014. t-values are reported in parentheses. Standard errors are fully robust toward arbitrary autocorrelation and heteroscedasticity (i.e., standard errors are clustered by home-host dyad with White-Huber corrections). All explanatory variables are one year lagged. *, ** and *** indicate statistical significance at the 10%, 5% and 1% levels, respectively.

1. The indicator has a spread of -2.5 (high political instability) to 2.5 (low political instability). It is rescaled to facilitate the interpretation of the results by deducting it from 2.5 so that a higher number represents higher political instability.
2. See Chinn and Ito (2006). Chinn and Ito Index is normalised from 0 to 100.
3. The original indicator measures statutory restrictions on FDI within an interval of 0 (low restrictions) to 1 (high restrictions). To avoid awkwardness in the interpretation of the coefficients, the indicator is rescaled so that a higher number indicates higher statutory restrictions on foreign direct investment by subtracting the original index from 1.

Source: OECD Bilateral Trade in Goods Database, International Monetary Fund's (IMF) World Economic Outlook and Direction of Trade Statistics (DOTS) databases, World Bank's Worldwide Governance Indicators database, OECD calculations.

2.2 The hollowing out of the middle classes in advanced economies

The hope that less-skilled workers would be sufficiently mobile to move between regions and industries to maintain or even improve their living standards over time is contradicted by outcomes across the OECD area. These and other related issues are discussed in the OECD (2015c). As a brief background on this issue for this *Outlook*, Figure 2.5 shows the changes in employment shares for high-skill, middle-skilled and less-skilled workers.[4] In nearly all countries, the share of middle-paying jobs fell between 2000 and 2015.[5] Relative employment growth has been strongest in the highest paying, more technologically demanding jobs. Lower skilled jobs are mixed, falling in some and rising in others.

There are competing explanations of these trends. One is the expansion of global trade and investment. It was always to be expected that employment of less-skilled workers would be affected in advanced economies as the workforces of emerging economies were integrated into global value chains. This is because unskilled labour is the abundant factor in less developed countries and capital is the abundant factor in advanced economies – without significant wage falls, employment of less-skilled workers in advanced countries would likely decline.

Figure 2.5. **Differences in share of employment between 2000 and 2015 by pay category**

(Percentage points)

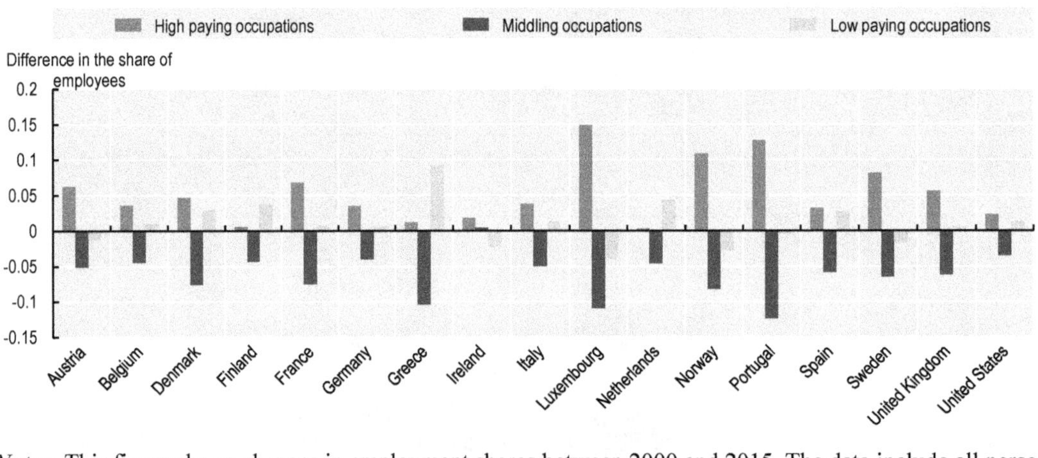

Notes: This figure shows changes in employment shares between 2000 and 2015. The data include all persons aged 15-65 who reported employment in the sample reference year, excluding those employed by the army. Occupations are first assigned by International Standard Classification of Occupations (ISCO) categories that are consistent over the whole period. These occupations are then grouped into three broad categories by wage levels, as in Goos et al. (2014).

Source: Eurostat, US Bureau of Labour Statistics, OECD calculations.

http://dx.doi.org/10.1787/888933476518

The other explanation is progress with digitalisation, new technologies and related innovations. Any activities that can be broken up into calculations and/or repetitive activities can be digitalised and linked up across the internet and ultimately applied to everything: production, innovation and design, inventory control and logistics, and driverless road, rail, sea and air transport. Robotics, cloud computing and the internet of things (where objects can communicate information about themselves to feed into the above processes) are platforms for innovation that are unstoppable in businesses that want to survive in the modern competitive world.

It is something of a "red herring" to think of technology and innovation as separate from trade. Indeed, new firm-based trade theories link the importance of economies of scale accessed by expanding sales abroad to the adoption of new technology and innovations that jointly drive productivity growth. Evidence from the global company database supporting this way of looking at trade is presented later on. As global competition becomes fiercer, the drive to better processes and efficiencies becomes essential for corporate success and indeed survival. Companies that do not adapt see productivity fall compared to successful firms and wages and employment adjust accordingly. Figure 2.6 uses the (updated) global company database used in previous editions of the *Outlook*. As before, Decile 1 companies refer to the weakest productivity growth companies while Decile 10 refers to the fastest.

The grouping of the best and worst deciles from companies across all of the non-financial sectors is shown in the top panel. The large "Materials" (i.e. chemicals, fertilisers, industrial gases, construction materials, metal (steel), glass containers, paper packaging, aluminium, diversified materials, mining, gold, precious metals and minerals, forest products and paper products) and "Industrials" (i.e. capital goods, transportation, and commercial and professional services) sectors are shown as examples in the middle and bottom panels, because they contain many of the most trade- and technology-exposed workers; i.e. they include large numbers of the lower skilled jobs where emerging market countries are making progress. They also include industries prone to the digitalisation of routine tasks (such as commercial and professional services where accounting, clerical, call centre services are examples and capital goods where robotics play such a key role). Previously-successful companies that do not adapt to the new trade and technology environment see productivity and wages per employee fall, while the best adaptors see productivity and wages growing. The pressures are particularly clear in the Materials and Industrials sectors. These heterogeneous within-industry outcomes lie at the heart of worker disgruntlement with their rapidly changing world.[6]

The impact of trade on employment in the United States

The very positive achievements of emerging economies on such a large scale were bound to affect lower-skilled jobs in other economies. Autor et al. (2016), and many cited articles therein, is one of the first serious economic studies to link the labour market developments noted earlier with the new firm-based trade theories, and to use them to analyse in depth what the authors term "the China shock". These theories focus on creative destruction forces within industries related to their (linked) successes and failures in innovation and expanding foreign sales to take advantage of scale economies, and are discussed more fully in the following section. Skilled wage premiums change via within-industry shifts in employment demand towards the more productive firms and away from the less productive (as illustrated in Figure 2.6).

Figure 2.6. **Productivity and wage trends of non-financial companies in advanced economies, 2002-2016**

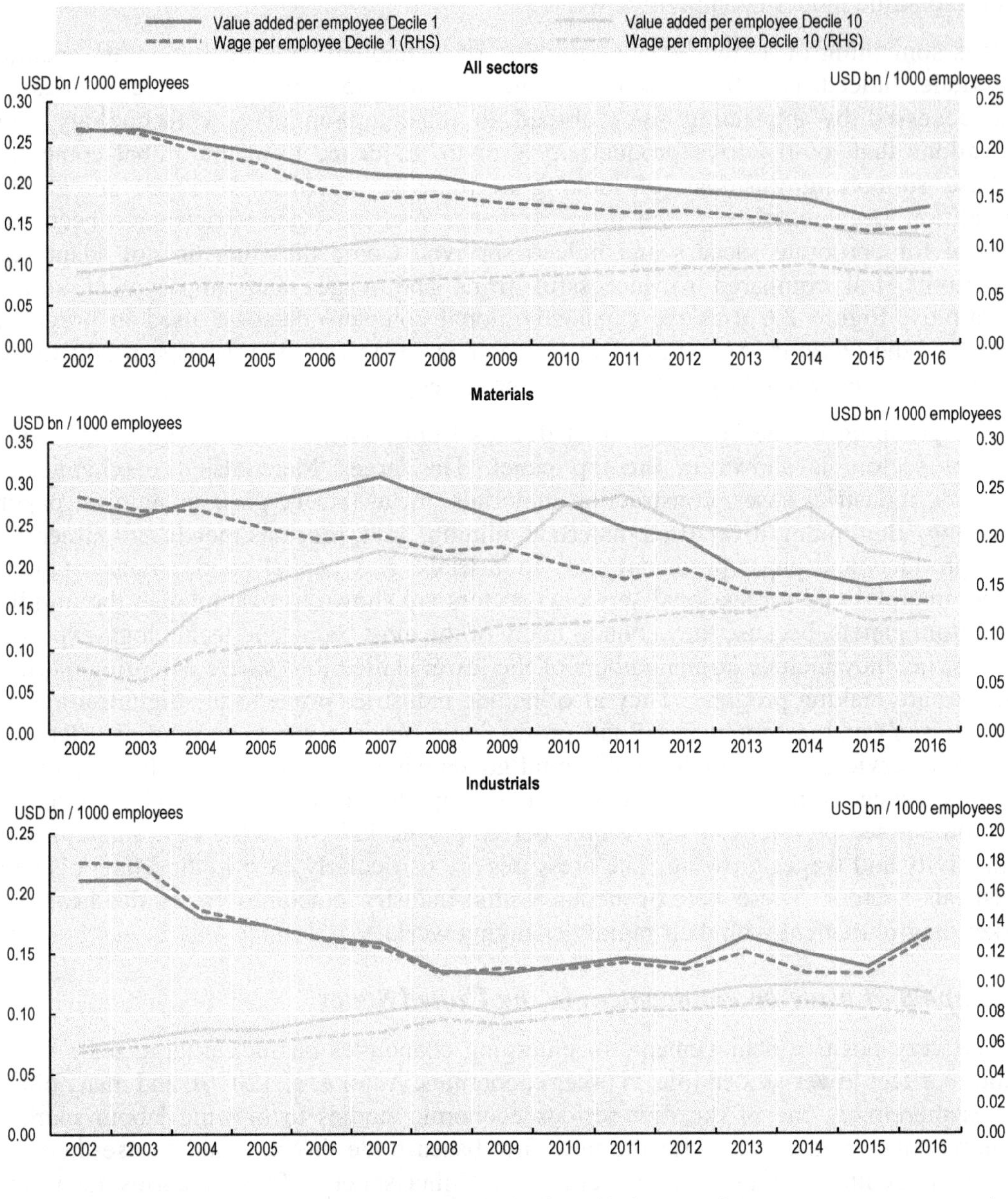

Note: The figure shows weighted averages of nominal value added per employee versus wages per employee. Decile 1 refers to companies sorted to be the lowest productivity growth within the shown group, and Decile 10 to the fastest growth companies. RHS stands for Right Hand Scale.

Source: Bloomberg, OECD calculations.

StatLink http://dx.doi.org/10.1787/888933476525

These firm-level theories make it easier to incorporate a greater richness to the analysis of the way in which local (regional) labour markets respond to trade shocks. Some of the main findings of the Autor study are summarised in Box 2.3. Very granular local data on import penetration from China into specific US industries and labour market commuting zones are used in this influential study.[7] It also includes detailed longitudinal analysis (what happens to the same workers through the years following the initial impact).

Box 2.3. **Studies on labour market impacts of import penetration**

Autor et al. (2016), and cited publications therein, together show that, at the firm and local labour market commuting zone levels most exposed to import penetration from China, some of the predictions of standard economic theory (as in Box 2.1) are contradicted. This is the case at most employee education levels. US companies and local labour market geographies most exposed to import penetration from China were found to be affected in the following ways:

- Trade-exposed localities suffered the largest falls in manufacturing jobs, which was accommodated by unemployment or withdrawal from the labour force (at all education levels) rather than reallocation to other firms and sectors.
- For workers with less than college education, employment also fell in non-manufacturing within the labour market commuting zone, suggesting that negative demand spill-overs magnify the loss of jobs.
- The working age population did not change much within local commuting zones and, tracing individual workers over time in longitudinal studies, there was very little geographic migration in response to the trade shock.
- Input-output studies confirm that the net supply chain effects are negative – thus (for example) the exit of a tyre making company reduces its demand for upstream steel fibre and synthetic rubber, and this effect outweighs any theoretical benefits that could arise from cheaper imports of these intermediate inputs from China that might benefit other surviving US producers of tyres.
- Workers so displaced move into job churning with fewer years working than non-displaced workers, and they remain in the same trade-exposed industry (since their industry-specific human capital is destroyed leaving them badly placed). After some 16 years, 43% are still "churning" in the same exposed industry.[1]
- The direct employment effects at the local commuting zone level are estimated to account for 2.4 million job losses due to import penetration in the 1999 to 2011 period. This effect based on micro analysis does not include aggregate demand effects and non-local input-output linkages – so the full impact over this period could be much larger.
- Some studies referenced by the authors suggest that these findings on the impact of import competition are not confined to the United States.[2]
- Studies of other trade shocks are also consistent with the above findings, though they are not based on the same degree of detail. Wage growth for US high school dropouts within industries most protected by tariffs was 17% lower than for comparable workers in other industries following NAFTA, and was 8% lower for locations (all industries) where the most exposed industries were situated. However, higher education workers did not suffer much wage loss.[3]

In summing up the literature the authors conclude that: "Employment has fallen in US industries more exposed to import competition. But so too has overall employment in the local labour markets in which these industries were concentrated. Offsetting employment gains either in export-oriented tradables or in non-tradables have, for the most part, failed to materialise. Input-output linkages between sectors appear to have magnified rather than dampened the employment effects of trade both within regions and nationally".[4]

1. "These results run counter to a precept of general equilibrium trade theory that the local employment effect of sectoral demand shocks should be short-lived, as the forces of wage and price arbitrage and labor mobility dissipate these shocks nationally.....That this neoclassical prediction does not appear to hold even approximately over the span of a decade suggests that the labor market impacts of trade shocks are likely to be amplified by slow and incomplete adjustment: rather than modestly reducing wage levels among low-skill workers nationally, these shocks catalyze significant falls in employment rates within trade-impacted local labor markets", (Autor et al. 2016, p26).
2. For Norway, see Balsvic, Jensen and Salvanes (2015); for Spain, Donoso, Martin and Minondo (2014); and for Germany, Dauth, Findeisen and Suedekum (2014). In the case of Germany, job losses to import penetration were substantial, but were matched by gains in the export sector. Germany has had a unique role of exporting high technology capital goods to China and other emerging market economies.
3. See McLaren and Hakobyan (2015) for Mexico. These finding are also similar in trade liberalisation impact studies in India, Topalova (2010), and Brazil, Kovak (2013).

4 Autor et al. (2016).

Manufacturing employment in the United States receives considerable attention in this study. Evidence on the more aggregate outcome for manufacturing is also clear in the data. Figure 2.7 shows the trend in the share of US manufacturing employment in the total. While manufacturing employment is broadly stable over the pre-2001 period, the rest of the US economy is growing more quickly, resulting in a steady trend decline in the share. The break in trend around 2001 shows up clearly. The level of employment is also shown in Figure 2.7. It is flat on average (following the re-absorption of manpower after the War), and it then moves in a business cycle pattern – it troughs in downturns and then always recovers in the upturns. After 2001, this cycle disappears. US manufacturing employment drops sharply, and does not recover with ups and downs of GDP. Formal econometric tests suggest a clear structural break.[8] While more research needs to be done, the suddenness of this decline (and occurring as it did at the time of the tech bust) suggests that the trade factors may have been quite important at first.

Figure 2.7. **US manufacturing: Share of total employment and the employment level, 1950-2016**

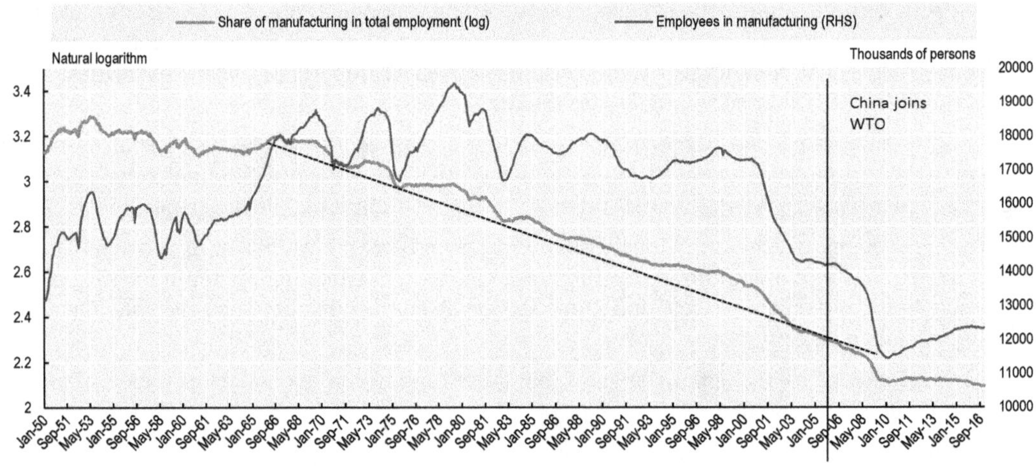

Note: RHS stands for Right Hand Scale.

Source: Federal Reserve Bank of St. Louis, OECD calculations.

StatLink http://dx.doi.org/10.1787/888933476534

New firm-based trade and productivity growth theory and evidence

The above discussion emphasises that both the expansion of trade and the digitalisation/technology revolution are both important in explaining the hollowing out of middle class jobs in advanced and emerging economies. These two factors need to be considered together. The reason for this is that trade and the adoption of new technology are inextricably linked processes. To understand the level-playing-field factors that might block productivity growth and/or distort the gains from trade, it is important to first understand how multinational firms succeed or fail in a more open environment. This section provides evidence supporting the new firm-level trade theories that drive productivity, providing a framework of understanding for the subsequent discussion of the different factors that contribute to uneven playing fields and their effects on trade, investment, and competition.

These new theories link trade and technology adoption in a dynamic manner at the firm level. Firms within industries are heterogeneous, based on management skill and innovations in their business models that drive leanness and efficiency levels. More productive firms expand within the industry and become more intensive in their use of high-skilled labour. This raises industry productivity by causing the exit of low- and falling-productivity firms. There are substantial overheads in developing export markets and foreign subsidiaries that allow economies of scale to be achieved. High-productivity firms are better able to manage these costs of establishing global value chains and they expand to enter foreign markets (via exports or investment).[9] These economies of scale further increase the return to productivity-enhancing investments in technology adoption and innovation in a competitive global environment where the successful firms from different countries compete for market share. This further increases the company's demand for skilled workers and reallocates resources within industries. Technology allows production processes to be broken into different skill categories and reallocated in global value chains. Operations, logistics and information technology are combined allowing boundaries separating business process tasks, research, design, finance, legal contracts, firms and consumers, to be crossed.[10] Trade, foreign investment in subsidiaries and the adoption of technology become correlated with each other and are reflected in the sort of relative productivity outcomes shown earlier.

Since new theories of trade and productivity were developed to explain observed patterns, it should not come as a surprise that OECD firm-level research lends support to the above propositions (as shown in Box 2.4).

The processes explicit in new firm-level trade theories affect labour markets directly and, as Autor et al. (2016) have shown, can explain the patterns in job shares and living standards such as those shown in Figures 2.5 and 2.6:

- Exiting firms within an industry shed labour. These workers need mobility between geographies and industries, which research shows, for whatever reason, they do not have.
- Merger and acquisition (M&A) processes extract synergies where domestic transactions are concerned; and cross-border M&A (the dominant component of FDI) facilitate outsourcing and global value chains, which again economise on duplication with implications for workers.
- Successful high-productivity exporting firms invest more in technology and innovation which can replace many repetitive lower-skilled labour activities.
- Skill premiums in wages will emerge which are often firm (not industry) specific. Inequality among workers in the same industry will emerge.

Trade and technology interactions also provide new avenues to explain why productivity growth may have slowed down during the post-2000 period. International sales for firms are critical to productivity growth in both advanced and emerging economies. These firm-specific mechanisms for sustainable productivity growth cannot be promoted by monetary and fiscal policies. Infrastructure investment is a key enabling factor, but firms still need to take advantage of it. Those that succeed are those taking advantage of technology and trade in the most creative ways. These firm-based insights help to inform subsequent discussion on why there is a need for a common set of cross-border rules.

Box 2.4. The empirical support for new firm-level trade and productivity theory

An important tenet of the new heterogeneous-firm trade theory is that it is based on company-level data within sectors where it is observed that trade participation defines the differences between firms – exporters being more productive (Melitz 2003). In this literature, globalisation through export liberalisation: "leads to within-industry reallocations of resources which raise both average industry productivity, as low-productivity firms exit and high-productivity firms expand to enter export markets. The increase in firm scale induced by export market entry enhances the return to complementary productivity-enhancing investments in technology adoption and innovation, with the result that trade liberalisation also raises firm productivity".[1]

FDI as an alternative to exporting is consistent with the new theories considered here. Helpman et al. (2004) expanded the Melitz (2003) model into one in which the productivity of exporting firms is lower than that of firms engaged in local production overseas. The decision of more productive companies to export or to produce in local markets depends in large part on transport and other costs (such as tariff walls and capital controls) as considered in gravity theories of trade and FDI. The theory in Helpman et al. is also based on the idea that only productive firms can cover the enormous fixed costs (local factory construction, distribution networks, and supply chains) entailed in local production overseas.

Following the methods used in OECD (2016a), Figure 2.8 shows productivity and international sales linkages at the micro level. International sales, as measured here, may be due to exports or local production abroad.

Figure 2.8. **Company productivity levels versus international sales by productivity growth decile, 2002-2016**

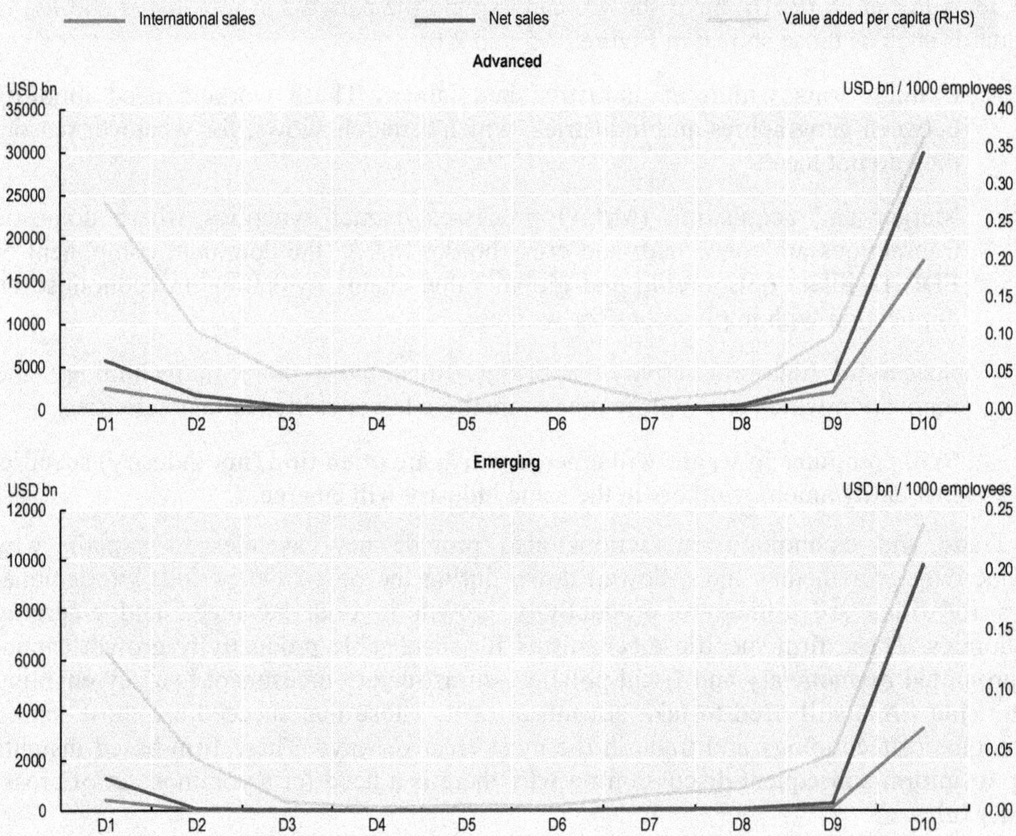

Note: RHS stands for Right Hand Scale.
Source: Bloomberg, OECD calculations.

StatLink http://dx.doi.org/10.1787/888933476544

Box 2.4. **The empirical support for new firm-level trade and productivity theory** (cont.)

Firms within each Global Industry Classification Standard sector are ranked according to their value-added-weighted productivity growth from 2002 to 2016. Then size-weighted firms from each bucket of productivity growth from each sector are grouped together (the lowest growth D1s from each sector, the D2s together, etc., to the highest-growth D10 grouping). Both firm and sector size weights are used. Thus, for example, decile 10 consists of the fastest (weighted) productivity growth companies across all industrial sectors.

The D1 slow growth companies often have relatively high productivity levels but are declining (negative productivity growth). These companies are failing to expand markets shown with the sales lines. The D10 companies have very high productivity levels and the most rapid growth in value added per worker growth. They also have very large shares of international and domestic markets.

Consistent with the new trade theory, the D10 firms (with high productivity levels and growth) also have the greatest average foreign sales. These high productivity firms also share the bulk of domestic markets – as trade costs fall and globalisation proceeds, these firms are best placed to take advantage and further raise productivity. This pattern of productivity growth and foreign sales of companies is also true of emerging economies. As shown in OECD (2016a), movements in and out of the middle ranking deciles to D10 is more difficult – there is some persistence in the winners. Where transitions do occur, merger and acquisition activity plays a strong role.

Granger causality tests for the international sales of firms as a causal influence on firm value added (employee remuneration plus earnings before interest, tax and depreciation) per capita (the productivity measure) are compared to other factors in Table 2.2. Research and development, mergers and acquisitions, capital expenditure and international sales are all tested. All influence productivity, as shown in the left column. In the bottom row, only in the cases of international sales and mergers and acquisitions is the hypothesis of no causation from productivity to the tested variables not rejected by the data. This absence of reverse causation is very consistent with the new-new trade theory hypotheses about most productive firms taking advantage of globalisation as the causal mechanism.

Table 2.2. **Granger causality test for international sales and firm productivity, 2002-2016**

Granger causality results using 2 Year lags: Hypothesis variable in the left column does not cause the variable in the row

Annual non-financial company data from 2002 to 2016. The dependent variable is the annual percent change in value added per employee.

	Value added per capita (%YoY)	R&D expenditure per capita (%YoY)	Capital expenditure per capita (%YoY)	Value of M&A deals per capita	International sales per capita (%YoY)
R&D expenditure per capita (%YoY)	reject ***	-	-	-	-
Capital expenditure per capita (%YoY)	reject ***	-	-	-	-
Value of M&A deals per capita	reject ***	-	-	-	-
International sales per capita (%YoY)	reject ***	-	-	-	-
Value added per capita (%YoY)	-	reject *	reject **	no reject	no reject

1. Melitz and Redding (2012).

Source: Bloomberg, OECD calculations

Globalisation that operates according to a common set of cross-border rules

Currently there is a consensus that monetary policy is exhausted as a source of support for growth and more fiscal expansion especially via infrastructure is needed for those countries with "fiscal room". A part of this consensus is that structural reforms to improve flexibility are important, and more active labour market policies (such as better matching of job seekers with vacancies, work experience programmes, use of social media and behavioural economics insights into what would encourage more active job search) may be helpful. Such policies need the full support of governments.

But it is also possible that the task posed for domestic policy is made greater by the conduct of cross-border activities on an uneven playing field that undermines the gains from trade, global investment and competition. These issues need to be dealt with before they become a part of the negative outcomes that domestic policies are trying to deal with. If the paths to better productivity and less inequality are to be found within industries at the firm level, where the interactions between trade and technology are driving the process, then a coherent set of rules to facilitate cross-border competition in a fair manner will be critical to improving outcomes. This is the subject matter of the rest of this *Outlook*.

2.3 Exchange rate and capital account management

> The first distortion to the level playing field considered in this *Outlook* concerns exchange rate, traded goods price and capital account management. Economies of scale might be achieved not on the basis of efficiency but instead through relative price and capital flow distortions. Evidence presented suggests most advanced economies tend to have overvalued exchange rates, and there is some evidence of pricing traded goods for market share. Empirical findings from a gravity model of exports suggest capital account management policies, which often accompany managed exchange rate regimes, are very important. Since 2001, when the vast Chinese market became better integrated into expanding global value chains, openness with respect to FDI and capital account portfolio flows has become more important in supporting foreign sales through trade and investment. This aspect of the level playing field opens the way for productivity growth through economies of scale. The OECD Codes of Liberalisation are designed to make capital account management policies more transparent and provide a framework for moving towards more openness (while still allowing for the different stages of economic development of adherents).

The first area of debate on "the level playing field" concerns exchange rate and capital account management. If a country holds its exchange rate at a level that is undervalued compared to fundamentals, it will favour its exporters and discriminate against imports. Economists sometimes refer to this as a "beggar-thy-neighbour" policy. Capital account management is often used to support such regimes, and these also affect trade. Companies have the choice to produce at home and export to a foreign country or, particularly where transport and tariff costs are high and when penetration of the market requires a local presence, they may choose to set up subsidiaries abroad. FDI controls restrict that choice. For example, restrictions on insurance and other financial service subsidiaries in the host country make it more difficult to serve that market. Economies of scale for the innovative foreign firms are blocked and the domestic consumer in the host country is denied a competitive service. More general capital account openness (including banking, portfolio and trade credit flows) is also an important supporting factor for trade.

Undervaluation

Undervaluation is difficult to define. In principle, a purchasing-power-parity (PPP) real exchange rate is compared to some fundamentals-based "norm" for where its level should be. For a price-taking commodity-exporting country, for example, this might be the terms of trade where, say, a rise would reflect a real income transfer from the rest of the world which justifies an equilibrating higher real exchange rate. Real GDP per capita is a more general measure of real living standards against which PPP real exchange rates might be compared over the longer term. Higher GDP per capita warrants a higher real exchange rate.[11]

Figure 2.9 shows a measure of average real exchange rate valuation for selected countries.

Figure 2.9. **Five-year rolling real exchange rate valuation for selected countries, 1990-2015**

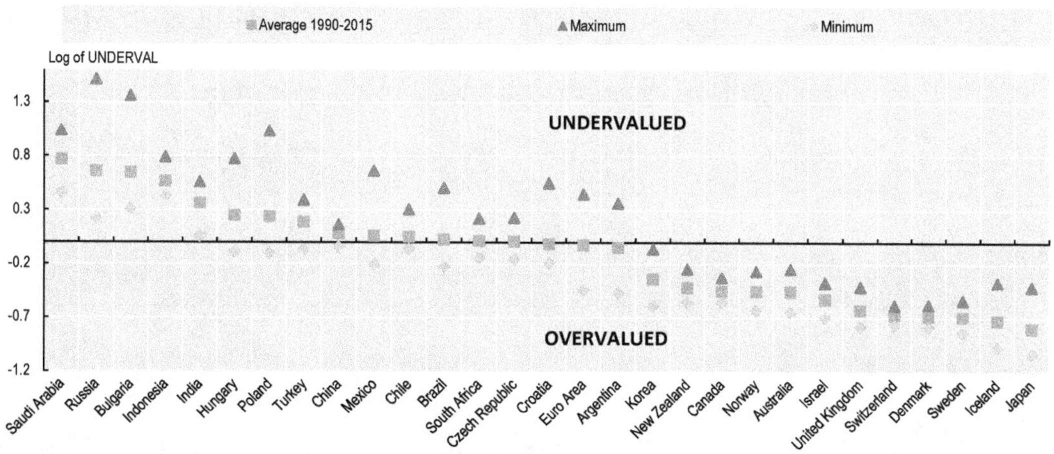

Note: Rodrik (2008). The overvaluation and undervaluation exchange rate measure is derived from the Rodrick (2008) model. It is an exchange rate measure based on domestic price level adjusted for the Balassa-Samuelson effect. Whenever UNDERVAL exceeds unity, it indicates that the exchange rate is set such that goods produced at home are relatively cheap in US dollar terms: the currency is undervalued. When UNDERVAL is below unity, the currency is overvalued. See Box 2.5 for definitions and details of the model used in these calculations. Selected countries included in the chart are OECD or G20 Members.

The statistical data for Israel are supplied by and under the responsibility of the relevant Israeli authorities. The use of such data by the OECD is without prejudice to the status of the Golan Heights, East Jerusalem and Israeli settlements in the West Bank under the terms of international law.

Source: International Monetary Fund, OECD calculations.

StatLink http://dx.doi.org/10.1787/888933476551

The squares show the average for the period since 1990, the triangles show the maximum and the diamonds the minimum (for 5-year rolling averages). "Undervaluation" in Figure 2.9 is a measure of the real exchange rate after allowing for GDP per capita in a panel regression model for 170 countries. As a country gets richer its real exchange rate would normally appreciate,[12] but policies can be used to force the real exchange rate to be undervalued (compared to the GDP per capita "justified" level).[13]

Policies that are often the subject of dispute between countries (e.g. US Dept. of the Treasury, 2016) include some combination of:

- Exchange market intervention to resist appreciation in the face of inflows.

- Capital account management (restrictions on inflows and more liberal attitudes to outflows – other than in crisis periods).
- More general "financial repression" policies to boost saving in relation to national investment.[14]

Together, such policies can help to undervalue the exchange rate (equivalent to a subsidy to tradables with a "tax" on consuming traded goods). Where countries carry out such policies while others do not (not everyone can be undervalued) then "beggar-thy-neighbour" outcomes may ensue.

The calculations in Figure 2.9 provide some interesting observations. First, amongst the BRIICS countries,[15]India, Indonesia and Russia have been significantly undervalued on this PPP measure, but Brazil, China and South Africa have on average been much closer to the level justified by fundamentals. Second, amongst OECD countries, only a few appear to have had undervalued currencies (Hungary, Poland and Turkey). Most OECD countries have overvalued currencies (compared to that justified by GDP per capita).

Figure 2.10. **Prices of US imports from China, 2003-2017**

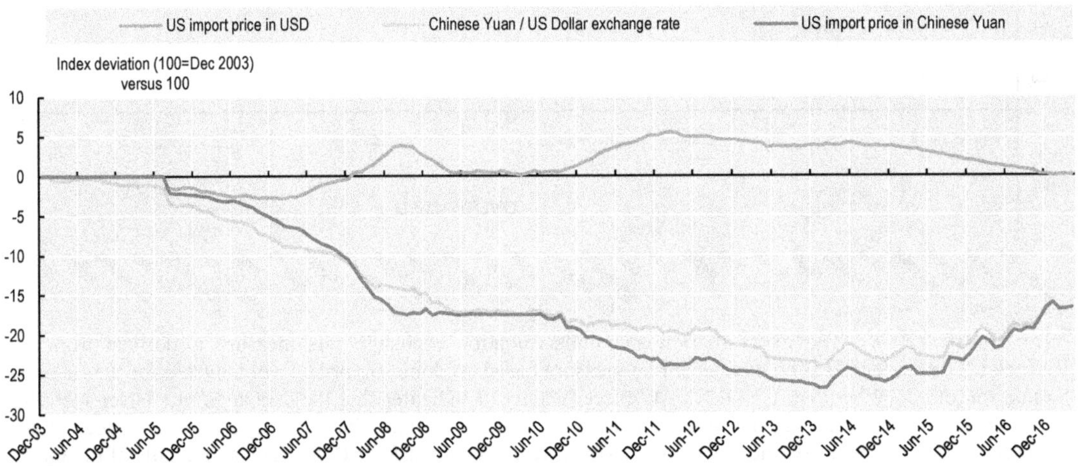

Note: If prices in Chinese Yuan fully offset the exchange rate appreciation, the green and blue lines would be fully aligned. Offsetting can lead to negative margins, so the USD price can be adjusted up to offset this in appreciation periods. This can be reversed again when the Chinese Yuan weakens.

Source: Thomson Reuters Datastream, OECD calculations.

StatLink http://dx.doi.org/10.1787/888933476569

For much of the 2000s, China resisted exchange rate appreciation due to significant capital inflows, accumulating very large quantities of foreign exchange reserves, but appears to have done so only to the extent necessary to prevent moving into over-valuation territory compared to its level of economic development. However, if China is not particularly undervalued on a PPP basis, then how has it managed to keep its prices competitive versus other exporters (the so-called "China Price")? This can happen if the price of domestic non-tradables rises faster than the price of tradables, where pricing policy applicable to the latter offsets exchange rate moves. The general price level would rise (PPP appreciation) while traded goods prices would be kept low.

Figure 2.10 shows the US price index for imports from China in US dollars, the yuan and the implied price received by exporters in yuan, all expressed as deviation from the

December 2003 base of 100. From 2003 to the end of 2016, there has been no net increase in prices, despite wage increases at home and a 24% appreciation of the exchange rate to 2016. This is consistent with export companies pricing for market share: in the face of a rising exchange rate, profit margins would have to fall, placing pressure on companies to contain costs in other areas. Cited factors include: low wages in the export sector; subsidies to state-owned enterprises in certain industries; network clustering for efficiency aided by permitted FDI; lower occupational safety and environmental protection costs; and use of counterfeit products. These observations may be systematic when imperfect competition and variable mark-ups are introduced into a model of international trade.[16]

Box 2.5. **Constructing an overvaluation and undervaluation measure**

The overvaluation and undervaluation exchange rate measure is derived from the Rodrick (2008) model. It is an exchange rate measure based on domestic price level adjusted for the Balassa-Samuelson effect (see Box 2.1). The advantage of this index is that it is comparable across countries as well as over time. This index is computed in three steps using IMF data, including 179 countries over the period 1990-2015. First, exchange rate data are extracted from the International Financial Statistics database. Power parity conversion factors (PPP) are extracted from IMF World Economic Outlook database. The "real" exchange rate (RER) is calculated as follows:

$$\ln RER_{i,t} = \ln(\frac{FX_{i,t}}{PPP_{i,t}})$$

Where i indexes countries[1] and t indexes five-year time periods. FX and PPP are expressed as national currency units per US dollar. Values of RER greater than one indicate that the value of the currency is lower (more depreciated) than indicated by purchasing power parity. However, in practice non-tradable goods are also cheaper in poorer countries (through the Balassa-Samuelson effect), which requires an adjustment. To account for this effect, in the second step, five year averaged RER is regressed on five year averaged real GDP per capita (RGDPC), taken from the IMF World Economic Outlook database.

$$\ln RER_{i,t} = \alpha + \beta \ln RGDPC_{i,t} + f_t + \varepsilon_{i,t}$$

where f is a fixed effect for time period and ε is the error term. This regression yields an estimate of β of −0.18 (with a very high t statistic of around -12), suggesting a strong and precisely estimated Balassa-Samuelson effect: when incomes rise by 10%, the real exchange rate falls (appreciates) by around 1.8%. Finally, the undervaluation index (UNDERVAL) is derived from the difference between the actual real exchange rate and the Balassa-Samuelson-adjusted rate.

$$\ln UNDERVAL_{i,t} = \ln RER_{i,t} - \widehat{\ln RER}_{i,t}$$

where $\widehat{\ln RER}_{i,t}$ is the predicted value from equation 1. Whenever UNDERVAL exceeds unity, it indicates that the exchange rate is set such that goods produced at home are relatively cheap in US dollar terms: the currency is undervalued. When UNDERVAL is below unity, the currency is overvalued.

1. Data for euro-area members are not available after 1999. Hence, aggregate data for the euro-area are considered in the regressions instead of individual country data over the period 1980-2015. Missing exchange rate data before 1999 are replaced by data for Germany. PPP conversion factor data are average PPP conversion factors of the 99 euro-area members. Real gross domestic product per capita is the ratio of the sum of real gross domestic product per capita of euro-area member states to total population in the euro-area.

Capital account management

Table 2.1 in Box 2.2 (the gravity model of bilateral exports) provides some insights concerning trade and capital account openness. The first two columns relate to the standard gravity model with the FDI restrictiveness index (FDIRI) included.

The positive sign implies that greater FDI restrictiveness blocks foreign subsidiaries so the company in the origin country is forced to export (incurring transport cost) rather than produce abroad. In the second column, the results of a difference-in-differences experiment is reported: the dummy variable equal to 1.0 post 2001 (and zero elsewhere) is applied to the FDIRI. The difference-in-difference coefficient is negative and strongly supported by the data. The sum of the 2 coefficients on FDIRI is moderately negative (and significant at the 1% level). The result is interpreted as follows: since 2001, when global value chains have become important and China joined WTO, FDI openness in the host country benefits global value chains and subsidiary structures to take advantage of scale economies and to reduce transport costs associated with exports. This is marginally negative for exports as production abroad becomes more important in foreign sales.

The third and fourth columns relate to the case where the overall capital account openness using the Chin and Ito index is used. The coefficient is positive and well supported by the data. This suggests that overall capital account openness (financing flows) supports stronger bilateral exports. The difference-in-differences coefficient is also positive and the sum of both coefficients is 16% higher post-2001 (and significant at the 5% level). This result is interpreted as follows: since 2001 general capital account openness has become more important as a positive influence on bilateral exports.

Box 2.6. **The OECD Code of Liberalisation of Capital Movements**

The OECD Code of Liberalisation of Capital Movements (OECD, 2016c) is an international agreement under which adherents commit to progressively liberalise capital flows. They may lodge reservations as regards operations they are not in a position to liberalise at the time of adherence and at any time as regards short-term capital flow operations. In situations of serious balance of payment difficulties or economic and financial disturbance, adherents can also avail themselves of the derogation clauses of the Code for new restrictions on other operations.

A system of notification and peer monitoring ensures transparency and mutual accountability in adherents' policies related to capital flows.

Countries have adhered to the Code in recognition of the fact that open capital accounts bring market disciplines that foster productivity, facilitate investment financing and provide opportunity to expand and diversify businesses abroad. By adhering to the Code, countries have agreed to abstain from a "beggar-thy-neighbour" approach to capital flow restrictions, including for the purpose of achieving competitive undervalued exchange rates, as this can prompt countermeasures and lead to negative collective outcomes in the end.

Today, the group of adherents to the Code have more open capital accounts than non-adherents. This situation contributes to imbalances and distortions in the global economy. The Code was opened in 2012 for adherence by non-OECD countries. Interested and able non-OECD countries are encouraged to join the Code. By doing so, non-OECD countries that are G20 members will also demonstrate strong adherence to G20 commitments to "refrain from competitive devaluation and not to target exchange rates for competitive purposes". They will build a reputation as responsible international players while enjoying the benefit of the protection provided by the Code against potential discrimination on the part of their peers.

The OECD Code of Liberalisation of Capital Movements

It is difficult to find strongly-supported exchange rate effects in this gravity model of trade. This may be because a large part of the world stabilises the exchange rate and uses more targeted policies on export pricing with a market share focus. The empirical evidence is clearer for capital account management. Indeed, one of the main benefits of moving away from exchange rate management may be the gradual removal of all the capital account management measures that accompany such regimes that are harmful to both origin and destination countries. This conclusion also applies equally to more advanced countries that have not sufficiently sequenced capital account reforms commensurate with their degree of economic development. The OECD Code of Liberalisation of Capital Movements (OECD, 2016c) provides a framework for transparent and cooperative policy approaches to capital account reform (Box 2.6).

2.4 Financial regulation and pushing risks into new areas

A second set of issues about the global playing field concerns uneven financial regulations which distort leverage between large and small banks, between banks and shadow banking and between countries. The aftermath of the crisis has seen deleveraging and a sharp pulling back of banks capital from cross-border activities in most advanced countries as re-regulation proceeds. The attempt (by "shadow banks" and countries previously dependent on cross-border banking flows) to deal with the effects of regulatory reform and bank business model changes in advanced countries is seeing a rise in contagion risk in emerging economies. The use of off-balance sheet special purpose vehicles (particularly so-called wealth management products managed by banks) has contributed to the emergence of significant contagion risk between emerging banks and shadow banks. This was not identifiable prior to 2008. Broad principles that would serve to level the regulatory playing field are discussed.

One of the most important aspects of globalisation has been deregulation and financial innovation that greatly increased the cross-border interdependence of banking in general and counterparty risk through derivatives in particular. The term global-systemically important bank (G-SIB) is a regulatory concept reflecting the size and interdependence of bank conglomerates that combine deposit banking with other more high risk businesses. In the lead up to the crisis, G-SIBs carried an implicit guarantee due to their size and links with retail accounts – they were too big and too interconnected to fail. Lax and inconsistent regulation in advanced economies prior to 2008 saw G-SIBs and large insurers at the very centre of the crisis. This has led to a regulatory reform process known as Basel III. The process of reregulation has swept up all banks, and the right balance might not have been achieved: small community banks, for example, should be subject to very different regulations compared to those needed for G-SIBs.

The globally-coordinated Basel III process should have been able to achieve one basic principle of financial regulation: that securities and institutions be treated in a similar way in relevant jurisdictions to avoid regulatory arbitrage. Much indeed has been achieved. The Basel III process has improved the quality of bank capital and leverage has been reduced – though not evenly between banks and countries. Liquidity and funding issues that were particularly problematic in the crisis have been addressed (consistently) via implementation of the Net Stable Funding ratio (NSFR) and the Liquidity Coverage Ratio rules. Total Loss Absorbing Capacity (TLAC) has also been agreed to bolster potential capital via bail-in mechanisms.[17] Rules concerning bank cross-border business models also serve to ensure better equality of regulatory applications. For example, foreign banks with subsidiaries in the United States must form an intermediate holding company (IHC) when consolidated assets are above USD 50 billion. The tougher US regulations must be followed by IHCs. In response, the European Union has recently introduced the capital requirements directive for prudential supervision (CRD) and the capital requirements regulation (CRR) that establish similar intermediate holding companies in the European Union.[18] Most jurisdictions have attempted to improve margin and collateral rules, and incentives to use central clearing platforms will help to reduce net risks (though many over the counter and risky derivatives are not suitable for this). But the level playing field principle remains elusive.

Two very important cross-border anomalies remain. One is that, from the outset, countries started from different financial system structures. Bank finance has been much more dominant in financing the economy in continental Europe, while capital markets have played a greater role in Anglo-Saxon countries. This means that a one-size-fits-all approach to regulation will not be able to fully satisfy policy makers in any jurisdiction. The same rule might be perceived to penalise banks and the economy too much in a bank-dominated region, compared to one where capital markets play a larger role. Regional competitiveness begins to creep into decision making. The writing of the rules and additional measures make for significant differences.[19] The United States has been better at moving to achieve its regulatory targets for capital than elsewhere, including with the Enhanced Supplementary Leverage Ratio.[20] Bank business model separation of risky activities has been implemented in some form in the United States and the United Kingdom, but this has not been seen as an imperative in the rest of Europe (where bank resistance to such measures so far has been successful).

The other issue is more technical in nature. Bank anticipation of the weak Basel II rules contributed to the crisis. Subsequently, fixing the system via Basel III kept the most problematic aspect of Basel II – namely the use of bank internal models to calculate risk weights, which introduces the moral hazard of putting into bank hands the means for them to affect the amount of costly capital they have to hold. Capital ratios, such as Basel Tier 1, apply not to bank total assets but to the smaller risk-weighted assets (RWA) that G-SIBs calculate with their own models – to determine a capital requirement that directly affects the return on equity for their shareholders. This moral hazard, together with different regulatory attitudes, results in diverging risk profiles between banks in different banking locations.

The RWA feature has been criticised by the OECD since the beginning of the crisis (see Blundell-Wignall and Atkinson, 2008 and 2010). G-SIBs have an incentive to use their internal models to minimise the holding of costly capital. Figure 2.11 shows the ratio of risk-weighted assets to total assets. A large sample of banks is used, consisting of G-SIBs and other large national banks. A fall in the ratio of risk-weighted assets to total assets (by definition) implies a rise in leverage[21], which is always the most attractive means for a bank to gear up its spreads (including synthetically via derivatives) for increasing profits. The G-SIBs in particular have targeted a reduction in this ratio (from 50% on average in 2003 to 34% by the time of the 2008 crisis, and much more extreme examples can be found on an individual bank basis). Non-G-SIB banks are less able to use internal models (the systems require sophisticated processes and derivatives for shifting exposures and "netting risks"). Quantitative impact studies have shown that each bank can have very different capital levels to support identical asset portfolios (all of their models differ, are used differently and cannot easily be verified and changed by supervisors).[22] This mechanism precisely precludes a cross-border level playing field.

Figure 2.11. **Ratio of risk-weighted assets to total assets: G-SIBs versus full universe of large banks, 2001-2016**

(Risk-weighted assets as a percentage of total assets)

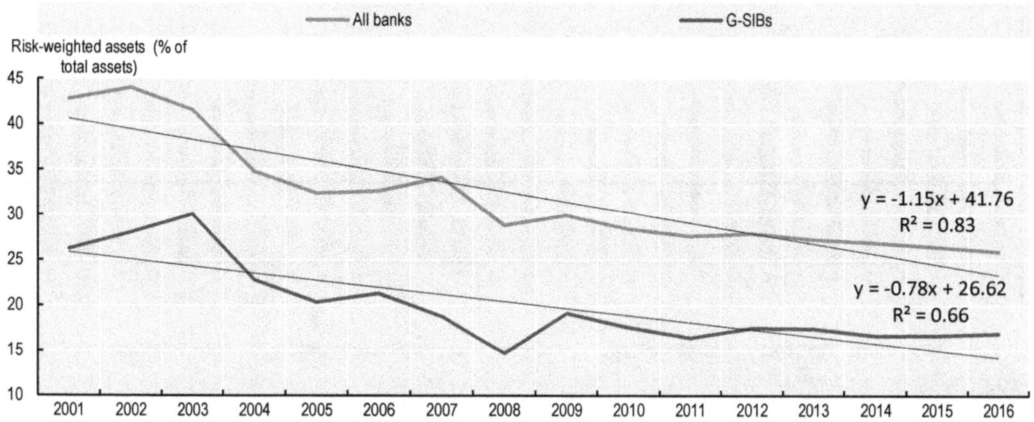

Notes: G-SIB stands for Global Systemically Important Bank. The sample includes 129 large global banks over the period 2001-2016. All G-SIBs listed by the Financial Stability Board (2016) are included. Based on Sarin and Summers (2016), the six US G-SIBs, the fifty largest US banks by 2016 assets, the fifty-five largest banks in the world ranked by market capitalisation (including European, Japanese and Australian G-SIBs and/or Domestic SIBs) and eighteen listed domestic systemically important European banks identified by the European Banking Authority. Following Ayadi et al. (2015), banks considered as systemic in this paper are the ones identifiable in the list of banks which are directly supervised by the ECB, non-Euro area EBA stress tested and Swiss banks with more than €30 billion. Chinese banks are excluded from the sample as state ownership involves different issues than for the ones relevant for the other banks considered in this paper. Financial statement data are collected from SNL Financials and Bloomberg. For consistency purposes, financial statements reported under GAAP accounting standards are adjusted to be comparable with IFRS basis.

Source: SNL Financials, Bloomberg, OECD calculations.

StatLink http://dx.doi.org/10.1787/888933476579

The United States depends less on banks and more on capital markets for funding companies, while national banks provide a larger share of US deposit and lending activities than G-SIBs compared to, for example, Europe. For this reason, and because Basel-favoured mortgages are often offloaded to Fannie Mae and Freddie Mac and not kept on bank balance sheets, the US banking system has a higher ratio of RWA/TA. It therefore has relatively more capital and less leverage. Converting US bank data on the basis of International Financial Reporting Standards (IFRS), so banks can be compared, the Core Tier 1 ratios (based on Basel RWA) and the simple leverage ratio (against total assets) are shown in the top and bottom panels of Figure 2.12, respectively, for the G-SIBs. The blue columns refer to 2008-2010 averages and the grey columns to 2015. For Core Tier 1 ratios (versus RWA), all G-SIBs comply easily. However, nearly half of the G-SIBs do not meet the OECD recommendation of a 5% minimum leverage ratio:[23] two investment banks in the United States, five universal banks in the Euro area, one in the United Kingdom, two in Switzerland, one in Sweden, and three in Japan.

This capital shortage in risky institutions remains a significant concern from a financial stability perspective. As Thomas Hoenig (2016) points out, US bank losses and the Troubled Assets Relief Program together were summed to be 6% of total assets of the US banks concerned (Hoenig, 2016). Since such an outcome actually happened in the recent past, even the OECD 5% rule would not have been enough to absorb the losses.

Figure 2.12. **Core Tier 1 risk-weighted capital ratio versus Basel III leverage ratio for G-SIBs, 2008-2016**

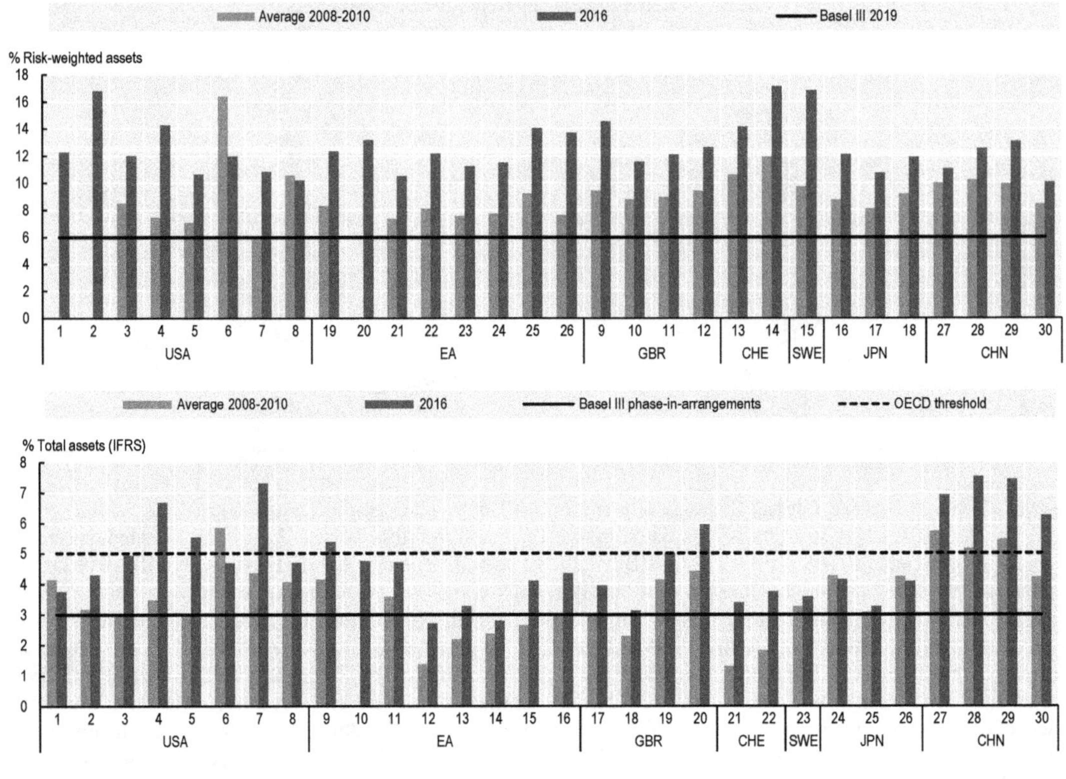

Note: USA: United States; EA: Euro Area; GBR: United Kingdom; CHE: Switzerland; SWE: Sweden; JPN: Japan; CHN: China. G-SIB stands for Global Systemically Important Bank. IFRS stands for International Financial Reporting Standards.

Source: Bloomberg, SNL Financials, OECD calculations.

StatLink http://dx.doi.org/10.1787/888933476588

Minimum floors that some market participants call "Basel IV"

For this reason, the Basel Committee has recommended a sensible modification (which some market commentators have begun to term "Basel IV"). The recommendation is that sophisticated banks using internal models should be subject to minimum floors versus the "standard approach" (based on external agency ratings of risk). For example, while models are always useful to assist banks in allocating capital according to the riskiness of loans (regardless of regulations), their use for the capital rule should be subject to floors in the ranges of 60% to 90% of the "standard approach".[24] In the recommendation, internal models should not be used at all for difficult-to-model activities (such as exposures to other financial institutions, to large companies, equities, and specialised lending). Floors are also to be used for market risk.

This proposal on "floors" and that to remove internal risk modelling as an option for operational risk[25] is contentious. The Basel Committee has been unable (at the time of writing) to obtain agreement on this modification, due to the opposition of virtually all of the larger global banks.[26] The Vice President of the European Commission in charge of (amongst other things) financial stability states in relation to this proposal:

> *"As things stand, the proposals Basel has issued for consultation would imply significant capital requirement increases in all areas. As far as the EU is concerned, there remains work to be done on a number of areas which are important for the EU economy. .... Latest data shows it undermines risk sensitivity and could lead to significant capital requirement increases. We want a solution that works for Europe and does not put our banks at a disadvantage compared to our global competitors. We believe such an agreement is in everyone's interest if we're to maintain a credible framework".*[27]

This statement, linking prudential policy to macroeconomic support and the competitive position of European banks, is not often stated as succinctly by a policy maker, but has long motivated lobbying for lighter prudential policy in Europe. Views expressed by EU banks include: European banks hold mortgages on balance sheet, whereas US banks offload them to the government-sponsored institutions Fannie Mae and Freddie Mac; US banks already use the standardised risk weights for mortgages, so Europe will suffer competitively compared to the United States by imposing floors; Europe is more dependent on bank finance than is the United States, with its deeper capital markets, and hence policy makers should be careful about imposing greater costs on the economy; that a binding higher leverage ratio would force banks to take on more risk (to meet ROE targets); and United States RWA capital rules for operational risk are more stringent and so they will suffer less than European banks from the proposed changes.[28]

The OECD has consistently recommended four key elements of crisis management and banking reform:[29]

- Insure all deposits in the crisis phase.
- Deal with any troubled assets first.
- Focus on a simple leverage ratio of at least 5% of the un-weighted (IFRS) balance sheet, and not to over-rely on the Basel risk-weighting approach.
- Separate derivatives and other high-risk investment banking activities from insured deposits on bank balance sheets, to avoid the latter subsidising the former activities (that contribute to the underpricing of risk).

The United States has more or less followed this sequence. Continental Europe chose not to use public money as aggressively to deal with troubled assets first and instead have seen non-performing loans rise in virtually every year since the crisis, in contrast to the United States where they have fallen. The US banking system is now safer and is lending to support the recovery and the Federal Reserve is raising interest rates. A stronger approach to dealing with bad loans and recapitalising banks is a prerequisite for sustainable growth.

More generally, bank capital requirements need to be based on the same accounting standards and a simple leverage ratio with a minimum of at least 5%. This would go a long way towards a level playing field that avoids regulatory competition and bank arbitrage based on regulatory differences. Arguments against this, on the grounds that internal models and risk-weighting are sufficient and the leverage ratio causes more risk taking, are not convincing. It is precisely because the leverage ratio does not distinguish between different levels of market, credit and operational risk (and instead focuses on banks having enough capital to absorb losses such as those of 2008 and to restrain leverage) that it is to be preferred. In an age where the scope for regulatory and tax arbitrage, financial innovation, cyber risk, fraud, bribery, corruption and money laundering are all very high, it is not plausible that banks' internal risk modelling can accurately capture this.[30]

Inconsistent regulation and balance sheet stress pushing risks into new locations

Inconsistent regulations give rise to incentives that cause cross-border holdings of banks and non-bank financial firms to move away from the more highly-regulated jurisdictions. Following a crisis, regions that permitted too much leverage beforehand find banks having to pull capital back from foreign subsidiaries in the presence of more balance sheet stress at home. This affects countries where cross-border bank finance had been important, and hence now requiring changes in business models there to "fill the gap". BIS data for cross-border banking business is shown in Figure 2.13.

The chart shows cross-border claims for banks by nationality (i.e. their cross-border counterparty claims by the "nationality" of the parent in their own country and by their own subsidiaries abroad), and by "location" (i.e. claims against all counterparties by local banks and by foreign subsidiaries operating in the home country location), all as a share of GDP. The difference between "nationality" and "location" in the United States is relatively small. The United Kingdom stands out with by "location" much higher than by "nationality", which is normal for a major financial centre like London.

The most striking feature of these data is the behaviour of cross-border claims of advanced banks before and after the crisis. Foreign claims of banks by nationality and by location rose strongly in the loose regulatory environment prior to the crisis, though this was more contained in the United States (rising by only 15% of GDP between 2000 and the peak of 25% in 2008 to 2009). Other countries expanded foreign claims much more rapidly, particularly the United Kingdom where they rose by around 100% of GDP on both measures, with the role of the City being a key factor. In Japan and Other Europe, a pre-crisis rise of around 60% of GDP is evident. Since the crisis, cross-border claims are falling in response to regulation and deleveraging: by 10% of GDP in the United States; and by about 60% to 70% of GDP on either measure in the United Kingdom, and 40% of GDP in Other Europe. Japan, whose financial crisis and related deleveraging was much earlier than 2008, appears to have been at least partly "filling the gap" left by the others in the post-crisis period, with cross-border claims rising by around 25% to 30% of its GDP.

The sharp fall in cross-border bank capital flows initially saw a fall in bank fund inflows into emerging markets. Subsequently, non-bank capital inflows picked up strongly to purchase emerging market debt in particular. At the same time, the credit stimulus in China required more domestic financing that has led Asian banks to do much more. Table 2.6 (in section 2.7 on underwriting activities) shows that investment banking activities in China and Asia, excluding Japan, are the big winners in taking global market share in debt and equity underwriting, syndicated loans and M&A. Falling market shares are seen in all main advanced country regions. As the authorities in China tried to rein in excessive credit demand in 2010, the strong financing needs of the economy caused an offsetting acceleration of off-balance sheet activity – shadow banking.

Figure 2.13. **External claims of banks by nationality versus location, 1990-2016**

(Per cent of GDP of each country or region)

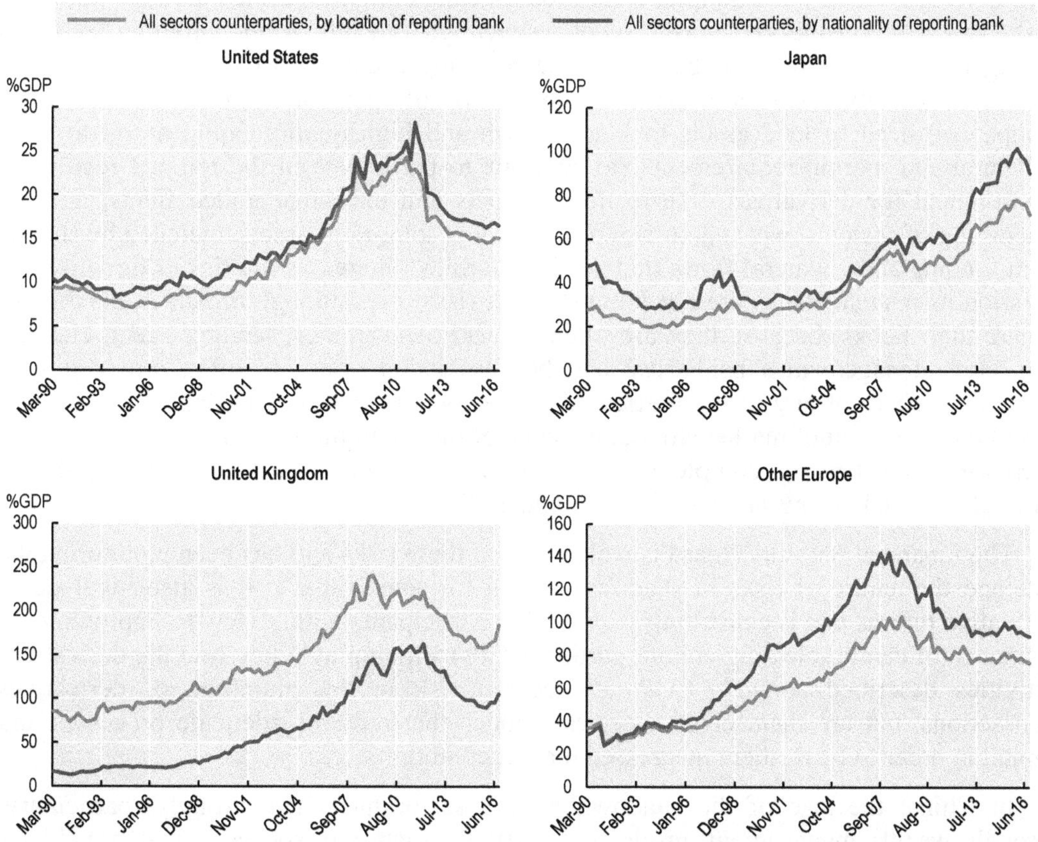

Notes: Other Europe refers to: Austria, Belgium, Cyprus, Denmark, France, Finland, Germany, Greece, Ireland, Italy, Luxembourg, Netherlands, Norway, Portugal, Spain, Sweden and Switzerland. "All sectors" means the cross-border positions of the reporting bank are vis-a-vis both banks and non-bank counterparties. By location of reporting bank refers to all BIS reporting banks operating in the country/region shown, both activities of the own-country and activities of foreign bank subsidiaries in that country. By nationality of reporting bank refers to own-country BIS reporting banks, activities in their own-country and those of their subsidiaries abroad.

Source: Bank for International Settlements, OECD calculations.

StatLink http://dx.doi.org/10.1787/888933476595

Re-regulation risks rolling into shadow banking and emerging markets

An increased shadow banking role has been important in advanced countries in response to the tougher regulations on banks. Banks are pressed by regulation, while investors are searching for higher yields. Banks have been forced to take less risk onto their own balance sheets, but lost revenue is made up via fees and/or margins associated with the increased role of and interaction with shadow banks. This latter term, for the purposes of this report, is defined as the main non-bank participants in the activities that might be described as the re-use of assets (i.e. asset managers and insurance companies involved in interacting with bank-related broker-dealers, lending agents, and custodians in securities lending, re-hypothecation, repurchase agreements and indemnification functions).

Non-bank financial institutions' attempt to lower costs and improve returns: buying more passive structured products; and via the re-use of assets through securities lending (see OECD, 2015c). For example, bank broker-dealers might intermediate between high-cash/low-yield businesses (cash funds, sovereign wealth funds, foreign reserves managers, etc.) that want to borrow higher-yielding securities to boost returns, while long-term-security businesses (investment arms of pension funds and insurance companies) need to lend assets to borrow cash and high quality liquid assets to meet collateral and margin requirements (to continue to participate in the tougher regulatory environment for derivatives,[31] structured products and exchange traded funds) and the smoothing of cash inflows and outflows. Lending of long-term assets, matched by shorter term funding and collateral flows that need to be rolled, increases the risk of liquidity and duration mismatch. Banks are not immune from risks, even though broker-dealers might square their books, because they are often owners of insurance, lending agent, clearing and asset management subsidiaries; and because indemnities are often provided with respect to failure of any of the parties. Many factors are involved in determining where risks lie in the event of market stress, and some of the "plumbing" for ETFs and securities borrowing and lending complexities are set out in more detail in OECD (2015c), particularly in Chapter 3 and Figures 3.13 and 3.18.

The Financial Stability Board is well aware of these risks and has been monitoring the size and the nature of risks in shadow banking for some time. [32] It is also involved in derivative refoms and is consulting with market participants with a view to improving the resilience of central clearing counterparties (CCPs) which play a key role the derivatives activities described above.[33] CCPs reduce net risk in the plumbing of derivatives transactions, but are themselves a central "node" that requires adequate processes and capital in order to be resilient in stressed market conditions.

In China, the size of the shadow banking sector has risen strongly, particularly through wealth management products (WMPs) which are special purpose vehicles managed by banks. WMPs allow banks essentially to shift assets and deposits off balance sheet in much the same way as occurred in advanced-country banks in the run up to the crisis (described in more detail below).

To examine how these developments might be shifting risks in the financial system, a set of tests were developed based on measuring the Distance-to-Default (DTD) for shadow banks in a manner parallel to the measure the OECD uses for banks – this compares the book value of a firm's liabilities with an estimate of the market value of its assets based on share price volatility characteristics.[34] The extent of contagion risk between banks and shadow banks in the post-crisis period is compared to that before 2008. The results are set out in full in Box 2.7. The findings suggest that contagion risk has been reduced in the tougher regulatory environment of the United States. This is not the case in other advanced countries, where contagion risk has either not been improved or deteriorated slightly (Australia, Europe, Japan and the United Kingdom). The most striking result, however, is the across-the-board deterioration of contagion risk in emerging markets. Before the crisis there were no statistically identifiable contagion links between banks and shadow banks (here taken to be asset management – including hedge funds – and insurance companies, which are investors in WMPs, and hence deal with bank sponsors and broker dealers). However, causation from banks to shadow banks, and vice versa, has become highly significant in the tests conducted for the post-crisis period.

Box 2.7. **Empirical evidence on risks being pushed into shadow banking**

A test on DTD relationships was conducted using Granger causality techniques for banks versus two shadow bank groupings: life insurance companies (with future liabilities such as annuities); and asset managers and hedge funds (that mix lending, retirement planning, investment management and insurance products). These are shown in Table 2.3 for the pre- and post-crisis regulatory periods. The hope is to see less causality between financial intermediaries in the post-crisis period.

Table 2.3. **Distance-to-default Granger causality tests for banks, asset managers, and insurance companies, 2000-2016**

Granger causality results using 30 days lags: Hypothesis variable in the left column does not cause the variable in the row. The dependent variable is the distance-to-default of banks.						
	Daily financial company data from 01-2000 to 12-2007			**Daily financial company data from 01-2008 to 06-2016**		
	DTD Assets managers	**DTD Life insurers**	**DTD Banks**	**DTD Assets managers**	**DTD Life insurers**	**DTD Banks**
United States						
DTD Assets managers	–	–	reject ***	–	–	no reject
DTD Life insurers	–	–	reject ***	–	–	no reject
DTD Banks	reject ***	reject ***	–	reject ***	reject ***	–
United Kingdom						
DTD Assets managers	–	–	no reject	–	–	reject ***
DTD Life insurers	–	–	reject ***	–	–	no reject
DTD Banks	reject ***	reject ***	–	reject ***	reject ***	–
Other Europe						
DTD Assets managers	–	–	reject ***	–	–	reject **
DTD Life insurers	–	–	reject ***	–	–	reject ***
DTD Banks	reject ***	reject ***	–	reject ***	reject ***	–
Japan						
DTD Assets managers	–	–	no reject	–	–	no reject
DTD Life insurers	–	–	reject ***	–	–	reject ***
DTD Banks	no reject	no reject	–	reject ***	reject ***	–
Australia						
DTD Assets managers	–	–	no reject	–	–	reject *
DTD Life insurers	–	–	no reject	–	–	reject **
DTD Banks	reject ***	reject ***	–	reject ***	reject ***	–
Brazil, Russia, India, Indonesia, China and South Africa						
DTD Assets managers	–	–	no reject	–	–	reject ***
DTD Life insurers	–	–	no reject	–	–	reject ***
DTD Banks	no reject	no reject	–	reject ***	reject ***	–

Source: Bloomberg, OECD calculations.

Box 2.7. **Empirical evidence on risks being pushed into shadow banking** (cont.)

For all countries the health of the banking system is (unsurprisingly) causal for all of the shadow banking sectors; but this is not always the case for the shadow banking groups versus banks.

- For the United States, the new regulatory environment is associated with reduced causality from banks to asset managers and insurance companies, in line with the objectives of financial regulation in general. This may be due to the tougher capital and separation rules.
- For Other Europe, two-way causation is present in the post-crisis period for all sectors, which may reflect some of the earlier discussion of the looser regulatory environment.
- In the United Kingdom, two-way causation is mostly present in the pre- and post-crisis period implying little improvement in contagion issues. Insurance companies appear to be less causal for banks since the crisis but asset managers more so.
- For Japan, there is a clear deterioration post-2008 from the bank DTD to both asset managers and insurance companies. Insurance companies DTD is causal for bank risk in both the pre- and post-crisis periods.
- In Australia, banks are a clear contagion risk for asset managers and insurance companies pre- and post-crisis. Contagion risk from asset managers and insurance companies to banks has increased to moderate significance since the crisis, though only at the 10% level for the asset manager sector.

The clearest deterioration has been in the BRIICS. Prior to 2008 there was no apparent causality from the shadow banking sector to banks or vice versa. Since the crisis there has been a marked change. In all cases, the hypothesis that the DTD of asset managers and insurance companies do not cause the DTD of banks is rejected at the 1% level. The causality from shadow banks to the banking system has increased. Similarly, the DTD of banks post-2008 is causal for the two shadow banking sectors. Consistent with the concern about rising debt in China discussed earlier, these findings suggest that the regulation and monetary policy processes are increasing risks more generally in the BRIICs economies.

The role of wealth management products in increased contagion risk

Chinese banks and shadow banks are by far the largest in the emerging country dataset and have a strong influence on the above findings. Increased contagion risk is a direct implication of the use of WMPs. According to the Peoples Bank of China Monetary Policy Implementation Report, off-balance sheet WMPs constituted CNY 26 trillion at the end of 2016, and has grown faster than social financing off-balance sheet items such as entrusted loans and bank acceptances (around CNY 25 trillion in 2016).[35] WMP assets constitute a large 35% of GDP. This activity took off after 2010 when the authorities tried to rein in credit expansion due to the crisis. Like advanced-country banks prior to the crisis, Chinese banks use WMPs to move deposits and loans off the balance sheet, thereby allowing them to avoid policy restrictiveness. It is also a useful way to shift doubtful loans out of reported bank non-performing loan (NPL) numbers. The higher yields are attractive to investors such as asset managers and insurance companies. WMPs are short-term in nature (3 to12 months) and must be rolled over to continue financing the longer-term and often illiquid asset side of the structure. There is little transparency on loan quality for investors who instead rely on the implicit guarantee that comes with management by state-owned banks. Other sources of contagion risk between banks and between banks and WMPs include strong cross ownership between the banks and shadow banks.

The acceleration of credit during the crisis and the off-balance sheet activity via WMPs has accommodated economic growth at a faster rate than otherwise. The total debt of non-financial companies, governments and households has grown explosively and is around 250% of GDP, almost in line with that of advanced economies (Figure 2.14). NPLs are rising and the inclusion of the China Banking Regulatory Commission "special mention" loans, plus those in WMPs, would push the numbers well above the officially acknowledged 1.81% NPL level at the end of Q4 2016. With respect to NPLs China has re-opened its non-performing loan securitisation market and is currently encouraging debt-for-equity swaps to try to reduce enterprise leverage. Many NPLs have been shifted to WMPs. There are many legal and practical issues to consider. Bank balance sheets include special mention loans rather than non-performing, and non-performing loans have been pushed off balance sheet to wealth management arms. A useful survey can be found in KPMG (2016).

Figure 2.14. **Indebtedness by sector in advanced and emerging economies, 2008-2016**

(Per cent of GDP of each country or group)

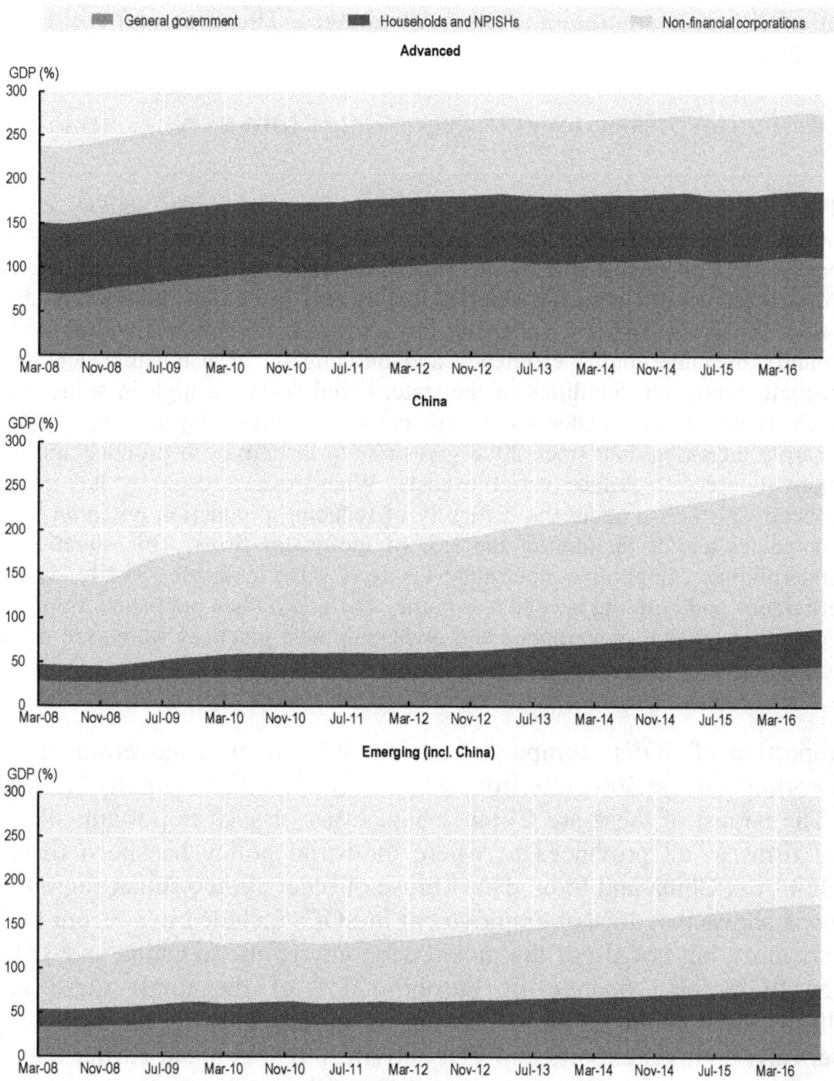

Note: NPISH stands for Non-Profit Institutions Serving Households.

Source: Bank for International Settlements, OECD calculations.

StatLink http://dx.doi.org/10.1787/888933476601

Dealing with the growing financial risks possibly explains the management of expectations for slower growth implicit in the new 5-year Plan. Financial measures under consideration to rein in WMPs, at the time of writing, include leverage caps and the setting aside of 10% of fees in a risk insurance pool. It will not be possible to deal with WMPs easily. In December 2016, the PBoC also decided, in its macro-prudential assessment to include off-balance-sheet WMPs for purposes of capital requirements in 2017.

In a sense, the Chinese economy with strong public investment drivers is bursting out of the financial repression constraints via WMPs, and dealing too quickly with them would be very damaging to the economy (for example a liquidity squeeze that interrupted the rollover process). A gradual approach, starting with future issues of WMPs, seems likely.

Implicit guarantees from state-owned enterprise (SOE) banks to WMPs give rise to moral hazard and the misallocation of investment. This theme is important more generally in the SOE sector when private-firm governance equivalence is not achieved because of government subsidies, guarantees and other advantages. This more general topic is taken up in section 2.5.

2.5 State-owned enterprises, level playing fields and excess capacity

> The third set of issues pertinent to fairness in cross-border activity concerns SOEs, which benefit from advantages of favourable funding from state-owned banks, most of them domiciled in Asia. This, and other forms of support, raises concerns about the terms on which SOEs are able to bid for global assets and set prices for market share in trade. But this also leads to problems within the home country by undermining efficiency and building up unsustainable debts which become contingent liabilities of the state. Fixed costs are high in some sectors, such as energy and materials, where emerging SOEs play an important role. Sharply increased debt since 2008 gives rise to incentives to produce and export more in order to reduce variable costs. Where excess capacity has emerged, concerns also arise about the difficulty of reducing production potential in these companies and/or facilitating the exit of inefficient firms. This situation risks undermining competitive neutrality vis-a-vis other countries, while damaging efficiency and building up debts at home. The OECD has published a number of guidelines for SOE governance and ownership best practices which are designed to deal directly with many of these issues.

The proportion of SOEs (companies having 50% or more government ownership) among the Fortune Global 500 grew from 9.8% in 2005 to 22.8% in 2014 (Kwiatkowski et al., 2015). The largest of these are Chinese banks that play an important role in funding state-owned firms in all provinces to where industrial policy has been delegated (see below). SOEs from China and India dwarf those of others in the Asian region: Chapter 3 in this *Outlook* shows that 46% of employment in SOEs included in a recent OECD study which covers most, but not all, of the global economy is due to China and 18% to India. While large SOEs also operate in Europe (21% of the total) these are mainly domestically-focused public utilities.[36] Asian SOEs are playing an increasingly large cross-border role, both via exports and FDI activities. It was noted earlier that China has increased its share of merchandise exports to 14% of the total in a short space of time and has also moved quickly to be 10% of global M&A outflows. India, Indonesia and Malaysia, which also have many domestic SOEs, have only managed together to capture 4% of world exports (shown in Figure 2.2).

Three issues are the "elephant in the room" when it comes to SOEs. First, they may benefit from an unfair edge in domestic as well as cross-border activities (via financial support that lowers the cost of capital, tax concessions, preferential treatment in public procurement, regulatory privileges that support monopoly advantages and legal immunities) that are not available to privately-owned competitors (competitive neutrality issues) at home and abroad. In terms of the firm-based trade theory discussed earlier, trade and investment economies of scale should favour the most efficient and innovative firms (and not be conferred by special advantages) if global productivity is to advance. Second, barriers to trade and investment mounted in response to perceived unfair practices directly block the expansion of firms through foreign sales also damaging the scope for productivity growth. Third, the incentives under which SOEs operate in some key sectors leads to excess capacity that becomes difficult to eliminate with potentially heavy costs for the home country in terms of efficiency and excessive debts. This undermines company returns, innovation and productivity. For these three reasons, it is in the interests of countries with significant SOE sectors to improve their governance with private company benchmarks for risk and return management in mind.

Figure 2.15. **Listed SOEs by sector in advanced and emerging economies, average 2002-2016**

(Per cent)

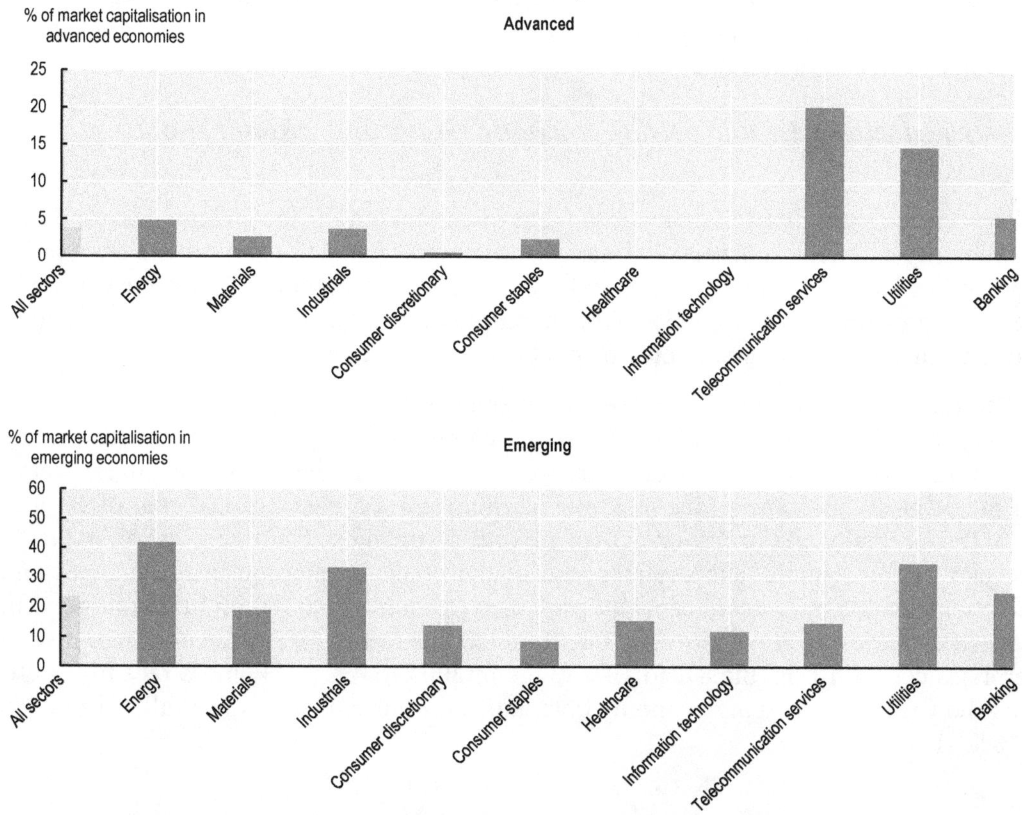

Note: These figures relate to listed companies where government holds 20% or more of the shares (for the most part, a lot more and often over 50%). Averages refer to the annual percent market cap shares over the period 2002-2016. Companies were drawn from a total pool of the 11 000 largest listed companies in the world and allocated to advanced or emerging economies.

Source: Bloomberg, OECD calculations.

StatLink http://dx.doi.org/10.1787/888933476611/

Figure 2.15 shows the share of the market valuations of listed SOEs versus the total market capitalisation (SOE and private companies) of the Global Industry Classification Standard (GICS) sector shown, for advanced and emerging economies.[37] In advanced economies (top panel) government ownership is fairly small outside of the natural monopoly sectors (utilities and telecommunications). On average, around 23% of the market capitalisation in emerging economies (second panel) are SOEs (defined as 20% or higher state ownership), and most industrial sectors are involved, in contrast to the advanced country SOEs.

The SOEs in China included in this sample (not shown individually) are closer to a 40% average share of the total market capitalisation of the companies in the China Bloomberg benchmark (with shares often owned by sovereign wealth and pension funds).[38] From 1978, China embarked on a process of reforms: combining capital account and exchange rate management policies with its own hybrid model of central planning for industries starting first with experiments in agriculture. While the Soviet Union chose economy-wide planning, China's reforms permitted a more flexible regional structure for governance of its SOEs, with self-contained local governments responsible for a wide array of production decisions (Qian and Xu, 1993). As economic liberalisation gained hold, and a large number of government activities were corporatised, this also became the model for the Chinese SOE sector. What began with agriculture was extended to other sectors with a success that has put China at the top of world growth league tables for a very long time (Allen et al., 2005).

State-owned enterprise and private company return and cost of capital comparisons

The return on equity (ROE) versus the cost of capital (COK, the weighted share of the cost of equity and debt in the firm's financial structures) for SOEs and private companies is shown in Figure 2.16 for both advanced and emerging economies.[39] This measure will reflect any pressures from two sides: that on margins caused by excess capacity (affecting ROE) and financial structure affected by debt and equity choices.

The return on investment is higher on average for both SOEs and private firms in advanced economies – companies with state shareholdings appear in line with private firms. Within the emerging economy group, returns versus the COK are lower overall than in advanced economies (due to lower margins and a higher average cost of capital) and SOEs normally perform worse than private companies. Chinese companies are a large part of this sample, and the response to the crisis in ramping up investment and production exacerbated excess capacity pressures (discussed below) on price margins. In advanced countries, ROE versus the COK for a large selection of private and state-owned enterprises declined from the 8% to 10% range in 2005 to 4% to 6% more recently. ROE minus the COK for emerging economy companies on the same basis has fallen from 4% to 6% to -1% to 1%.

Figure 2.16. **Return on equity minus the cost of capital for private non-financial companies versus SOEs in advanced and emerging economies, 2002-2016**

(Per cent)

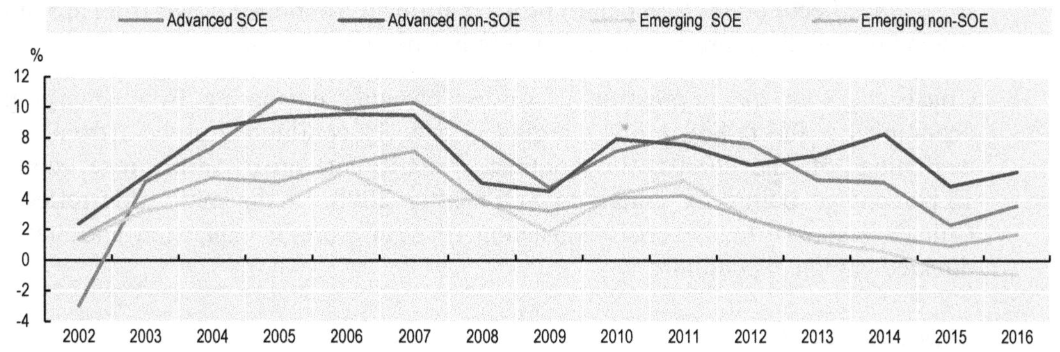

Source: Bloomberg, OECD calculations.

StatLink http://dx.doi.org/10.1787/888933476628

Figure 2.17. **Profit margins and leverage for private non-financial companies versus SOEs in advanced and emerging economies, 2002-2016**

(Per cent)

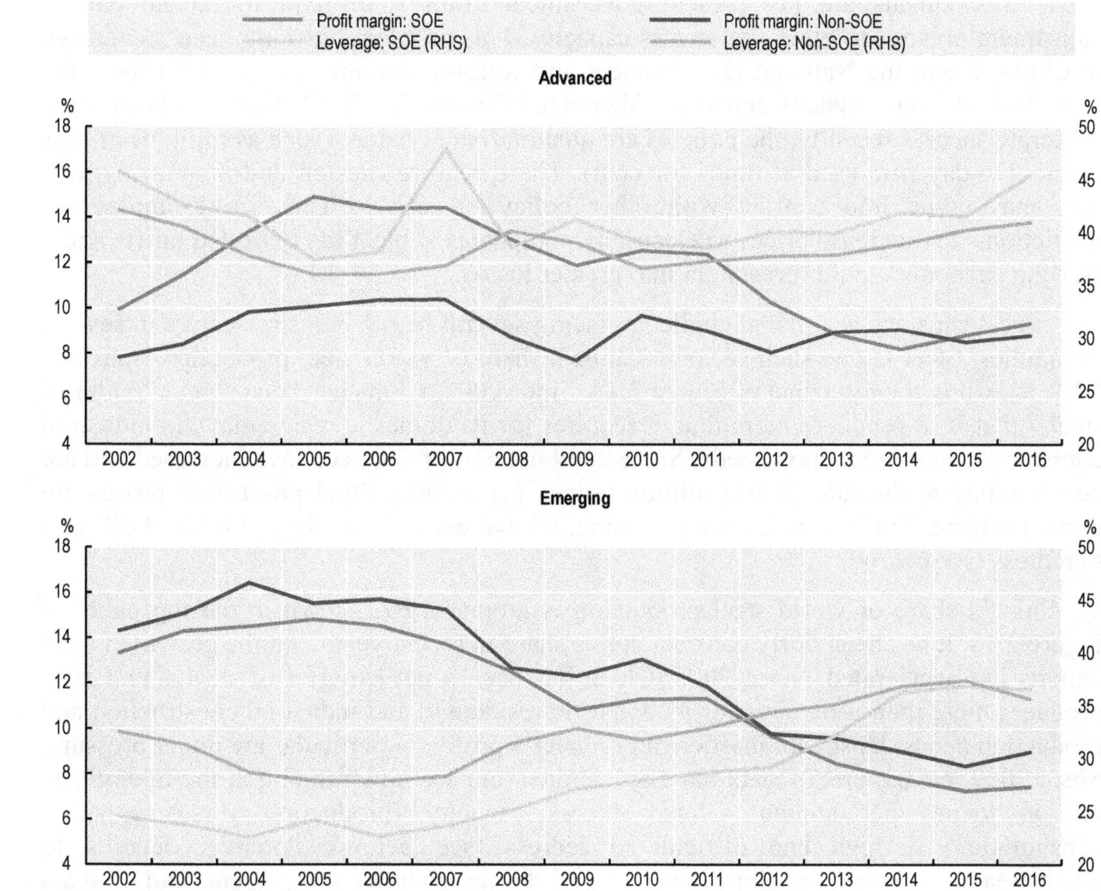

Note: RHS stands for Right Hand Scale.

Source: Factset, Bloomberg, OECD calculations.

StatLink http://dx.doi.org/10.1787/888933476634

Company profit margins (net income divided by total revenue) and company leverage (long-term debt divided by enterprise value)[40] are shown in Figure 2.17. Advanced and emerging economies are shown in the two panels:

- In advanced economies (top panel) profit margins have moved down from around 8% in 2005 to 4% more recently, and debt has been reasonably stable.
- Consistent with the impression of excess capacity emanating from emerging economies is the falling profit margins in a fairly continuous process from the beginning of the 2000s. In contrast, debt-to-enterprise value rose some 13 percentage points for emerging SOEs after 2008. In the main, this reflects China's response to the crisis consisting of strong credit expansion and state-directed capital expenditure.

Excess capacity issues

Exits of inefficient firms from industries and/or bankruptcies are expected consequences of sound competitive processes. If there are barriers to exit of inefficient firms because of inherent market failures or as a result of the actions of governments, then there will be adverse implications for domestic and international competitors. China's institutional set-up relies on local government implementation of the central government industrialisation mandates.[41] The problem is that when market-based efficient "exit" mechanisms are not present governments find it difficult to dictate painful adjustment policies to eliminate excess capacity. This problem has long been recognised in China, where the National Development and Reform Commission (NDRC) for some years looked to cut capacity across a wide range of industries. While there has been some moderate success recently, the policies are quantitative in nature (such as millions of tons or the 276-day rule used at times for coal). These require suasion and monitoring, and they may come into conflict with other policy objectives. Thus for example coal restrictions that increase prices to electricity companies subject to controlled tariffs and a slowing economy would force them into greater losses.

Excess capacity is a global challenge facing several heavy industry sectors in several economies. Steel is one such sector.[42] China's share of world steel production is around 50%, shown in the top panel of Figure 2.18. Since 2005, China has been a net exporter of steel – that is, it produces more than it requires for its domestic residential and industrial construction and production needs. Since 2009 net exports of steel have increased and are now running at the rate of 100 million tonnes per annum. Steel producers' profits are under pressure. Trade frictions are mounting. Global excess capacity is high and difficult to redress (see below).

China's share of world steel production is around 50%, shown in the top panel of Figure 2.18. It has been fairly constant at this share in recent years, but the growth of steel exports has accelerated. Since 2005, China has been a net exporter of steel – that is, it produces more than it requires for its domestic residential and industrial construction and production needs. Upstream inefficient producer's profits in particular are under pressure. Since 2009, net exports of steel have accelerated and are now running at the rate of 100 million tonnes per annum. Global excess capacity (production versus apparent consumption) is high and difficult to redress (see below). Potential benefits to downstream producers are limited where anti-dumping duties are present, and China's export destinations have had to be redistributed to places like the Middle East and some parts of Asia.

With respect to petroleum, in 2015 China produced around 215 million tonnes of crude oil and imported 336 million tonnes. Normally, such a high level of imports would be required to meet excess demand for running the fuel needs of the domestic economy. However, China has become a net exporter of refined petroleum products (distillates) as shown in the bottom panel of Figure 2.18 – a trend that accelerated for kerosene and diesel after 2011. The refining industry is dominated by Sinopec and PetroChina, and their trading arms (ChinaOil and Unipec) have stepped up their presence in global trading platforms with a view to becoming more dominant in global benchmarks (see Oxford Institute for Energy Studies, 2016). Part of the reason for this is that, since 2013, competition has been encouraged in the regional independent producers ('Teapots') to create more competition for Sinopec and PetroChina – granting them licences to import crude oil (allowing them to produce petrol and jet fuel instead of refining only low-quality fuel oil). The success of this (and the absence of an exit strategy for weaker producers) has led to over-supply, causing the government to increase the export quota for all petroleum products in general (see United States Energy Information Administration, 2016).

Figure 2.18. **China's production and export of steel and refined petroleum, 2004-2016**

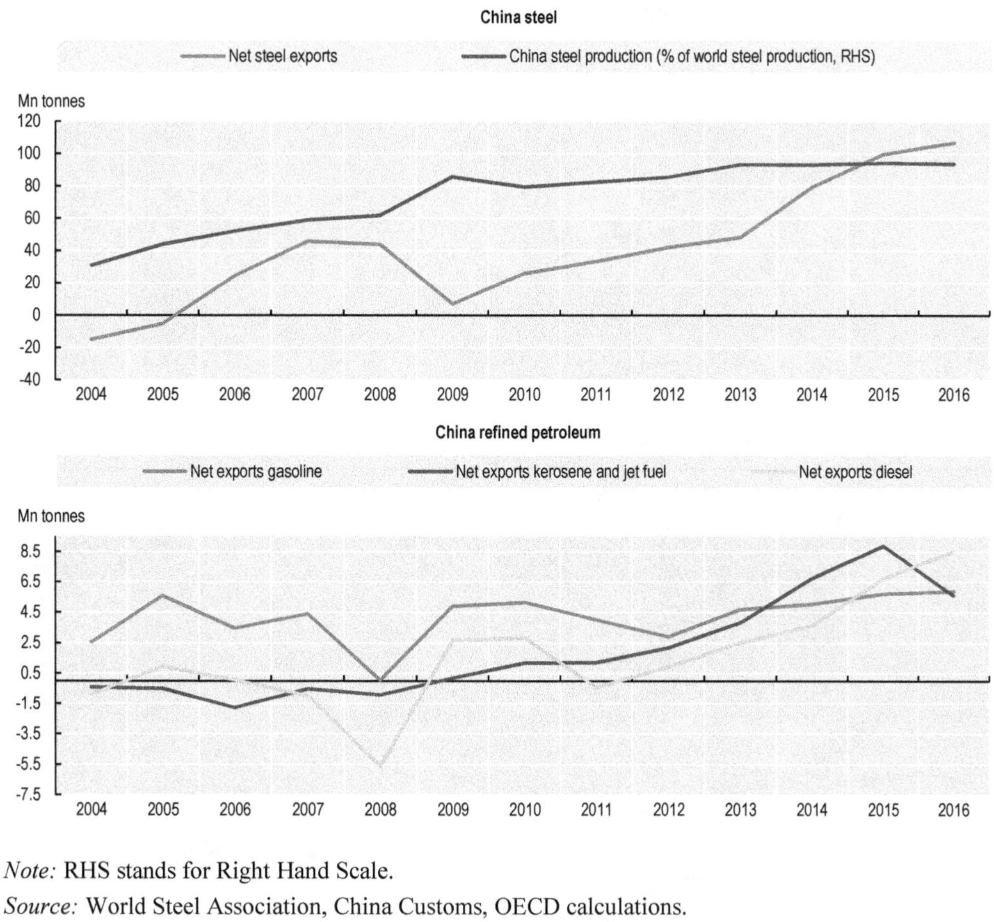

Note: RHS stands for Right Hand Scale.

Source: World Steel Association, China Customs, OECD calculations.

StatLink http://dx.doi.org/10.1787/888933476642

It is in the energy and materials sectors that profit margins have declined the most in the global company database since 2007, as shown in Figure 2.19. For the energy sector the sharp dip in the most recent years was partly due to the fall in oil prices which affected all players. In the case of China, SOEs in the Materials Sector (that includes steel) have profit margins at around zero.

The issues are more generic than steel and petroleum problems alone. The development of China's solar photovoltaic panel industry is an instructive example of a few years ago, but most industries are subject to similar dynamics.[43] China's Ministry for Industry and Information Technology (MIIT) has had targets for removing excess capacity across around 19 industries in recent years, and particularly in steel, ferrous alloys, iron, paper, flat glass and coking coal. For example, by 2020 steel capacity is to be cut by 100-150mt while upgrading the industry, according to Government plans. Cuts are hard to enforce. High fixed costs and SOE debt obligations give rise to incentives to increase production in order to reduce variable costs. There is concerted resistance to reform from SOE managers, trade unions and local politicians in regions which would have to face the employment and financial consequences of shutting down plants. This suggests there is a need for the reform of the governance of SOEs along more market-oriented lines.

Figure 2.19. **Profit margins for non-financial companies operating in the sectors of energy and materials (incl. steel), 2002-2016**

(Per cent)

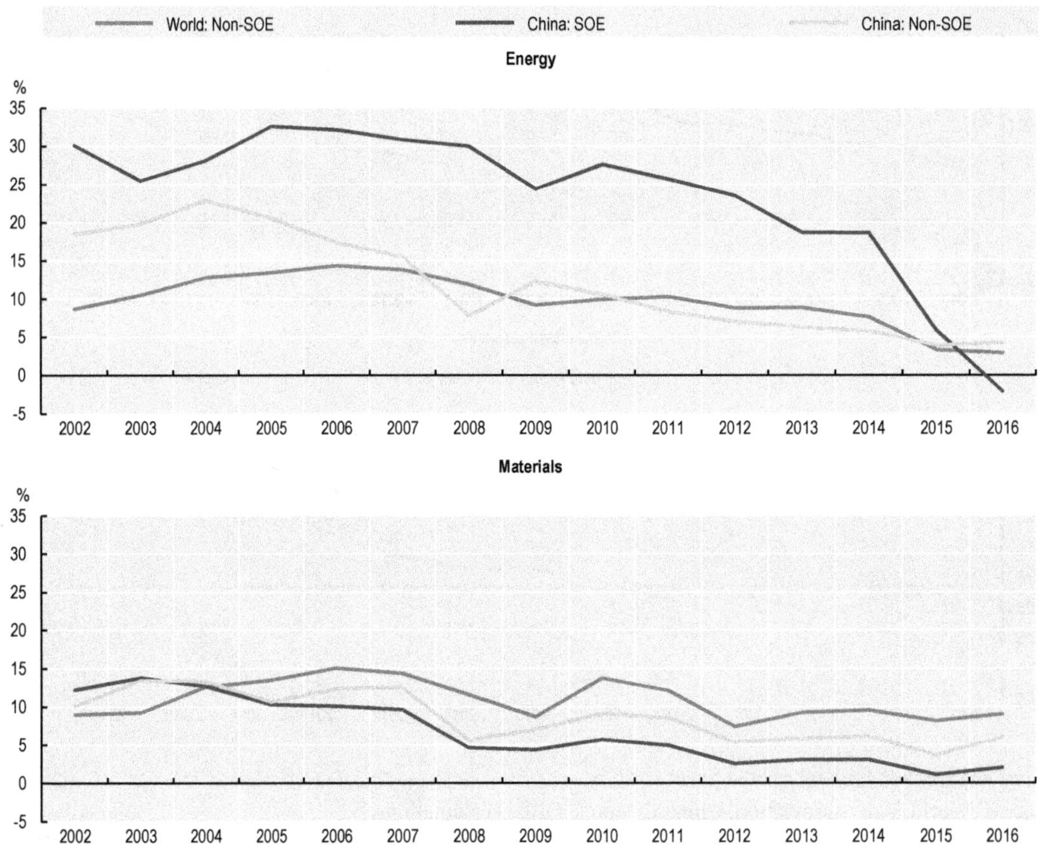

Note: The free market non-SOEs are affected more by the decline in oil prices in 2015.

Source: Factset, Bloomberg, OECD calculations.

StatLink http://dx.doi.org/10.1787/888933476653

Anti-dumping indications

Data on anti-dumping initiations and measures taken by reporting WTO members against the exporters, shown on the left side of Figure 2.20 (for the period 1995-2015) suggest that excess capacity pressures have been building. Steel is a large concern. Economies targeted in more than 100 anti-dumping initiations (all sectors, included) since 1995 include Brazil, China, European Union, Germany, India, Indonesia, Japan, Korea, Russia, Chinese Taipei, Thailand, the United States, . Some of these are retaliatory in nature. Initiations and measures against China make up by far the largest group and they have been accelerating – 46 new initiations were taken against China in the first half of 2016.

Figure 2.20. **Global anti-dumping trade initiations and measures taken, 1995-2015**

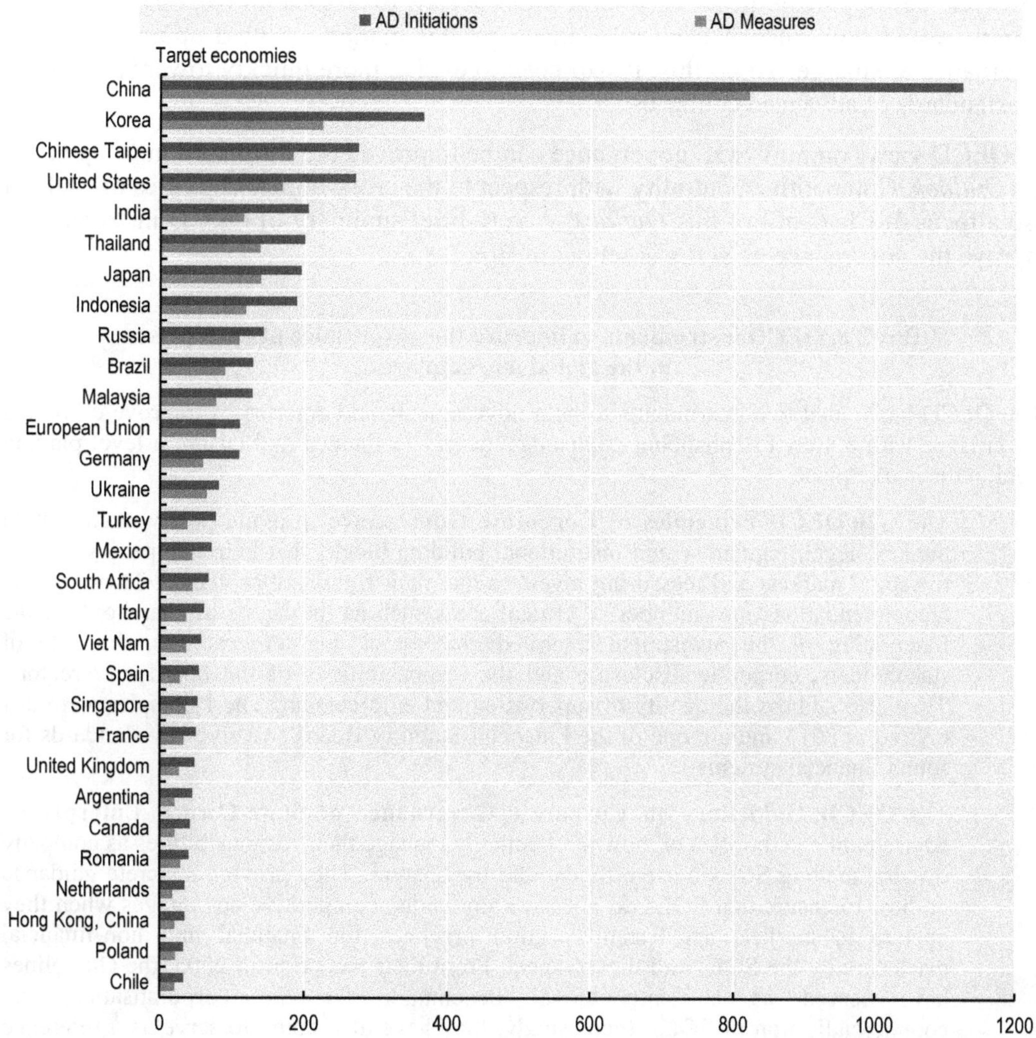

Source: World Trade Organization, OECD calculations.

StatLink http://dx.doi.org/10.1787/888933476665

It is unclear how the export orientation of excess capacity sectors in China will be dealt with from the 13th Five Year Plan. According to the Oxford Institute for Energy

Studies (2016), as a part of the "Openness" guiding principle of that plan, the government intends to promote more outbound investment through the "Belt and Road Initiative". This is likely to see many over-capacity industries pursue more overseas opportunities.

The governance of SOEs in the global marketplace

SOE reform in a number of countries has further to go before a level playing field, and the ability to exit markets in the manner of fully private companies, is achieved.[44] Policies that provide artificial state support to companies competing in the global market place and which do not allow for market discipline and the exit of less efficient firms hurt their own economies and those of their neighbours through the misallocation of resources, excess capacity and the deterioration on returns on investment.

China is a highly successful and increasingly developed country on many criteria. However, developments in its very large SOE sector, discussed above, suggest that the country would now benefit from allowing a greater market-oriented approach to their governance to emerge. To do this, it will need to evolve more quickly towards the norms and standards of advanced countries.

OECD views on how SOE governance can be improved are discussed in Chapter 3 of this *Outlook*. Competitive neutrality with respect to the cross-border activities of SOEs, is also a focus of Chapter 4 of this *Outlook*. A very brief summary of OECD instruments to improve the governance of SOEs is set out in Box 2.8.

Box 2.8. **OECD instruments to improve the governance of enterprises in the global marketplace**

The OECD has issued two instruments to help governments and enterprises improve corporate governance with a view to enhancing companies' access to finance and ensure a level playing field in the marketplace:

- The **G20/OECD Principles of Corporate Governance**[1] provide policy makers with the key, legal, regulatory and institutional building blocks that help companies' access to capital markets and reassuring investors that their rights are protected. They provide recommendations in a number of critical areas such as the rights of shareholders, the functioning of the investment intermediation, stock market practices, the role of stakeholders, corporate disclosure and the responsibilities of the board of directors. They also address the quality of supervision and enforcement. The Principles were last revised in 2015 and are one of the Financial Stability Board's twelve key standards for sound financial systems
- The **OECD Guidelines on Corporate Governance of State-Owned Enterprises**[2] advise public authorities on how to effectively manage their responsibilities as company owners, making SOEs more efficient and transparent. They provide concrete guidance on how to ensure that SOEs do not have any undue competitive advantages when they operate in markets and establish good practices for financial and non-financial disclosure by the SOEs and their owners. From their inception in 2005, the Guidelines have served as an international benchmark for the corporatisation and commercialisation of SOEs. Increasingly, they have also come to serve as a reference for international trade and investment regulators for assessing internationally active SOEs. The Guidelines were last revised in 2015.
- A full discussion of SOE and state aid issues is presented in Chapter 3.

1. www.oecd.org/corporate/principles-corporate-governance.htm
2. www.oecd.org/daf/ca/guidelines-corporate-governance-soes.htm

2.6 Globalisation, competition and cross-border cartels

> The fourth set of level playing field issues concerns the interplay between multinational firms (benefitting from trade, technology and economies of scale) and the consumers of their products. Sometimes collusion through cross-border cartels can deny the benefits of globalisation being passed on to consumers and instead artificially high prices will mostly benefit profits and share owners. Cartel overcharges are substantial. They hurt consumers (overcharges often involve necessities) and contribute to poor perceptions of globalisation. The import competition-exposed worker is hit twice in a sense: via employment and wage remuneration, while paying higher prices for essential goods and services. OECD instruments on dealing with hard core cartels, bid-rigging and ways to enhance co-operation between competition agencies are designed to help level the playing field.

Open markets with heterogeneous firms are, in principle, pro-competitive. International sales and the deployment of technology allow these firms to expand, take advantage of economies of scale and compete with each other in global markets. This competition between multi-national firms should discipline monopoly elements in the domestic economy, improve competition there and reduce prices (squeezing excess margins and promoting business restructuring). Successful firms drive out inefficient firms, and their exit creates more scale opportunities for the more efficient companies that remain or dynamic new firms that enter. This constant "scaling" causes productivity to rise further.[45] These mechanisms have introduced competition and reduced prices in most major traded goods (automobiles, clothing, textiles footwear, electronics, etc.). Consumers also benefit from greater choice from international suppliers. From the perspective of the rebuff to globalisation, however, two issues are of particular relevance. The first concerns cross-border cartels which deny consumers the benefits of globalisation. The second concerns the implications for competitive neutrality of cross-border activities of SOEs.

Cross-border cartels

Companies that benefit from openness may also block the gains from trade accruing to consumers by forming international cartels. Cartels are designed to keep prices higher than they should be and extract rents that hurt consumers. In terms of the globalisation debate, this affects low-income families least able to afford higher prices on necessities relatively more (such as banking, pharmaceuticals, transport, retail services and white goods). In a sense, the import competition-exposed worker would be hit twice: via job and wage pressures as well as by paying higher prices for essential goods and services. Addressing the issue of competition is therefore also important to ensure the appropriate governance of globalisation: i.e. companies should not divert the gains from trade and investment via monopolistic practices and cartels.

This is no small issue:[46]

- 240 cross-border cartels were detected and fined between 1990 and 2015 (Figure 2.21).
- Total sales affected by cross-border cartels from 1990 to 2015 (and hence in injury to customers) were approximately USD 7.5 trillion.[47]

- Cartel overcharges are, on average, a very high 20% of sales.[48] Applying this overcharge to USD 7.5 trillion sales, would amount to USD 1.5 trillion in rents extracted and passed on as a direct injury to consumers. This likely understates the total amount, as cartel conduct that ceased as a result of commitment decisions, where no fines were levied, is not included. Furthermore, average overcharges have been estimated in some studies to exceed 50% of sales.[49]
- Detecting and dealing with cartels is both difficult and time consuming. In the European context, 113 cases dealt with by the EU Commission and analysed by Hellwig and Hüschelrath (2016) over the period 2001 to 2015, involved 600 firm groups, an average cartel duration of 87 months (with typically long investigation periods) and an average of around 5 countries involved in cartels in any one year. The complexity and cross-border nature of cartels make them difficult to analyse and the need for comity and co-operation is essential.
- The income distribution and wealth effects are substantial – global cartels essentially impose a regressive tax on consumers. They transfer the income from consumers to the managers of the companies involved and their shareholder owners. These take the form of stock dividends, management salaries and bonuses, and stock price appreciation.

Connor (2016) states:

"In sum, global cartels are the worst of the worse: bigger in sales size, covering more territory and jurisdictions, and causing greater injuries to their customers. Although antitrust authorities are moving in the right direction, global schemes are penalised less severely on average by antitrust authorities than their greater injuriousness would warrant." (See fines in Figure 2.21)

Figure 2.21. **Cross-border cartels detected and fined between 1990 and 2015**

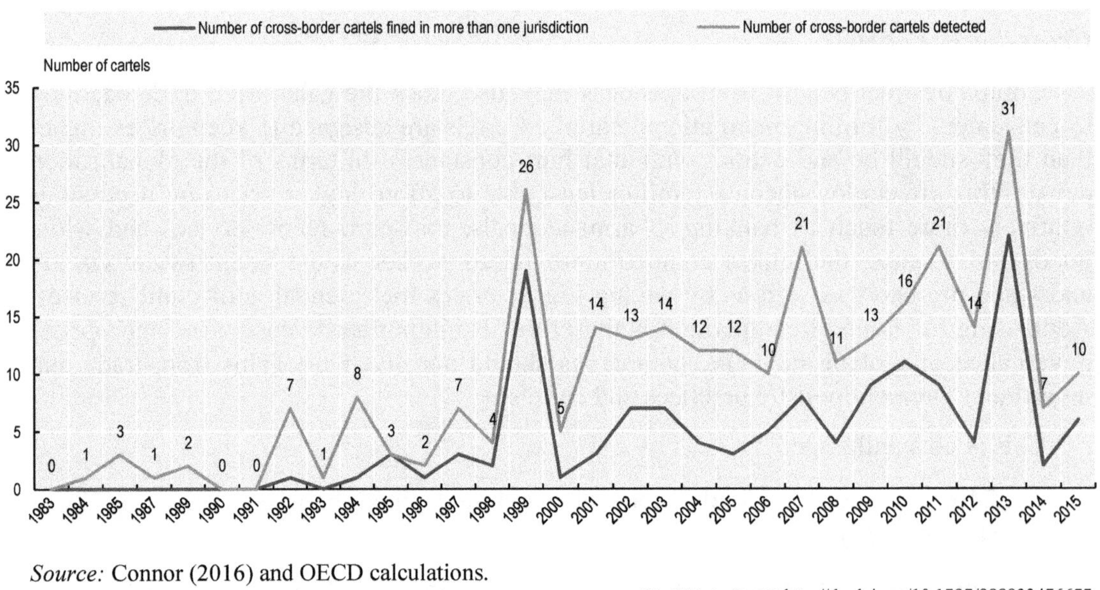

Source: Connor (2016) and OECD calculations.

StatLink http://dx.doi.org/10.1787/888933476677

Global cartels, trade patterns and rent extraction

The issue of corporate collusion then is also a critical factor affecting the face of globalisation: as firms expand internationally to take advantage of scale economies and improve their efficiency, the scope of potential collusion, which prevents efficiency gains from being passed on to consumers, will also expand.

These global cartels are more likely to be formed when goods are homogeneous, there are multi-market interactions, fixed costs are high and demand is relatively inelastic. The implications for trade structures can take any number of forms.

- Large firms may act collusively via geographical specialisation in markets adjacent to where production facilities are set up (for example, in Asia, North America and Europe) due to the standard "gravity" factors (proximity which reduces transport costs and GDP size). These may appear as domestic oligopolies when, in fact, they exist via global collusion.
- Transport costs have fallen (standardisation of container shipping and the growing importance in value of trade in technology and pharmaceutical products that can be shipped by air, while financial services have no "hauling" costs at all). This may encourage other forms of geographic collusion – replicating collusive agreements in multiple markets and geographies tacitly or explicitly.[50]

Many categories of homogeneous goods permit multi-market interaction between competitors. Cross-border cartels are particularly common in the industries set out in Table 2.4. This excludes OPEC, which is an agreement between sovereign states (not a typical cartel), and is outside the scope of competition law. In the European region, manufacturing constitutes 89 of the 113 European Commission cases studied by Hellwig and Hüschelrath (2016). "Transport and storage" and "finance and insurance" were the next most frequent industry groups where cartels were investigated.

Table 2.4. **Cross-border cartels by industry, 1984-2015**

(Per cent of total cases)

Sector	%
Machinery, including electrical and parts	17.6
Organic chemicals, other than pharmaceuticals	13.4
Transport services	11.4
Finance, insurance, banking	7.2
Rubber and plastic	7.2
Electronic devices, including computers	5.9
Stone, clay, graphite, glass products	4.5
Fabricated metal products	4.5
Others	28.3

Source: OECD analysis of the cartels contained within the Private International Cartels Dataset.

The finance sector has some characteristics that make it a favourable environment for collusion – transport costs are zero, product components are perfectly homogeneous, there are potential multi-market interactions between firms, and demand by ultimate consumers is inelastic in many instances (e.g. mortgages, credit cards). Furthermore, since open competition in provision of financial products would drive out all excess returns, the attraction of collusion is also very high. The cases of high identical fees in underwriting initial public offerings and the increasing dominance of the multiple lead underwriter model (involving several large cross-border financial institutions) is discussed in section 2.7. Such behaviour drives the cost of capital up for investors, which works against capital expenditure and productivity growth (see Figures 2.16 and 2.17). LIBOR fixing and suspected collusion in the pricing of some derivatives (credit default swaps and foreign exchange derivatives) are other cases in point. Bank collusion in such pricing directly diverts income from clients to dividends and bonuses, while at the same time affecting the cost of mortgages, personal credit, student loans, pension fund fees and the cost of capital.

Detailed studies of cross-border cartels, with respect to trade sharing and price overcharging, are not available for all industries, but pharmaceuticals have been studied in some depth. Pharmaceuticals are a particularly important item of household consumption which affects the cost of healthcare insurance. Patents sometimes give rise to accusations of "gouging" – sometimes justified and sometimes not.[51] There is always ample scope for collusion, since the products are characterised by inelastic demand, multi-market interactions and homogeneity. The viability of healthcare systems can be affected by high pharmaceutical prices. A recent detailed study of chemicals and pharmaceutical products illustrates some features of the interaction between trade and cartel activity (Levenstein et al., 2015). The products studied were chosen because the cartels were detected and broken up by authorities, allowing sufficient detailed information to be accessed by researchers (summarised in Table 2.5).

Table 2.5. **Examples of cartels and trade patterns in pharmaceuticals**

	% Price decline after breakup	HHI concentration index: scale 0-1 (above 0.18 implies concentrated market)		Mean number of partners (3-6 cartel members but produce from multiple locations implying greater number of "partners")	
	Post-breakup	Pre-breakup	Post-breakup	Pre-breakup	Post-breakup
Citric Acid	-7.6	0.29	0.28	15.5	15.0
Methionine	-29.0	0.44	0.35	9.3	9.8
MCAA	-31.3	0.45	0.45	9.1	9.2
Vitamin A	-29.5	0.42	0.37	11.6	11.9
Vitamin B1	-39.6	0.43	0.54	8.9	9.8
Vitamin B2	-30.8	0.42	0.43	9.6	10.4
Vitamin B3	-36.4	0.42	0.36	11.1	11.9
Vitamin B4	-23.3	0.45	0.42	10.2	10.3
Vitamin C	-51.3	0.29	0.31	14.4	14.3
Vitamin A	-86.8	0.37	0.32	12.1	14.3

Note: HHI refers to the Herfindahl-Hirschman concentration index (a number of above 0.18 is usually taken to be high concentration). Methionine is an amino acid important in the growth of new blood vessels and is used in treatment for: Parkinsons, alcoholism and drug withdrawal, various classes of depression, radiotherapy, asthma, etc. MCAA refers to the chemical monochloroacetic acid which is used in crop protection amongst others.

Source: Levenstein et al. (2015), OECD calculations.

In the event of detection and remedies, the prediction from such arrangements is that breaking up the cross-border cartel should: (i) cause prices to fall; and (ii) have little impact on the structure of trade and concentration (since overheads, the size and proximity of markets and agglomeration linkages remain as relevant export and FDI factors). This is consistent with the results in Table 2.5. The price falls in the four years following the breakup of the cartel, shown in the left column of Table 2.5, are (with the exception of citric acid) within a 23% to 87% range, mostly well above the average over-charge of 20% for all identified global cartels noted earlier. The columns to the right show that the trade and concentration measures are broadly unchanged (detection can leave scale economies in place but without collusion).

Competition policy and competitive neutrality

SOEs and the problem of competitive neutrality, mentioned earlier in section 2.5, also raise important issues for competition policy. Domestic competition laws can be enforced with respect to domestic SOEs, provided governments choose not to promote national champions and insist on governance standards equivalent to those of private firms. However, this may not apply to the presence of an SOE operating in a foreign jurisdiction. It is extremely difficult to assess the benefits available to such firms through financial, tax and regulatory privileges that generate artificial scale economies and a less-than-market cost of capital. Instruments are available to address the issues, such as "public interest reviews" in merger control (that can be requested by domestic competitors) and "foreign investment reviews" that can be used to block FDI. Achieving the right balance between outright protectionism and competitive neutrality is extremely difficult without comity, accounting transparency and full regulatory co-operation.

Difficulties in the administration of competition policy have increased with globalisation. Large firms that operate in global markets are harder to monitor since, historically, competition law and policies (the European Union notwithstanding) have been organised on a national basis. Consequently, international firms will be subject to the competition laws of other countries and this complexity increases the scope for anti-competitive activities. When the scope for cartel activity is greater than the coverage, cooperative arrangements and resources of competition authorities to detect and deal with them, cartels will continue to flourish and divert income from low-income consumers to share owners. Similar comments apply to cross-border SOEs and competitive neutrality.

OECD instruments to deal with cartels and the related issue of bid rigging are summarised briefly in Box 2.9. Chapter 4 of this *Outlook* takes up these issues and others in more detail, including:

- The extent to which detection and prosecution gaps may be due to jurisdictional challenges, barriers to competition authority information collection, and limitations to competition authority cooperation in cartel investigations.
- The need for governments to address competition distortions through taxation, and SOE policies that are not consistent with competitive neutrality. Export cartels are also discussed.
- Public interest review mechanisms for foreign investment.

Box 2.9. **OECD instruments that tackle cross-border anticompetitive business conduct**

The OECD has developed several instruments to help governments better detect and prosecute cartel conduct:

- The OECD Recommendation concerning Effective Action against Hard Core Cartels[1] sets out a common approach to cartels which, as the Recommendation notes, is important because of the market power, waste and inefficiency in international trade that cartels create. This Recommendation calls for adherents to ensure their competition laws effectively halt and deter hard core cartels by providing for effective sanctions, and ensuring enforcement procedures and institutions are adequate to detect and remedy hard core cartels (including powers to obtain information and impose penalties for non-compliance).
- The OECD Guidelines for Fighting Bid Rigging in Public Procurement[2] contain practical tools to assist governments with the detection and prevention of bid rigging, where firms conspire to raise prices or lower the quality of goods or services they provide to governments. Without established processes and a clear understanding of bidder behaviour, laws against bid-rigging can be challenging to enforce. The *Guidelines* illustrate common bid rigging strategies, and identify aspects of goods, services or industries that facilitate collusion. They also include checklists for designing procurement processes to reduce the risks of bid rigging, and for the detection of bid rigging.
- The OECD Recommendation on Fighting Bid Rigging in Public Procurement[3] contains a detailed set of practices for public procurement officials at all levels of government to follow. These measures, in addition to the *Guidelines* described above, include: techniques to promote competition through tender design, procedures and selection criteria, using electronic bidding systems, and encouraging awareness of the signs of collusion. These recommendations are equally applicable to local or cross-border situations.
- The Recommendation of the OECD Council concerning International Co-operation on Competition Investigations and Proceedings[4] calls for adherents to commit to effective international co-operation including, where appropriate and practicable, providing each other with relevant information that enables their competition authorities to investigate anticompetitive practices. The Recommendation also states that competition authorities of the adherents should support each other on a voluntary basis in their enforcement activity by providing each other with investigative assistance (as appropriate and practicable, taking into account available resources and priorities).

1. www.oecd.org/daf/competition/2350130.pdf.
2. www.oecd.org/competition/guidelinesforfightingbidrigginginpublicprocurement.htm.
3. www.oecd.org/competition/oecdrecommendationonfightingbidrigginginpublicprocurement.htm.
4. www.oecd.org/daf/competition/2014-rec-internat-coop-competition.pdf.

2.7 Global banking, high underwriting fees and the cost of capital

> A fifth set of level playing field issues (related to those discussed in section 2.6) concerns the pricing power displayed by large global banks in their underwriting of equity (initial public offerings) for non-financial companies that would use these services in their strategies to innovate and expand in global markets. Equity finance is preferable to debt for a long-term focus on investment projects, since innovation and expansion entails risk taking. Unfortunately, however, corporate debt issuance has dominated equity since the crisis (particularly in emerging markets). This has been associated with US, UK and European investment banks losing market share to China and other parts of Asia. High levels of fees and parallel pricing (akin to tacit collusion) appear to have increased. This increases the cost of equity and works against long-term productive investment. Reinforcing competitive conditions in these markets could contribute to better outcomes for globalisation.

The supply of investment banking services is fairly concentrated at the global level. These activities are a key source of revenues for the banking sector. They include underwriting of debt and equity issuance, syndicated loans, and advisory services in M&A.[52] Such intermediation services constitute an important part of a well-functioning capital market as they help to channel financial resources from savers to corporations who put them to productive use. It is in the public interest to ensure that excessive market power does not raise capital costs unnecessarily.

The market shares of the top three, ten and 20 largest investment banks, in terms of total USD value of transactions in different market segments, are shown in Figure 2.22. The non-investment grade corporate bond market, which was the smallest market segment in terms of total transaction value in 2016, had the highest degree of concentration with 85% of total value attributed to the top 20 banks. In other markets segments, the market share of the 20 largest banks varied between 63% and 75% of total transaction value.

Figure 2.22. **Share in global total transaction volume of largest investment banks, 2016**

(Per cent)

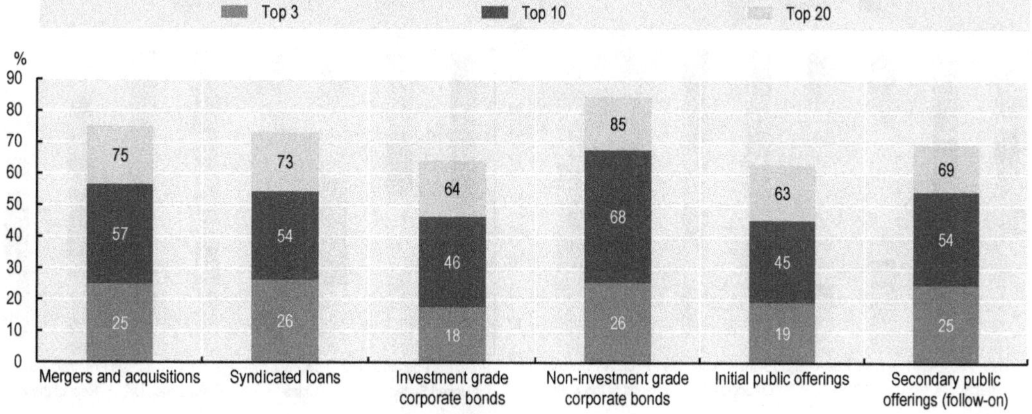

Source: Thomson Reuters, OECD calculations.

StatLink http://dx.doi.org/10.1787/888933476686

Traditionally, investment banks headquartered in the United States have dominated all segments of investment banking activities. However, during the post-crisis period (2009-2016) they lost market share in all segments except for M&A activity, compared to the pre-crisis period (2000-2006). Also European banks, excluding the United Kingdom, lost market share in all segments of investment banking activities, notably in equity issuing and in M&A transactions (Table 2.6).

As shown in Table 2.6, it is primarily banks in China that have gained in terms of global market shares, particularly with respect to equity issues and investment grade bonds. The shift in favour of banks from China, and to some extent other Asian countries, is the combined effect of the relative growth of their capital markets and a decline in the share of US banks in these markets (Figure 2.23). This may be due in part to advanced-country divestment from Asia, noted in OECD (2016a), China's post-crisis stimulus and the likely stronger relations Chinese banks have for purely domestic business funding.

Table 2.6. **Changes in market share of investment banking activities of top 100 banks worldwide, pre-crisis versus post-crisis**

(Percentage points)

	Corporate bonds	Initial public offerings	Syndicated loans	Mergers and acquisitions
United States	-5.36	-1.24	-6.68	1.48
United Kingdom	-1.99	-1.85	-1.85	2.02
China	7.91	13.53	1.81	2.12
Japan	0.24	-3.17	5.67	-0.46
Europe (excl. United Kingdom)	-3.27	-9.84	-2.66	-6.24
Asia (excl. China and Japan)	1.24	2.21	2.14	0.24
Rest of the World	1.23	0.37	1.57	0.83

Source: Thomson Reuters, OECD calculations.

StatLink http://dx.doi.org/10.1787/888933476988

Figure 2.23. **Market share of investment banks in underwriting, pre-crisis versus post-crisis**

(Per cent)

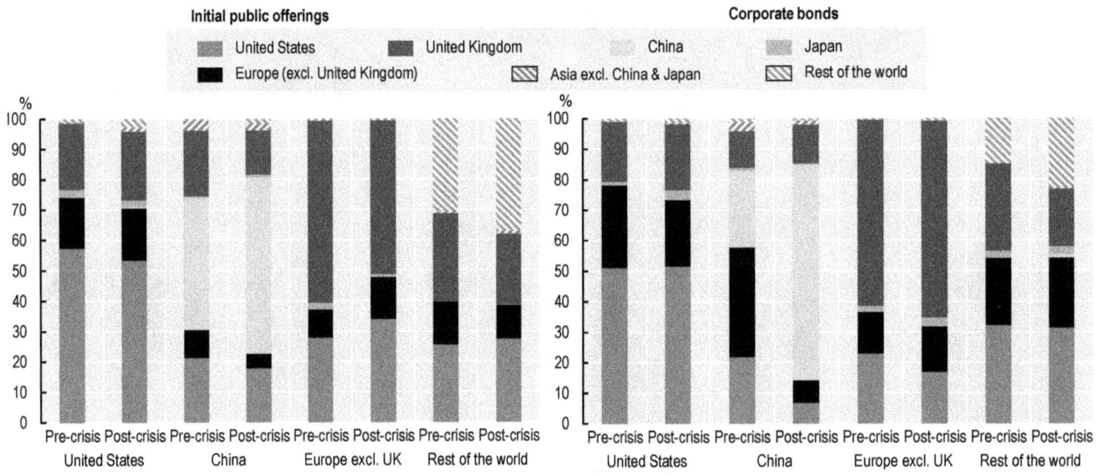

Source: Thomson Reuters, OECD calculations.

StatLink http://dx.doi.org/10.1787/888933476692

In order to finance themselves through public equity markets or corporate bond markets, companies typically pay an underwriter (usually investment banks) that will manage the offering of the securities. Traditionally, one underwriter used to assume a leading role in the offering with greater responsibilities and coordinated the transaction with other investment banks. This "lead underwriter" also received the lion's share of the underwriting fee paid by the company. However, since 2000, the traditional "one-lead-underwriter" model has, in the US market, successively shifted to a model that relies on a consortium of multiple underwriters. This is true both for initial public equity offerings and corporate bond offerings (Figure 2.24). During the last few years, most equity and bond offerings have been underwritten by three or more investment banks. The practice is most prominent in the corporate bond market where three out of four transactions in 2016 included three or more banks in lead positions. With respect to public equity issues, about half of all transactions have three or more lead underwriters.

Figure 2.24. **Market shares of lead underwriters in the United States, 2000-2016**

(Per cent)

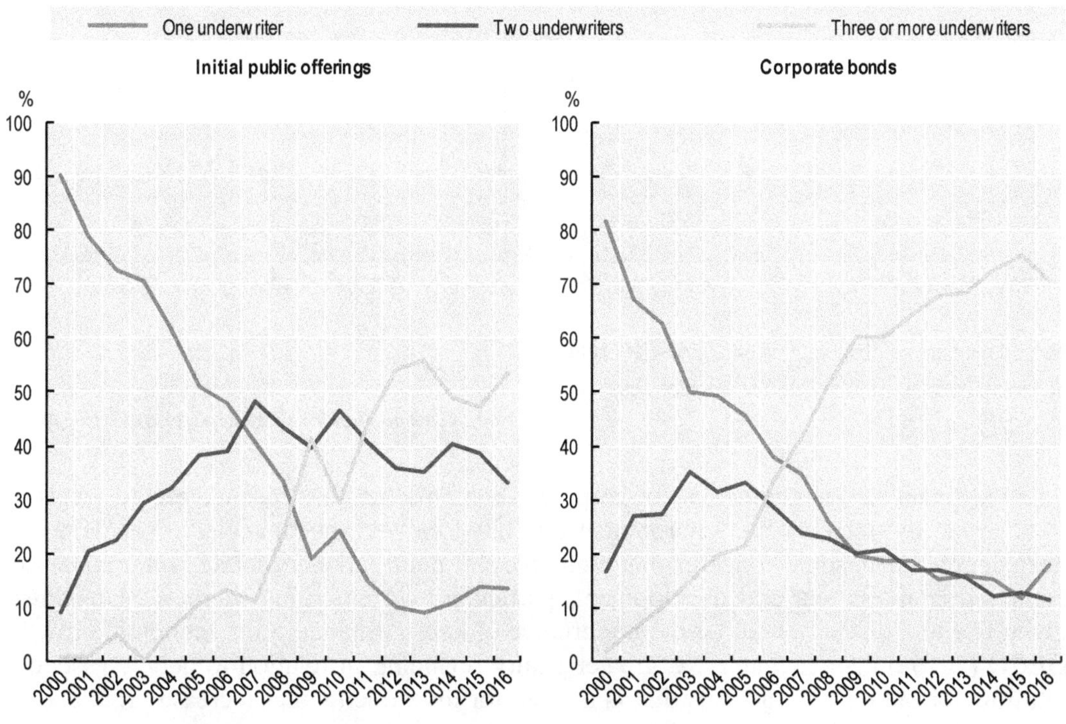

Source: Thomson Reuters, OECD calculations.

StatLink http://dx.doi.org/10.1787/888933476702

Together with the increasing dominance of the multiple-lead-underwriter model, a key feature of the US capital markets has been the "one-fee" model, particularly for smaller issues. In all years since 2000, the median underwriter fee paid by US companies for an initial public equity offering was always 7% of the total proceeds. With the sole exceptions of 2008 and 2016, and with a lesser degree of clustering, the fee was 0.65% for undertaking a corporate bond issue. An important observation from Figure 2.25 is that the Japan data is also consistent with a "one-fee" model, but at a somewhat higher level of 8% for initial public equity offers. A further striking observation from the figure is that European issuers have been paying about half of the fees paid by US and Japanese companies. Underwriting fees for initial public equity offerings in China have more than doubled in the last seven years with a median fee of 7% in 2016.

Figure 2.25. **Underwriting fees as a percentage of total proceeds, median values, 2000-2016**

(Per cent)

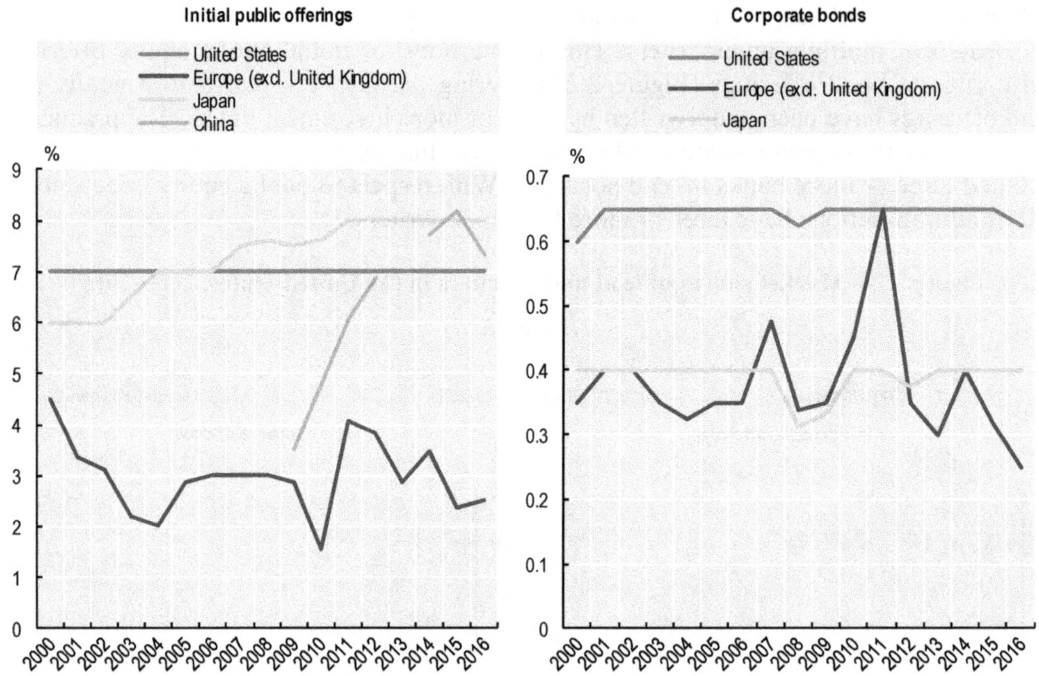

Note: There are no observations on Chinese IPOs for 2013.

Source: Thomson Reuters, OECD calculations.

StatLink http://dx.doi.org/10.1787/888933476710

Non-financial companies' use of corporate bond markets has reached record levels in the current low interest rate environment that has followed the financial crisis. This has been coupled with some concerns that high levels of debt in the corporate sector constrain companies' investment and development, particularly in emerging markets. It has also given rise to a discussion about the importance of equity financing for economic growth. OECD (2016a) demonstrated that greater equity financing in relation to debt is essential to allow for the long-term focus that is needed for investments that increase productivity and thereby long-term economic growth.

Against this background, concerns have been raised about the substantive decline in the number of non-financial companies in advanced economies that, during the last decade, have raised equity capital through stock exchange listings. Explanations for this decline are often focused on increased costs of equity finance after the so-called dot.com bubble. In particular, increased costs have resulted from new reporting and compliance requirements for listed companies that followed some high-profile corporate governance scandals of the early 2000s. A neglected aspect, however, is the fee that companies pay in relation to an initial public offering. These underwriting fees constitute, by far, the largest direct cost for an initial public offering (IPO).

Figure 2.26 provides a breakdown of IPO costs into underwriting and other costs for small and large company equity issues in the US, Japan and China. In all three countries, and both for small and large companies, underwriting fees constitute more than 60% of total costs. For IPOs with a size less than USD 100 million, the average cost is between 9 and 11% of total proceeds. This means that, on average, the cumulated fees from ten IPOs correspond to the market value of one new company. Not shown in the figure, but still important to note, is that underwriting fees for secondary public offerings by companies that are already listed in the United States and Japan have been over 5% in recent years. Hence, being already listed for public trading does not result in any significant reduction in underwriting costs.

Figure 2.26. **Cost of median initial public offerings as a share of total proceeds, small versus large companies, 2015**

(Per cent)

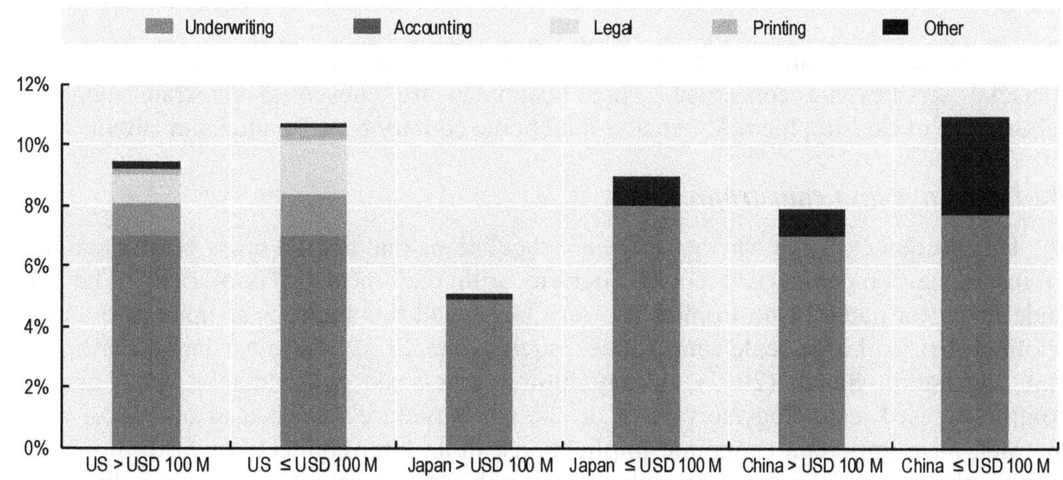

Source: Thomson Reuters, OECD calculations.

StatLink http://dx.doi.org/10.1787/888933476723

The failure of underwriting fees to adjust after the crisis raises important questions about the competitive structure of investment banking and regulatory attitudes towards it. A deeper assessment of the competitive conditions in these markets may be valuable. Should the high costs of IPO and bond underwriting involve collusion, instruments are available to deal with the issue (see Chapter 4 of this *Outlook*).

2.8 Cross border barriers in trade in financial services

> Direct cross-border barriers through regulation of trade in financial services need little motivation as a level playing field issue. Three examples which work against a well-functioning global economy are discussed. The first concerns the ability of international reinsurance companies to absorb the burden of large-scale catastrophe losses. This depends on pooling, the full benefits of which may not be realised if (unwarranted) regulatory impediments are placed in the way. The second example concerns domestic rules and regulations for pension funds that encourage them towards a home-country bias, reducing benefits from the diversification of risk. The third example concerns Brexit, where there is uncertainty about what (if any) barriers to trade in financial services could apply in the future. Best practice OECD guidelines for insurance and pensions are relevant for the first two examples, while commitments under the OECD Codes of Liberalisation provide ample room for a pragmatic approach to the United Kingdom's exit from the European Union.

The issue of regulations that constitute cross-border barriers can be problematic where financial services are concerned. Three examples are chosen to illustrate the issue: reinsurance of catastrophic risk; pension fund home country bias; London and Brexit.

Re-insurance and catastrophic risk

This section explores whether there are regulations that restrict cross-border activities of insurance companies that could interfere with their need to pool risks. The risks undertaken for natural catastrophes are very large, and this requires re-insurance and the pooling of risks. Large-scale catastrophes, such as the 2011 Great East Japan Earthquake and Superstorm Sandy (2012), or any future large-scale cyber-attacks, such as on a commonly-used technology/service or on the infrastructure that ensures operation of the internet, have important economic implications. In an inter-connected world, these local catastrophes can quickly become global catastrophes as a result of supply-chain linkages.

The liberalisation of capital markets and co-operation on the supervision of international insurance companies have allowed for the development of global reinsurance and capital markets. These markets provide a critical mechanism for sharing the burden of catastrophic risks when they materialise and reduce the financial burden on any individual countries affected. For example, in the United States, non-US primary insurers and reinsurers paid a significant share of the insured losses after major catastrophes – including more than 60% in the aftermath of September 11th (2001) and just under 50% in the case of Superstorm Sandy (see Figure 2.27).

Capital markets are playing an increasing role in managing the financial impacts of large-scale catastrophes as alternative reinsurance market instruments, such as catastrophe bonds, sidecars and industry loss warranties. These have increased the overall property catastrophe market capacity by close to 20% (Wolfrom and Yokoi-Arai, 2015). These markets are also supporting the management of emerging catastrophe risks, such as cyber risk. For example, the UK-based Lloyd's insurance and reinsurance markets may have boosted the capacity for stand-alone cyber insurance coverage for US companies by as much as 80% in 2015.[53]

The benefits of international reinsurance and capital markets, in terms of absorbing the burden of large-scale catastrophe losses, may not be realised where (unwarranted) impediments are placed on insurance companies' ability to transfer these risks to international markets. According to the Global Reinsurance Forum, a number of countries around the world have imposed various types of constraints on reinsurance companies' ability to "freely conduct business on a cross-border basis."[54]

Figure 2.27. **Share of claims paid by international insurance and reinsurance markets**

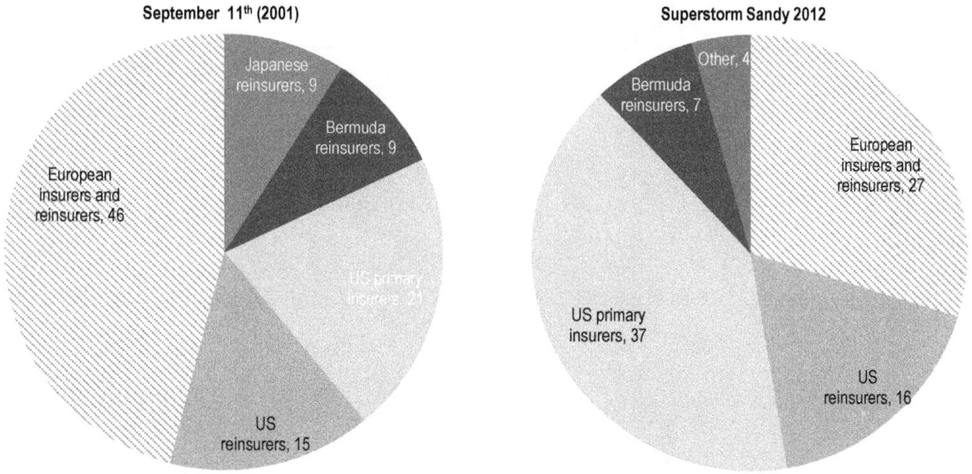

Note: The claims payments in the case of Superstorm Sandy exclude claims paid by the US National Flood Insurance Program.

Source: Global Reinsurance Forum (2014).

StatLink http://dx.doi.org/10.1787/888933476732

These restrictions include: controls on the ability to operate freely in a region (the African Union, Argentina, China, Ecuador, Egypt, India, Indonesia, Korea, Malaysia, Nigeria, Philippines, Poland, and South Africa); requirements for reinsurers to collateralise or localise their assets (Brazil, Canada, China, Ecuador, France, Portugal, Singapore, South Africa and the United States); barriers relating to the establishment of branches if local businesses used in helping to write business (Brazil, China, Egypt, India, Indonesia, Malaysia, Nigeria, Russia, South Africa, Thailand and the United Kingdom); and compulsory cessions (the proportion of insurance that can be put to reinsurance) and/or first right of refusal rules (the African Union, Argentina, Brazil, China, Egypt, France, India, Malaysia, Nigeria, Philippines, Sri Lanka and Thailand).

Pension funds and home country bias

This section explores whether national regulations create artificial cross-border barriers to appropriate global asset diversification. Pension funds, insurance companies and managers of assets earmarked for retirement have the duty of managing those assets in the best interest of their members, current and future retirees (OECD Core Principles of Private Pension Regulation, 2016e). This requires using a prudent person approach and investing assets in financial instruments that are expected to provide the highest return at the lowest risk possible, that is, the highest risk-adjusted returns on a sustainable basis. Additionally, portfolio investment should take into account principles related to risk diversification. Moreover, investing abroad should be permitted, subject to prudent management principles (Core Principles 3 and 4).

Table 2.7. **Share of foreign assets in pension fund portfolios, domestic market capitalisation and government debt in global debt markets, 2015**

A. Selected OECD countries			B. Selected non-OECD countries		
Country	Pension fund actual foreign investments	Domestic shares and government bonds	Country	Pension fund actual foreign investments	Domestic shares and government bonds
	% portfolio	% world		% portfolio	% world
Australia (1)	30.0	1.3	Brazil	0.2	1.5
Canada	34.2	2.6	Bulgaria	52.0	0.0
Chile	44.2	0.2	Colombia	3.5	0.2
Denmark (2)	25.8	0.4	Costa Rica (6)	5.8	0.0
Estonia	75.8	0.0	Dominican Republic	0.0	0.0
Germany (3)	12.0	3.3	Egypt	0.0	0.2
Iceland	23.8	0.0	FYR Macedonia	27.8	0.0
Israel	16.1	0.3	India	0.0	2.5
Italy	57.6	2.3	Jamaica	8.4	0.0
Japan (4)	20.2	12.1	Kosovo	91.9	0.0
Latvia	61.6	0.0	Lithuania	68.8	0.0
Mexico	12.7	0.7	Mauritius	23.4	0.0
Netherlands	81.3	0.8	Namibia (5)	61.4	0.0
Norway	29.7	0.3	Nigeria	0.0	0.1
Portugal	58.5	0.2	Peru	40.2	0.1
Slovak Republic	72.0	0.0	Romania	6.5	0.1
Slovenia (5)	43.0	0.0	South Africa (5.9)	20.1	0.5
Switzerland	39.8	1.4	Tanzania	0.0	0.0
Turkey (6.7)	0.6	0.3	Thailand	0.7	0.5
United Kingdom	26.8	4.4	Trinidad and Tobago (7)	10.4	0.0
United States (8)	29.2	35.0	Zambia (5)	9.7	0.0

Notes: (1) The share of foreign investments only refers to the share of the portfolio invested in international fixed income, international listed equity and International unlisted infrastructure by APRA regulated funds with more than four members. (2) Data on pension fund investments refer to defined contribution plans only. (3) Data on foreign investments come from PwC report "Beyond their Borders – Evolution of foreign investment by pension funds". (4) Data on pension fund investments come from Bank of Japan. (5) Data on pension fund investments refer to 2014. (6) Data refer to personal plans only. (7) Data on pension fund investments refer to 2012. (8) The share of foreign investments of pension funds in the United States is a weighted average of the share of foreign investments of four large pension funds in 2014 (Illinois SURS, NYCRS, LACERA and United Nations Joint Staff Pension Fund) and of one other pension fund in 2012 (CalPERS), weighted by assets of these funds (*Source:* OECD Annual Survey of Large Pension Funds). (9) data on pension funds only refer to the funds supervised under the Pension Funds Act.

Source: OECD Global Pension Statistics, International Monetary Fund, Bloomberg, OECD Calculations.

StatLink http://dx.doi.org/10.1787/888933476996

Investors should build their portfolios taking into account foreign investment opportunities to improve risk diversification: the idea is that investors should invest according to global market capitalisation.[55] In this sense, a pension fund should have a portfolio allocation to global equities equal to the market capitalisation of the global market relative to the home market. Investors who have a portfolio allocation to home securities larger than the global market capitalisation of the home market are showing "home bias". Several studies have shown that home bias in investment exists in all countries.[56] However, investors may be investing more domestically as a result of better risk-adjusted returns of home investments relative to foreign investments, or because of additional costs.[57] Risk-adjusted return analysis may still miss the risk associated with lack of global diversification.

Pension funds invest abroad but there is a strong home bias. Table 2.7 shows pension funds' investment abroad as a share of total investment in 2015 in selected OECD and non-OECD countries, compared to global averages as a benchmark. This shows that pension funds invest abroad much less than they should if they were to follow financial theory. For example, pension funds in Australia, the Netherlands and the United States invest abroad on average 30%, 81.3% and 29.2%, respectively, compared to their share in global equities and debt of around 98.7%, 99.2% and 65%.

Pension funds investing abroad fail to get higher returns. Figure 2.28 reports five-year average annual real returns, net of investment expenses, by country and the share of their portfolio that pension funds invested abroad in 2015. There seems to be no correlation between returns and investing abroad. If any, there is a slight, statistically insignificant, negative correlation. The case of the Netherlands is interesting: high share of the portfolio invested abroad and high returns.

Figure 2.28. **Average annual returns (2010-2015) and share of investment abroad (as of 2015) of pension funds in selected countries**

(Per cent)

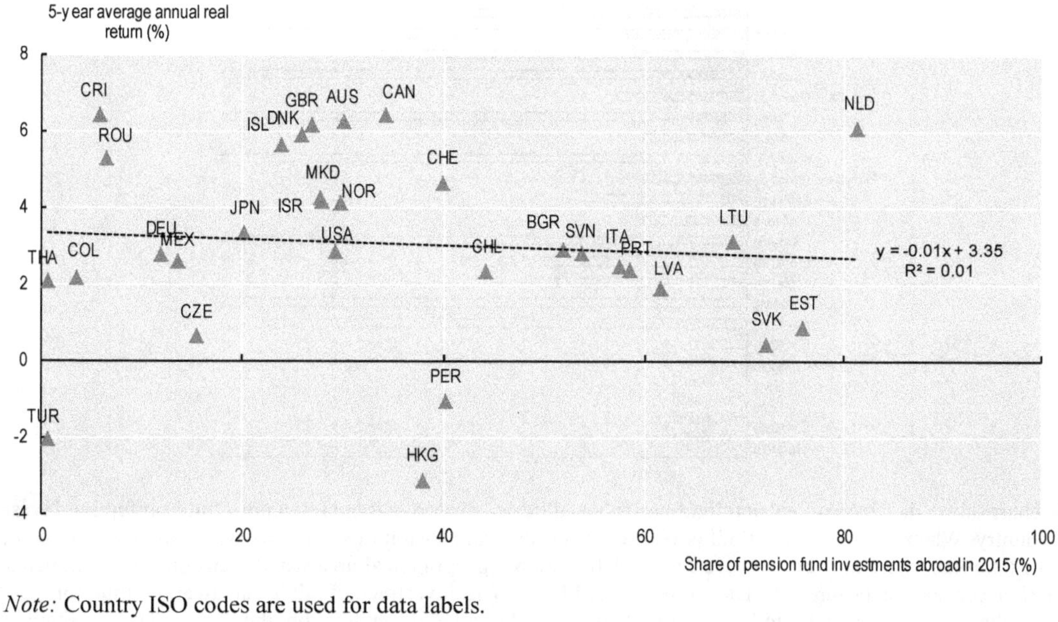

Note: Country ISO codes are used for data labels.

Source: OECD Global Pension Statistics, OECD calculations.

StatLink http://dx.doi.org/10.1787/888933476743/

Investing abroad can be constrained by a home bias but it can also be constrained or influenced by investment regulations. A number of countries do have investment regulations that restrict the amount of assets pension funds can invest abroad (particularly emerging economies), though these have tended to be loosened over time. In most OECD countries, pension funds could hold all their portfolios in foreign instruments in theory, but not in all jurisdictions. While there is room for a number of adherents to do more and a need to get more countries to adhere, commitments under the OECD Code of

Liberalisation of Capital Movements on institutional investors' portfolio investment abroad have helped to make progress by locking in adherents' levels of liberalisation achieved through the standstill obligation of the Code and by encouraging the removal of remaining restrictions through the peer pressure mechanism embodied in the Code.

Figure 2.29. **Pension fund investment abroad and restrictions in selected countries, 2015**

(As a percentage of total investment)

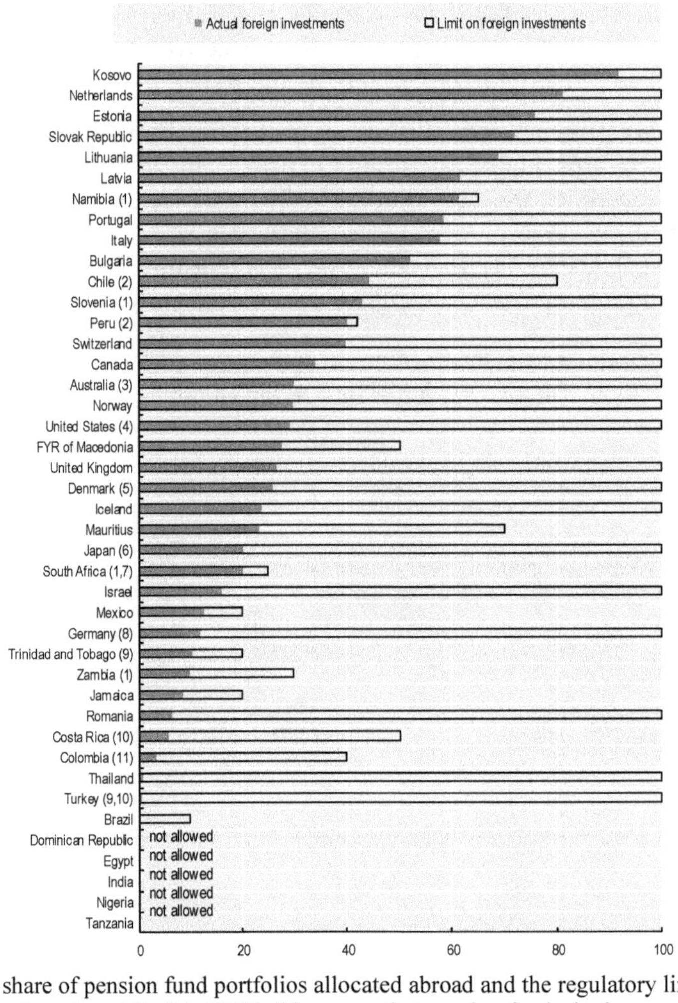

Notes: This chart shows the share of pension fund portfolios allocated abroad and the regulatory limit on foreign investments set up by each country. When the investment limit is 100%, this means that pension funds, in theory, could invest all their portfolios in assets issued abroad. There may be, however, a restriction on the geographical area where pension funds can invest in and a limit on foreign currency exposure. (1) Data refer to 2014. (2) The investment limit is an overall limit for pension fund administrators that manage several funds and invest assets differently, depending on the fund. (3) The share of foreign investments only refers to the share of the portfolio invested in international fixed income, international listed equity and International unlisted infrastructure by APRA regulated funds with more than four members. (4) The share of foreign investments of pension funds in the United States is a weighted average of the share of foreign investments of four large pension funds in 2014 (Illinois SURS, NYCRS, LACERA and United NationsJoint Staff Pension Fund) and of one other pension fund in 2012 (CalPERS), weighted by assets of these funds (*Source:* OECD Annual Survey of Large Pension Funds). (5) Data refer to defined contribution plans only. (6) Data on the actual share of investments abroad come from Bank of Japan. (7) Data only refer to the funds supervised under the Pension Funds Act. (8) Data on foreign investments come from PwC report "Beyond their Borders – Evolution of foreign investment by pension funds". (9) Data refer to 2012. (10) Data refer to personal plans only. (11) The limit given in this chart is the most binding limit (that applies to the conservative fund and the programmed retirement fund). The limit is higher for the moderate fund (60%) and the great risk fund (70%).

Source: OECD Survey on Investment Regulation, OECD Global Pension Statistics, OECD calculations.

http://dx.doi.org/10.1787/888933476750

Figure 2.29 shows that actual foreign investments in most countries are below investment restrictions, suggesting that those restrictions are not binding, though this does not show the restrictions on specific segments and locations.[58] Nevertheless, the data shows a correlation of 0.6 between the share of investment abroad and the ceiling. This suggests that regulation influences the ranges chosen by pension funds for their foreign allocations. Restrictiveness is extreme in most of Africa (bottom of figure), and is significant in Mexico, Brazil and the Caribbean.

Pension funds in many countries may be encouraged to invest domestically, especially in domestic government bonds.[59] In emerging economies, government bonds may provide the higher real return of any investment opportunity available. Unfortunately, the risk assessment of those investments may not take into account the risk that governments will use those funds to finance current expenditure instead of using those funds to promote public investment (e.g. public infrastructure) that may increase the productivity and potential growth of the country. This may negatively affect the likelihood of being able to pay the coupons. Moreover, the lack of diversification, even if returns on government bonds are high today, increases the risk of volatility.[60]

The criteria to invest in the best interest of members (OECD, 2016e) rest on risk-adjusted returns and diversification. Home bias, investment restrictions and inadequate risk management all may go against investing in the best interest of members.

Brexit

The United States and the United Kingdom have a great advantage over other parts of the world as they have huge financial centres with agglomerations in New York and London. Agglomerations give rise to economies that are external to the firm but internal to a specific geographic area. These economies encompass specialised labour supply, proximity to supply chains, and technical knowledge spill-overs and infrastructure. Other countries invest vertically and horizontally in these agglomerations to take advantage of skill endowment factors and economies that reduce costs.[61] Nowhere is this more important than in the highly-interconnected area of banking and finance. Within European geography, London is a key agglomeration:

> *"The United Kingdom is the venue for 40% of foreign exchange trading, half of trades in over-the-counter interest rate derivatives and more than two-thirds of trading in international bonds. It is home to more than 250 foreign banks, and more international banking activity is booked in London than anywhere else. The United Kingdom hosts the world's third largest insurance sector and the second largest investment industry." (Bank of England, 2015)*

Agglomerations and the cultures to which they give rise take many decades to build up, bringing scale economies via trade in financial services. The research about productivity growth and trade presented earlier suggests that erecting cross-border barriers blocks paths towards scale economies and efficiency. This applies to trade in financial services as much as it does to the activities of non-financial firms. If these theories are correct, then erecting new barriers to financial services in the post-Brexit environment will not be in the collective interest of the global economy, where London plays such a key role in international banking, bonds and foreign exchange. For OECD countries, international obligations in the form of the OECD Codes of Liberalisation should present no legal barriers to operating in the collective interest in the post-Brexit environment (see Box 2.10).

Box 2.10. **Brexit, cross-border financial services and the OECD Codes of Liberalisation**

EU countries have been entitled to accord each other preferential market access under the OECD Codes of Liberalisation[1] by virtue of their Article 10 providing for an "exception to the principle of non-discrimination for special customs or monetary systems". There is a similar situation under WTO agreements that allow for regional economic integration exemptions from the "most favoured nation" (MFN) principle.

From the moment the United Kingdom exits the European Union, the United Kingdom and EU countries will no longer be in a position to benefit from these provisions, unless the United Kingdom and the European Union enter into a new agreement that would pass the test of the MFN exception of Article 10 of the Codes. The alternative – to force the United Kingdom and European Union to re-erect barriers against each other for the sake of meeting MFN obligations – could be worse than the remedy from a collective interest standpoint.

However, selective market access rights in financial services can have legitimate prudential justifications and may not in themselves pose a MFN problem. As stated in the Codes User's Guide,[2] "selective recognition agreements, which may affect the right to carry out operations covered by the Codes, are in general based on objective technical criteria. In other words, different treatment is based on different circumstances and thus does not violate the non-discrimination provisions of the Codes". This has several implications under the OECD Codes:

- The EU passport facility for financial services is not treated as a "preferential treatment" which EU countries would have granted each other, but rather an arrangement which recognises that EU countries' financial services regimes have reached a level of regulatory and prudential equivalence such that a financial services provider authorised to operate in one EU country does not need to be licensed again to operate in another EU country. As a result, no reservations have been lodged by EU countries for the fact that, for instance, banks incorporated in an EU country can operate branches in any other EU country without the need for a licence from the host country while third country banks do need to obtain this licence.
- For the same reason, no breach of the MFN principle results from EU Directives that allow the European Commission to take the so-called "equivalence decisions" by which third country service providers can be entitled to access European financial services markets without incorporation. Such third countries identified so far include Japan and the United States, for example, and the financial service operations concerned relate to such areas as capital market prospectus, credit rating, statutory audit, insurance and reinsurance, credit institutions, or investment firms.
- Where market access for third country financial services providers is left to the decision of individual EU member states under EU regulations, the presumption under the Codes is that so long as the third country meets comparable prudential standards and accepts an appropriate supervisory co-operation arrangement with the individual member state concerned, this third country should be accorded the licence to operate in this member state.

Therefore, unless UK and EU financial services regimes diverge significantly after Brexit, it can arguably be expected that the United Kingdom would benefit from the sort of selective recognition arrangements provided for by the Codes. The converse – recognition of EU financial service providers by the UK authorities as meeting UK standards – is also to be expected, even though the material significance of this may be smaller (the United Kingdom already generally provides access to its financial services markets with no discrimination between EU and non-EU providers, with some exceptions such as depository services to Undertakings for Collective Investments in Transferable Securities).

1. OECD Codes of Liberalisation of Capital Movements and Current Invisible Operations, www.oecd.org/investment/codes.htm.
2. OECD Codes of Liberalisation of Capital Movements and Current Invisible Operations: User's Guide www.oecd.org/daf/inv/investment-policy/38072327.pdf.

2.9 Responsible business conduct and due diligence in global supply chains

> The seventh set of issues that bear on globalisation outcomes concerns responsible business conduct (RBC). While most of the previous sections have focused on distortions to pricing or inconsistent regulations that raise "fairness" issues, RBC pertains to global business outcomes in the context of the sustainability of supply chains. It is shown that for the average multinational firm financial performance (such as the return on equity) is improved by responsible behaviour. Gains from trade and international investment apply to all points (upstream and downstream) in the supply chain, and sustainability requires companies to do due diligence on their suppliers. The interruption of supply (via disputes, damage to the local environment or over-exploitation of resources) is a major company risk. Responsible business behaviour and supply chain due diligence have a strong potential to improve trust and reduce disruptions to trade and international investment which block firm-level paths to better productivity and sustainable growth. OECD instruments for multinational enterprises and supply chain due diligence are well suited to this task.

One of the important paths to productivity growth, discussed earlier in this report, is increased scale and innovation through foreign sales. This theory applies at all levels of the production chain – both upstream resources and intermediate products and downstream goods and service supplied to final consumers. While not an explicit part of these theories, the sustainability of these supply chains is an equally important consideration for long-term productivity growth. Indeed, the 2017 Risk Barometer (Allianz, 2017), published by the insurance giant Allianz (and based on the insights of more than 1 200 experts from more than 50 countries) identifies business interruption (including supply chain disruption) as the number one business risk for the fifth successive year. Concern about interruptions in supply chains is seen to be shifting increasingly towards events that require better risk-management of societal and environmental factors.

Companies have a responsibility to manage this risk. Cross-border interactions between companies are often not subject to any one set of laws, as with the domestic affairs of a sovereign government and, indeed, many different standards of responsibility may apply at different points in the supply chain. It is, therefore, both in the interest of and responsibility of companies to navigate those cross-border complexities. Negative impacts on human rights and the environment can result in unsustainable supply chains, which is bad for productivity growth and long-term investor returns.

RBC refers to the expectation that companies: avoid causing or contributing to negative impacts of their activities; address them when they occur; and make a positive contribution to economic, environmental and social progress in the countries where they operate. Supply chain (risk-based) due diligence is a key element of RBC: i.e. an ongoing proactive and reactive process through which companies can demonstrate that they do not contribute to harms to people, to societal conflict and to environmental degradation.[62]

Operating with RBC as part of a core business decision making is socially desirable but also makes sense from a risk management point of view. A company's primary responsibility is to earn profits for its shareholders. Similarly, under fiduciary duty and prudent person rules, agents must act in the financial interests of their shareholders. Environmental and social issues are also "financially material". If these are not reflected in risk management practices, the company can be subject to losses and investors' expectations will not be met.

Examples of RBC issues, some of which may be material to the risk management of companies include:

- *Climate change*: the owners of companies face three types of risks, (i) physical risks, such as the direct impact from climate and weather-related events; (ii) liability risks, or the compensation for parties who have suffered loss or damage from the effects of climate change; and (iii) transition risks whereby policy and technology changes prompt a reassessment of a large range of asset values, some of which may become "stranded" (Carney, 2015). Company boards and institutional investors need to be in a position to understand and act effectively on the opportunities and risks presented by climate change.
- *Abuse of human rights*: the ILO estimates that almost 21 million people are victims of forced labour. Moreover, an estimated 168 million children are trapped in child labour, accounting for 11% of the overall child population, with more than half doing hazardous work (ILO, 2015 and ILO, 2016). Freedom of association and the right to collective bargaining are suppressed in some countries, and working conditions can be unsafe. Upstream supply from companies abusing rights is not sustainable in the longer run.
- *Damage to the environment*: there are many specific examples of degradation of air, land and water by companies that have huge clean-up costs. Contributions to more global problems also come back to haunt the firm: for example, ill health and early death due to air pollution[63] affects productivity and the building up of a pool of efficiency of skilled labour.
- *Over-exploitation of resources:* The disappearance of resources is the ultimate supply chain disrupter. The United Nations Environment Programme (UNEP) estimates that, of the total production of the top-ten traded fish species, 74% are categorised as "fully to over-exploited", while the remaining ones are "fully exploited", or "depleted" (UNEP, 2009). According to the Global Environment Facility, three widely traded commodities (soy, beef and palm oil) are responsible for close to 80% of tropical deforestation worldwide and for 12% of greenhouse gas emissions globally (Global Environment Facility, 2014).

The evidence is mounting that sound risk management through RBC practices is correlated with stronger financial performance in the longer run and many companies and investors have begun to embrace them.

Company financial performance and sustainable supply chains: empirical evidence

A key enabling factor for sustainable supply chains is how companies manage their upstream supply chain providers accordingly – as a competitive strategy. Financial performance payoffs may derive from a number of sources:

- Sound risk management of the company avoids periods of concentrated losses.
- An integrated approach to sustainability may improve understanding and co-operation between stakeholders, improving productivity and reducing labour disputes.

- Intangibles such as corporate brand image, quality reputation, customer satisfaction and loyalty may improve sales.
- Organisational training and learning about sustainability within a company may result in innovations in operations, logistics, inventory control, diversification of supply and the adoption of new technologies.
- Bottom line cost savings via energy efficiency, waste disposal reduction, and positive revenues from recycling.
- Meeting regulatory requirements and obtaining licenses to operate are enabling factors for participating in and augmenting foreign sales.

Some of the empirical evidence that sustainable supply chains and better financial performance can go hand-in-hand includes:

- One early study of French companies found "reliability" places at the top of company considerations when selecting upstream suppliers (alongside "quality" and "price").[64]
- In a German meta-study of 2 200 papers, 90% had a nonnegative correlation between the strength of their environmental, social and governance systems and practices (ESG) and corporate financial performance, while the large majority was associated with positive correlations.[65] The positive ESG impact on corporate financial performance is stable over time.
- A Harvard Business School study which tracked the performance of companies for over 18 years, found that "high sustainability" companies outperformed "low sustainability" companies (as measured by stock performance and in real accounting terms) (Eccles et al., 2015).
- A 2016 study covering 8 500 French enterprises noted there was a 13% difference in economic performance, on average, between enterprises that implemented responsible business conduct and those that did not (Benhamou and Diaye, 2016).
- In a meta-study based on 190 sources, 88% of them found that companies with sound sustainability practices demonstrate better operational performance, ultimately translating into better cash flow (Clark, et al., 2015).
- A study reviewing research on company practices found that better business responsibility has the potential to build customer commitment, increase revenues (by up to 20% in some cases), raise market valuations of the company in the longer term, and reduce the cost of debt by up to 40% (Rochlin, et al., 2015).
- Evidence from the 2015 World Bank assessment of the *Better Work Programme*, which has been implemented in the garment and footwear industry in eight countries, concluded that participating factories, in general, see a positive correlation between investing in better working conditions and profits, productivity and survival rates. On a country level, participation in the programme is associated with significant increases in apparel exports (see World Bank, 2015 and BFC, 2016).

Box 2.11. OECD empirical evidence on financial performance and responsible business conduct factors

A parsimonious panel data model is postulated to study the impact of responsible governance practices on company's performance over the period 2008-2015.[1] The sample includes US companies listed in the S&P500 and European companies listed in the STOXX 600. The sample is restricted to large companies since 2008 for which ESG score data start to be more frequently and extensively reported in standard databases. In the model, company financial performance is regressed alternately on four Thomson Reuters environmental, social and governance (ESG) scores, while controlling for some other important factors. The model specification is outlined below:

$$Performance_{i,t} = \propto + \beta_1\, ESG\ score_{i,t} + \beta_2\, Debt\ ratio_{i,t} + \beta_3\, Log\ of\ total\ assets_{i,t} + Years + Industries + \varepsilon_{i,t}$$

Where Performance is either the return on equity (ROE) or the return on assets (ROA); the debt ratio is the ratio of total debt to total assets; and the natural logarithm of total assets. The following four ESG z-scores in the range of 0 to 1.0 are based on ethical screening of 6 000 companies and 400 metrics. Examples of screening metrics include: protecting health (accident records); avoiding bribery and corruption; guaranteeing freedom of association of its workers, avoiding child and forced labour; investing in the community, etc.[2]

- **Governance:** measure of a company's systems and processes, which ensure that its board members and executives act in the best interests of its shareholders.
- **Social:** measure of a company's capacity to generate trust and loyalty with its workforce, customers and society.
- **Environmental:** measure of a company's impact on living and non-living natural systems, including the air, land and water, as well as complete ecosystems.

"Years" and "Industries" represents year and industry fixed effects. Financial statement data and ESG score data are extracted from Datastream. The results are shown in Table 2.8.

Table 2.8. **The effect of RBC scores on company performance, 2008-2015**

	[1]	[2]	[3]	[4]	[5]	[6]
	Return on equity			Return on assets		
Total debt (%total assets)	-0.026 (-0.59)	-0.024 (-0.55)	-0.027 (-0.61)	-0.089*** (-9.16)	-0.089*** (-9.10)	-0.090*** (-9.15)
Log of total assets	-0.032*** (-7.31)	-0.034*** (-7.53)	-0.033*** (-7.22)	-0.015*** (-12.15)	-0.015*** (-12.18)	-0.015*** (-11.88)
Governance score	0.054*** (3.30)	–	–	0.011** (2.44)	–	–
Social score	–	0.050*** (2.73)	–	–	0.011** (2.43)	–
Environmental score	–	–	0.029 (1.64)	–	–	0.005 (1.12)
Constant	0.698*** (9.44)	0.739*** (9.75)	0.730*** (9.58)	0.344*** (17.17)	0.353*** (17.47)	0.350*** (17.31)
R-squared	0.090	0.089	0.086	0.223	0.222	0.221
Observations	7838	7845	7840	7906	7913	7908

Note: Standard errors are robust from heteroscedasticity. * Indicate statistical significance at the 10% level. ** Indicate statistical significance at the 5% level. *** Indicate statistical significance at the 1% level. t-values are reported in parenthesis.

Source: Thomson Reuters Datastream, OECD calculations.

Box 2.11. **OECD empirical evidence on financial performance and responsible business conduct factors** (cont.)

For the control variables, the results suggest a positive effect of the share of value added in total sales for both ROE and ROA. Debt-to-enterprise value is insignificant for the ROE model and negative for the ROA. The economic score always has a positive effect on the financial performance. The social responsibility score is positive and supported by the data at the 1% level. The environment score is supported at the 10% level for the ROE measure of performance.

1. Wang et al. (2013), using an earlier sample period, reports broadly similar findings.
2. A full description of the methodology can be found in http://financial.thomsonreuters.com/content/dam/openweb/documents/pdf/tr-com-financial/methodology/corporate-responsibility-ratings.pdf.

The OECD examined the issue of RBC and the financial performance of companies (return on equity and return on assets) in a panel regression study with over 6 500 observations, which is set out in more detail in Box 2.11. Controlling for value chain structure, economic and financial factors, the overwhelming finding is that the social score (a measure of a company's capacity to generate trust and loyalty with its workforce, customers and society) has a highly-significant positive effect on companies' return on equity and return on assets.[66]

These OECD results lend support to the proposition that investing in and implementing RBC practices throughout the supply chain enhances financial performance in the long-run, on average, while supporting social goals.

Closing sustainability gaps and moving forward

It has already been noted that the notion of a level playing field in international competitiveness is often at the heart of trade and foreign investment disputes. These include the role of exchange rates and subsidies, something particularly relevant for SOEs. RBC factors also play a role in this same sense. The "cheapest" sources of supply, if derived from irresponsible behaviour are unlikely to be sustainable: negative impacts on human rights and the environment in favour of short-term profits result in the failure to generate sustainable supply chains. The interruption to supply (via labour disputes, government intervention, the exhaustion of resources, etc.) is bad for productivity growth and long-term investor returns.

While governments, businesses, trade unions and civil society hold a shared responsibility to foster sustainable supply chains, it is businesses that have to implement risk prevention and management systems, to engage meaningfully with stakeholders and to account for their impacts and actions. Working towards sustainable supply chains, including by incorporating a thorough due diligence process into management systems, helps enterprises gain improved knowledge of operations and detect risks. The due diligence process envisaged in the OECD Guidelines for Multinational Enterprises comprises steps that enable enterprises to identify, prevent, mitigate and account for how they address their actual and potential adverse impacts. Since 2011, the OECD has developed due diligence guidance in the minerals, agriculture, extractives, and garment and footwear sectors. In addition, the OECD is currently developing a general, cross-sector guidance on how to implement due diligence and foster sustainable global supply chains.

Undertaking due diligence has the potential to change conditions in the supply chain. Progress can be rapid. Since it was set out in 2011, there has been significant uptake of *OECD Due Diligence Guidance on Responsible Supply Chains of Minerals from Conflict-Affected and High-Risk Areas* by industry, governments, civil society and other experts (see Chapter 5 in this *Outlook*).[67] The *Guidance* has now become the international standard and reference for responsible mineral supply chains. The European Parliament, on 16 March 2017, adopted a new EU regulation laying-down due diligence obligations in line with the *Guidance* for EU importers of tin, tantalum, tungsten and gold from conflict-affected and high-risk areas. In 2015, the same approach was adapted by the China Chamber of Commerce of Metals, Minerals and Chemicals Importers & Exporters (Chinese Due Diligence, 2015), while the Chinese General Administration of Quality Supervision, Inspection and Quarantine is developing a standard on responsible mineral supply chains that is expected to come into force in 2017. The *Guidance* is also referenced in the Securities and Exchange Commission's Rule on Section 1502 of the 2010 Dodd-Frank *Wall Street Reform and Consumer Protection Act*.[68]

Finally, finding the right balance for a win-win outcome (between social goals and company responsibility to shareholders) is a complex issue. Promoting RBC requires the right balance of legislation and support by governments and leading companies; i.e. international co-operation to design and promote broadly-supported standards for a globalised and interconnected world, with consistent legislation that imposes disincentives for irresponsible behaviour. On the other hand, the business case for RBC, which appears to be present, needs to be supported by governments in this context. Appropriate standards will recognise that over-regulation, or bad regulation, is not a good thing either, because it would raise costs too much and fail to reinforce the actual business case for RBC.

Box 2.12. **The OECD Guidelines for Multinational Enterprises**

These are the most comprehensive set of government-backed recommendations on responsible business conduct. They include recommendations addressed by governments to businesses operating in or from their territories in all areas of business responsibility. They are aligned with International Labor Organization conventions and the UN Guiding Principles on Business and Human Rights, but cover a broader range of areas, including employment and industrial relations, human rights, environment, information disclosure, bribery, consumer interests, science and technology, competition, and taxation. They are open to adherence by non-OECD members; the current 47 adherents include 14 G20 members. This means that a large majority of global supply chains are covered by the OECD Guidelines, as the enterprises in adhering countries accounted for 75% of FDI outflows and 58% of global FDI inflows between 2010 and 2015, as well as 81% of global FDI outward stock as of end 2014.[1] Each country sets up a National Contact Point to promote the implementation of the Guidelines and to handle issues related to their implementation, including non-observance of the Guidelines in enterprises' supply chains. Currently, National Contact Points are the only state-based non judicial mechanisms which provide a platform for discussion and resolution of a wide range of issues related to business conduct arising throughout global supply chains.

1. OECD Direct Investment Statistics (database), www.oecd.org/investment/statistics.htm and IMF Balance of Payments and International Investment Position Statistics (database), www.imf.org/external/np/sta/bop/bop.htm.

Source: OECD Guidelines for Multinational Enterprises, http://mneguidelines.oecd.org/guidelines/.

2.10 Bribery and corruption, international investment and productivity

> The final level playing field issue discussed in this Outlook concerns the bribery of foreign officials. Large sums are paid into corrupt hands to win contracts and gain access into businesses that are not based on merit. This reduces value for money and the bribes paid or income streams shared serve private rather than national interests (such as more investment in social infrastructure) reinforcing resource misallocation. The evidence shows that corrupt countries also receive less foreign direct investment from adherents to the OECD Anti-Bribery Convention (which includes all of the world's largest foreign investors other than China). Productivity growth is reduced as a consequence of such factors. Furthermore, the populations of corrupt countries tend not to see globalisation as working in their interest and corruption is a facilitating factor for money laundering.

Bribery and corruption are vast global industries. For the purposes of this chapter, corruption is concerned with the abuse of public office for private gain. This includes the demand side (soliciting or extorting pecuniary or other benefits) and the supply side (the offering of bribes and other advantages to public officials). Corruption is often involved in investment in countries where governance and property rights are weak and where economic rents are perceived to be potentially high. On the supply side, companies attempt to improve their odds of winning contracts in what should be an open competition by: gaining inside information; getting the details of competitor's bids; and eliminating stronger rivals from the bidding process (on the basis of the bribe rather than merit). They may attempt to obtain: subsidies, lower taxes, required licenses, faster approvals, equity allocations in privatisations and favourable legal outcomes. In short, the aim is to go around markets and legal processes to extract private benefits at the expense of competitors, and citizens more generally in some parts of the world.

The OECD Convention focuses on the (supply-side) bribery of foreign public officials. It is understandable that some commentators feel that there is little reason to punish companies that do what is allowed in other countries – it is the price of doing business. Some go as far to argue that one country taking the lead in proactive enforcement of anti-bribery laws could encourage corruption elsewhere.[69] On this view, the world could move backwards to days before the OECD Anti-Bribery Convention (that followed the US Foreign Corrupt Practices Act). Bribe frequency, amounts and its tax-deductibility could be allowed to rise. This would be a contrary view to those wishing to promote a level playing field in global commerce and potentially damaging to productivity growth through investment and trade:

- Rent-seeking behaviour through bribery and corruption wastes significant resources that could otherwise be invested productively.
- Bribery laws affect the pattern of foreign investment – directing it away from rent-seeking corrupt regimes and towards countries with stronger property rights and better potential for sustainable growth.

With respect to the size of wasted resources, and based on a World Bank micro survey data for households and companies, Kaufman (2005) estimated the total amount of bribes globally to be in the range of USD 830 billion to USD 1.5 trillion per annum in a study centred on 2002 (2.4% to 4% of world GDP). On a conservative view, a USD 1 trillion estimate would have been 2.9% of world GDP.[70] Such estimates are disturbing – i.e. each year individuals and companies pay bribes in the vicinity of the size of France's GDP. In today's prices, that conservative estimate would be around USD 2 trillion per annum. More recent whistleblower evidence in the Unaoil scandal and the Panama Papers suggests that use of offshore entities is a primary conduit for corrupt transactions.

To place the size of this misallocation of resources in perspective, the per annum amounts involved in bribes paid is more than half of the global economy's needs for productivity-enhancing infrastructure investment to 2030.[71] Nor do bribes help growth in host countries where foreign investment is concerned, but instead money disappears into shelf companies and foreign bank accounts of corrupt politicians and officials.

With regard to the second major issue – the pattern of FDI – the firm-based view of productivity growth discussed earlier relies critically on foreign sales, which can be achieved via exports or via local production abroad. Countries that carry out FDI abroad are the main productivity beneficiaries – the most productive companies do it and gain via scale economies and technology deployment.[72] Figure 2.30 shows average annual outflows of FDI over the period 2000-2015, versus the average World Bank corruption index for the same period (a higher index indicates more corruption). Large offshore banking hubs that act as pass-through centres for investment elsewhere (e.g. Hong Kong, China; Ireland; Luxembourg; the Netherlands; Singapore; Switzerland, etc.) are excluded. Adherents to the OECD Anti-bribery Convention are shown in blue triangles, and non-adherents are shown in squares.

Amongst adherents, it is clear that less corrupt countries (with the exception of a small southern country on the bottom right) invest more (not less) abroad.[73] Less-corrupt countries therefore are more likely to benefit (than corrupt countries) via foreign sales and scale economies. Amongst non-adherents, there is a bunching around very high-corruption and low-investing countries, with only two countries to the right that are very corrupt, but their SOEs invest significantly abroad.

Figure 2.30. **Corruption and foreign direct investment of adherents versus non-adherents to the OECD Anti-Bribery Convention, 2000-2015**

(World Bank corruption index, larger figure implies more corruption)

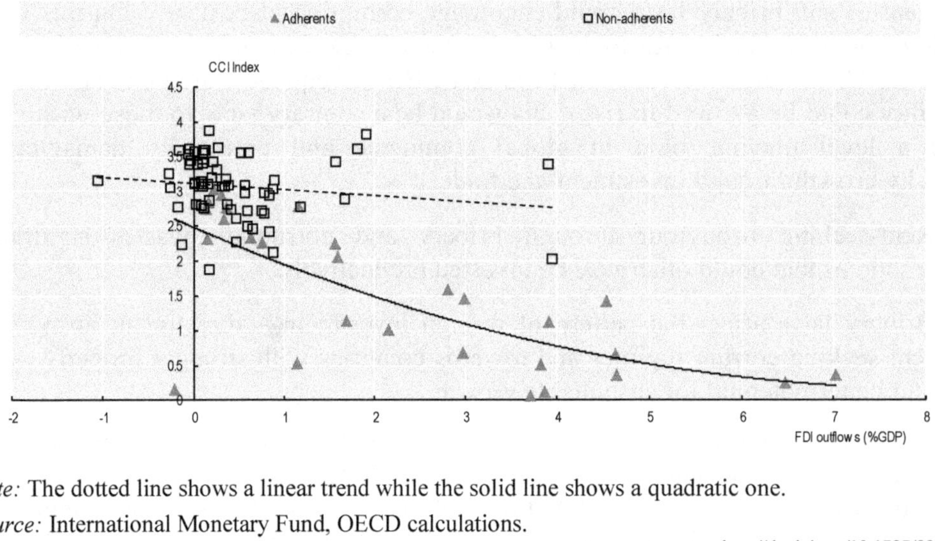

Note: The dotted line shows a linear trend while the solid line shows a quadratic one.

Source: International Monetary Fund, OECD calculations.

StatLink http://dx.doi.org/10.1787/888933476761

The causes of corruption are complex. In a survey of the literature, Svensson (2005) shows that it is driven by a country's wealth (the richer the less corrupt), its culture (different legal systems, etc.), citizens having a voice in a democratic process; and good governance structures, such as freedom of the press.

Box 2.13 sets out the results of an empirical study on the determinants of FDI and the impact of the OECD Anti-Bribery Convention. This shows that being an adherent to the Convention has a very strong and robust negative empirical impact on the ability of corrupt countries to attract FDI (which promotes rent-seeking behaviour and wastes resources). Since financial firms have a history of involvement in bribery and corruption and they play a key role in laundering the proceeds of bribery and corruption by others, some case studies are also set out in Box 2.14.

A group of large countries with high perceived corruption have also had strong GDP growth via mechanisms discussed elsewhere in this *Outlook*. This has meant that the size of economic activity affected by corruption in the world economy is likely to be growing. Figure 2.31 shows an aggregation of each country's perceived corruption (using the World Bank's corruption index which is comparable between countries) weighted by the country's GDP (at PPP exchange rates). This began to rise after the year 2000. Or, put more simply, global economic activity appears to be shifting to economies perceived to be relatively more corrupt. This suggests that opening the world economy to trade and investment without better control over corruption and good governance leaves all countries with links to the global economy more exposed to higher levels of corruption. A strategy of encouraging large countries that are not already adherents, particularly where they have a strong role in world trade, to join the OECD Anti-Bribery Convention would be most conducive to productivity growth, as would better enforcement of the requirements of the Convention.

Figure 2.31. **GDP per capita and the World Bank Corruption Index, 1997-2015**

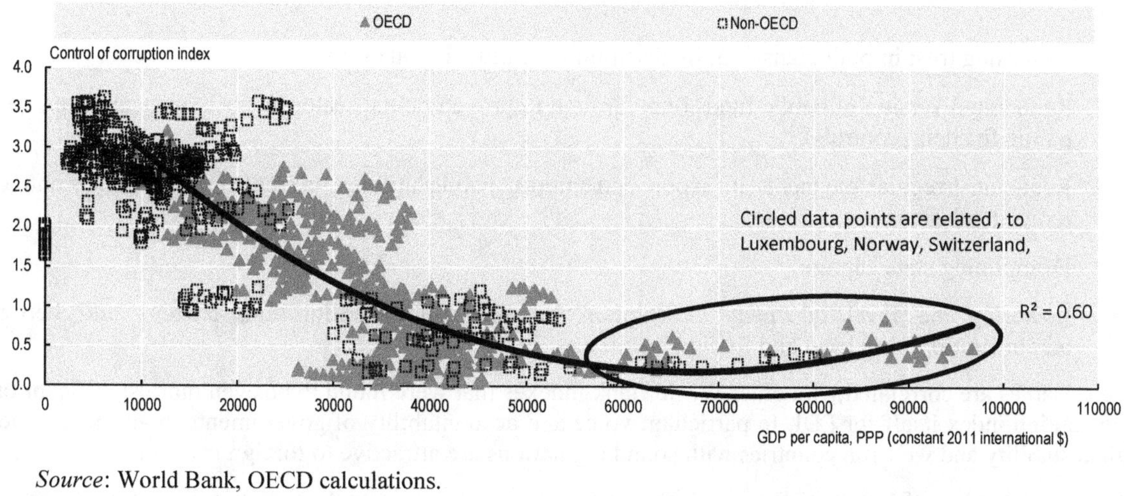

Source: World Bank, OECD calculations.

StatLink http://dx.doi.org/10.1787/888933476775

Box 2.13. **Foreign direct investment and the OECD Anti-Bribery Convention**

The OECD has estimated a dynamic FDI gravity model using ordinary least squares fixed effects and Arellano and Bond General Method of Moments (GMM) estimators. To account for the differential impact on bilateral investment flows of ratification of the OECD Anti-Bribery Convention in various years by the 41 Parties, an interaction effect between a dummy for the period of adherence and host country corruption is considered. This enables comparison between the coefficient for the general population, including non-Parties, and the marginal impact for the adhering group.

The estimations support the view that perceived corruption in host countries is generally positive and, if anything, is consistent with the "helping hand" view – that bribes help smooth the way for investment. In addition to these effects, the study looks at the differential impact of ratification of the OECD Anti-Bribery Convention. This effect is both statistically and economically significant. The coefficients on the products of the dummy for ratification of the OECD Anti-Bribery Convention and the two measures of perceived corruption (the World Bank and Transparency International) can be interpreted as the differential impact elasticity of ratification (that is, when the home country becomes a Party to the OECD Anti-Bribery Convention) on the sensitivity of international investment flows to one point changes the two perceived corruption measures.

The estimations show that a 1 point rise in the Transparency International Corruption Perceptions Index will have the "helping hand" FDI parameter reduced by about 40% via adherence, as captured by the interaction term. For the preferred World Bank index, there is no significant "helping hand" effect, so that a 1 point rise in corruption in the host (in a 0-10 range) will see FDI fall by between 4 and 9% in absolute terms for countries that have ratified the OECD Anti-Bribery Convention (depending on which corruption measure is used). These results reflect the compliance risks that host countries with high perceived corruption pose for both investors based in countries where foreign bribery has been criminalised.

The corruption perception indices that are used to characterise corruption in these estimated equations are not policy variables upon which governments can act directly. One might, therefore, ask: what policy changes need to be enacted to get declines in these corruption perception indices?

While this is a complex question that is necessarily linked to country-specific characteristics (e.g. the level of development and the relative importance of different sectors), a broad approach might still involve improving performance in the policy areas that underpin these indices. For the Corruption Control Index (CCI), these include:[1]

- Increasing trust in politicians (e.g. by disciplining political financing).
- Reducing diversion of public funds (e.g. through improved public sector integrity measures and better public financial controls).
- Reducing irregular payments in export and import, public utilities, tax collection, public contracts, judicial decisions.
- Disciplining state capture.
- Lowering the level of "petty" corruption between administration and citizens and between administrations and local and foreign businesses.

These variables are correlated with other World Bank indexes that were found to be even more significant than the corruption index itself for FDI. In particular, voice and accountability of governments in an open society, political stability and well-run countries with sound regulations are attractive to foreign investors.

With respect to the OECD Anti-Bribery Convention, the apparent impact of criminal laws suggests that increasing the number of Parties and better enforcing laws in countries that are Parties to the OECD Anti-Bribery Convention could begin to turn the tide further against corruption.

1. See http://info.worldbank.org/governance/wgi/pdf/cc.pdf.

Source: Blundell-Wignall and Roulet (2017).

Figure 2.32. **World Bank Corruption Index weighted by GDP, 1996-2015**

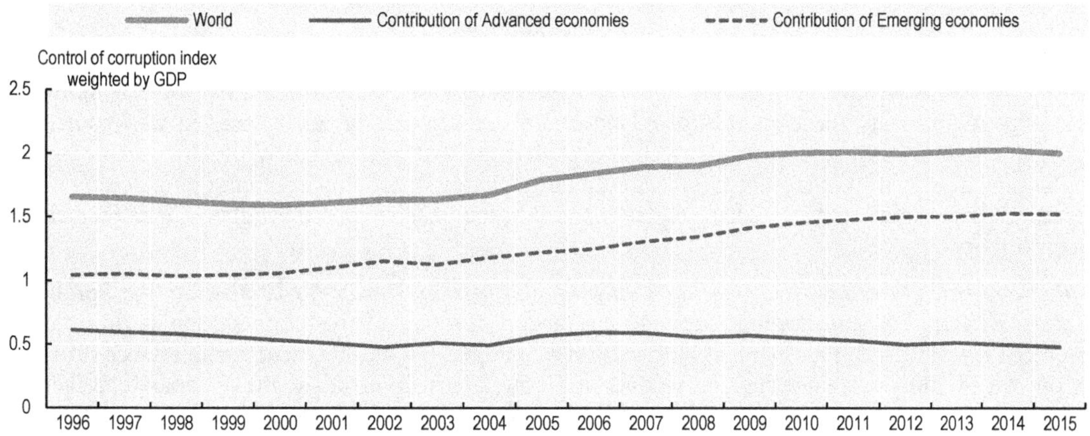

Source: World Bank, Thomson Reuters Datastream, OECD calculations.

StatLink http://dx.doi.org/10.1787/888933476787

Box 2.14. **Bribery by financial intermediaries**

The financial sector plays a crucial role in identifying both new and declining business activities and in allocating capital across sectors in order to create dynamic and productive economies. It also helps manage business and financial risks by providing diversification possibilities and risk pricing. The financial services industry needs to do its job well if global resources are to be allocated in an efficient, welfare-enhancing way. In order to succeed in this, the resource and risk allocation process needs to be free from the harmful influences of bribery and corruption.

Unfortunately, recent law enforcement actions would appear to add to an already-long list of concerns about how some financial institutions conduct their business. The present examination of law enforcement actions against banks traces out a specific sub-set of the broader misconduct that has rattled public trust in financial intermediaries. Specifically, it looks at the role of financial intermediaries in the bribery of foreign public officials.

Financial intermediaries can play several roles in foreign bribery transactions. First, they can facilitate or enable acts of bribery by others through the provision of financial and advisory services (money laundering or advice on hiding beneficial ownership). This Box focuses on another type of misconduct: financial intermediaries' role as active givers of bribes to foreign public officials. In order to do this, a survey is conducted of completed law enforcement actions that resulted in sanctions on financial intermediaries for bribery. These sanctions mean that the intermediaries have been found responsible for offering, giving, or promising bribes to a foreign public official. The 41 Parties to the Anti-Bribery Convention commit to making such misconduct a criminal offence.

These cases involve 10 major financial intermediaries (banks, insurance companies and hedge funds) and 8 smaller businesses providing various financial services. By examining these 18 completed cases, the OECD has explored the anatomy of supply side bribery in the financial sector using the same methodology as that of the 2014 OECD Foreign Bribery Report (OECD, 2014). The Foreign Bribery Report provides a clear picture of the crime of foreign bribery in all sectors (e.g. extractive industries, construction, transportation) and documents how it has been committed to date. It measures such characteristics as: who is bribing and who is being bribed; where the bribes are being paid; where law enforcement actions are taking place and the kinds of sanctions these actions produce.

Box 2.14. **Bribery by financial intermediaries** (cont.)

These cases constitute a rather special subset of all the bribes given by financial intermediaries in that the perpetrators have been caught and sanctioned. The cases were brought by WGB countries (the large majority by the United States).Undoubtedly, there are far more cases in the financial sector that have never been detected, much less prosecuted and sanctioned. While this sample may not be typical (e.g. it over-represents financial intermediaries in actively enforcing jurisdictions), it nevertheless provides some insights – indeed, possibly the only available insights -- into financial sector bribery.

Which countries have imposed sanctions on financial intermediaries for bribery? In the Foreign Bribery Report, US enforcement agencies accounted for about two-thirds of the anti-bribery enforcement actions. In the financial intermediaries' sample, US enforcement agencies account for 18 out of 28 sanctions targeting individuals and companies involved in the18 separate bribery schemes. The total enforcement actions include actions by the US Securities and Exchange Commission, the US Department of Justice, the UK Serious Fraud Office and Financial Conduct Authority and actions by three other law enforcement agencies in Korea, Japan and Germany. Thus, in both samples, US enforcement agencies account for the bulk of cases. It is perhaps normal, given the size of their financial sectors, that the United Kingdom and the United States dominate the enforcement activity against financial intermediaries. The three other sanctioning countries were Germany, Japan and Korea, each of which sanctioned one bribery scheme.

In which countries are the bribes given? The Foreign Bribery Report uses these data to conclude that there may be a need to revisit the "common perception of bribery in international business transactions" as consisting of "business people and companies from the wealthiest, most developed economies who only bribe officials from least developed countries to win lucrative contracts." In contrast to the Report's findings for the general sample, the financial intermediaries sample suggests that the "common perception" is correct. All of the companies involved in these bribery schemes had their headquarters in one of three G7 countries (Germany, the United Kingdom or the United States), though the schemes often took place with the involvement of host country subsidiaries and other foreign business partners. Of the 22 countries where bribery took place, 11 were in very poor countries (e.g. Chad, Democratic Republic of Congo, Myanmar, Tanzania and Vietnam) defined as having medium or low human development indexes by the UN Development Programme.

Of course, financial intermediaries from other countries engage in bribery and do not show up in samples of completed cases for a variety of reasons (e.g. because they are not caught, prosecuted and sanctioned or because reporting of concluded cases is sketchy or non-existent). That being said, a principal characteristic of these detected and sanctioned cases fits well with the "common perception" – it is one of financial intermediaries from highly developed countries bribing public officials in countries that, on average, have much lower development levels and pressing needs for better infrastructure, better public services and enhanced trust in government. Thus, they contribute to creating an investment climate in which globalisation fails to work for important segments of the world's population.

Why and to whom do financial intermediaries give bribes? Obtaining and retaining government contracts is, by far, the most common motivation for financial intermediaries' bribes to public officials (it motivated 73% of the cases). Interestingly, bribes that aim to influence prudential monitoring are largely absent from the sample. This confirms – indeed, reinforces – the Foreign Bribery Report's finding that public procurement was the aim of bribery in 57% of the all-sector sample. Thus, the desire to obtain or retain government business was the dominant motivation for foreign bribery in all sectors, and even more so in the financial sector.

Box 2.14. **Bribery by financial intermediaries** (cont.)

This motivation is linked to the question of who – that is, what category of public official – is being bribed (Figure 2.33). As in the OECD Foreign Bribery Report, officials working in state-owned enterprises – accounting for 8 of the 18 bribery schemes (44%) – were the most common receivers of bribes by financial intermediaries. Other receivers of bribes were sovereign wealth funds (two cases) and public pension or insurance officials (three cases). All of these bribes were oriented toward obtaining or retaining business.

Figure 2.33. **Bribes targeted which category of public official?**

(Number of enforcement actions)

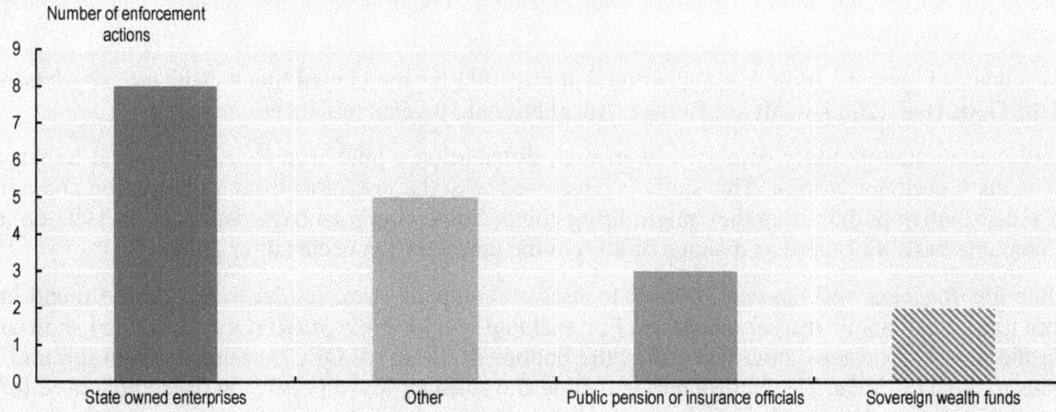

Source: (OECD, 2014), *OECD Foreign Bribery Report.*

StatLink http://dx.doi.org/10.1787/888933476799

Which corporate actors are involved in bribery schemes? The Foreign Bribery Report (page 22) states that "in the majority of cases, corporate management (41%) or even the CEO (12%) was aware of and endorsed the bribery, debunking the "rogue employee" myth …". This finding of various forms of top management involvement in bribe schemes is reinforced in the sample of financial intermediaries – in the sample, 67% of the bribes involved top corporate officials and virtually all involve a class of employees that could be categorised as "management". There were no cases in which only non-managerial staff were involved in the bribery. Thus, bribery in the financial sector is conducted by high level, managerial staff and, more often than not, by top management and corporate officers. Given that these financial sector actors are usually subject to high powered incentives created by these organisations' bonus culture, sanctions for foreign bribery needs to include sanctions on individuals (such as prison sentences) to counter-balance the effects of these incentives.

Notes

1. Agricultural subsidies have been the main point of conflict.

2. Just as a state within a country does not finance its investment by savings within that state, so too should countries that do not repress financially not see national investment heavily correlated with national saving. For emerging economies this correlation is around 0.7, compared to 0.3 for OECD countries. See Figure 6.6 in Blundell-Wignall, Atkinson and Roulet (2013), p. 209.

3. See Liu (2005) and Cai et al. (2008). China chose a regional organisational structure for its SOEs, with self-contained local governments responsible for a wide array of production. This had begun with the Deng Xiaoping agriculture reforms, where experiments with small-scale price liberalisation were highly successful, and this approach was extended to other sectors and notably steel and other intermediate inputs.

4. This updates Figure 11 from Acemoglu and Autor (2011) for the United States, which is also based on the Goos et al. (2009) study for Europe. An additional 10 years of data are included.

5. While these patterns imply employment income distribution would worsen, after tax and transfer payments it need not worsen. This study is concerned with the pressures from globalisation and not the redistributive policies that they might bring about. Some countries have data back to 1993 on a comparable basis. For these an average of 80% of the deterioration occurs after 2000.

6. While this *Business and Finance Outlook* focuses on company data, similar trends can be found in more traditional labour market databases. For example, *Divided We Stand* (OECD, 2011b) showed that the top decile wages grew faster than the bottom decile in all OECD countries from the mid-1980s to the late 2000s. The inclusion of part-time and self-employed persons in the sample used for this study worsens the overall picture.

7. It is a focus at the OECD, is referenced by the IMF (www.imf.org/external/pubs/ft/fandd/2016/12/obstfeld.htm), and has been written up by the Economist magazine of 10 March 2017.

8. A Chow test for a structural break from December 2001 confirms the highly-significant presence of such a break for both of the series shown.

9. See, for example, Melitz (2003) and Melitz and Redding (2012). The underlying idea in Melitz (2003) is that only highly productive firms are able to make sufficient profits to cover the large fixed costs required for export operations.

10. Unmanned factories are already operational in North America. Amazon is about to launch unmanned stores, so that even lower skilled service sector jobs are at risk. Any activities that can be broken up into calculations and/or repetitive activities can be digitalised and linked up across the internet and applied to everything in the end: production, innovation and design, inventory control and logistics, and driverless road, rail, sea and air transport. Robotics, cloud computing and the internet of things (where objects can communicate information about themselves to feed into the above processes) are platforms for innovation that are unstoppable in businesses that want to survive in the modern competitive world.

11. As in the Harrod-Balassa-Samuelson effect. In a survey of the empirical literature to 2006, Tica et.al (2006) found that 49 out of 58 empirical studies supported the presence of the effect. More recently Berka et al. (2014) found evidence for the effect in the context of European data. Rodrik (2008) uses this approach.

12. Domestic currency per unit of the US dollar, so the measure here falls when the domestic currency is appreciating; i.e. the US dollar would buy less of it.

13. Alternatively, crises resulting from poor macro-economic management might bring this about.

14. For example, studies based on OECD's trade input-output data suggest that the often-mentioned policy goal of China to move towards a greater focus on domestic consumption, were it to happen, could actually worsen the trade imbalance. This is because investment in China is much more import intensive than for its consumer goods sectors. Without major relative price shifts in the direction of Chinese Yuan appreciation, there would be additional headwinds for exporting to China. See Roberts and Kelly (2016).

15. BRIICS consist of Brazil, Russia, India, Indonesia, China, and South Africa.

16. Atkeson and Burstein (2008) are able to explain the large (and variable) swings in the PPP real exchange rate (implicit in Figure 2.9) with pricing to market (as is implicit in Figure 2.10), in a model of international trade. Markets are separated by trade costs and imperfect competition with variable mark-ups. Pricing to maintain market share by large firms drives observed wider swings in PPP real exchange rates. Separately, Navarro (2006) focuses on the "China price", where an attempt is made to quantify some of the drivers of pricing to market share. Undervaluation ranks only fourth in his analysis.

17. G-SIBs must hold 16% TLAC (versus RWA) by the start date of 1 January 2019. This threshold rises to 18% by 2022. TLAC is to consist of Tier 1 and Tier 2 capital, made up to the requirement with at least 6% additional plain vanilla long-term unsecured non-callable debt with at least one year of remaining maturity (that can be bailed in). There are some problems with this idea: forcing banks to take on more leverage for an instrument that has not been tested and may not prove useful as bail-in capital in an actual crisis raises questions about the reasoning. This may be a way for banks to avoid raising equity capital.

18. For any two or more institutions owned by a non-EU parent with assets of branches and/or subsidiaries greater than EUR30.bn. See European Commission (2016).

19. These include leverage reforms in the United States, rule writing under the Dodd-Frank Act and the continuing amendments to the European Union's CRD IV (capital requirements directive for prudential supervision) and CRR (capital requirements regulation).

20. A buffer of 2% versus the Basel leverage ratio of only 3%—for Bank Holding Companies with USD 700 billion of assets or USD 10 trillion under custody. This must be a 6% leverage ratio for insured depository institutions (IDI's) within the group. These rules will be effective from 1 January 2018. Smaller foreign IHC's will have to undergo stress testing if consolidated assets are USD10 billion.

21. If capital is a proportion λ of RWA and leverage (L) is the ratio of total assets (TA) to capital, then it follows that $L=TA/\lambda RWA$. A 1% rise in TA/RWA is a 1% rise in leverage. Banks make profits by leveraging spreads. It is in the banks interest to target a fall in the ratio of RWA/TA using internal models and derivatives to do so. It is because some regulators have continued to think of this as purely a risk ratio that banks continue to exploit it. They fight hard to keep risk-weighting and to be against the leverage ratio that was noted in earlier OECD publications. During the crisis the banks with the lowest ratio of RWA/TA proved to be the most risky.

22. See Bank for International Settlements (2013). An identical set of assets required some 300% more capital at the most demanding bank than at the least demanding one.

23. For example, in Blundell-Wignall, Wehinger and Slovik (2009).

24. For smaller banks not able to use internal models, external (agency-based) riskweightings are used.

25. See BIS (2016a) and BIS (2016b). Operational risk would revert to the standard approach.

26. See www.bis.org/bcbs/publ/comments/d362/overview.htm.

27. See Dombrovskis (2016). The European Banking Federation republished the speech under its own banner.

28. See Ames et al. (2015). This appears to be true. The United States uses the loss distribution approach, stress testing under the Comprehensive Capital Analysis Review does not allow expert overrides, and banks have not used insurance mitigation.

29. See Blundell-Wignall et al., (2008, 2009, 2010, 2011, 2012, 2013), and OECD (2009).

30. These risks have nothing to do with those associated with the global macro cycle, which is the common risk factor in the formal underpinning of the Basel framework. The correlation between these risks is at best unknowable and at worst non-existent. Legal risks are fat-tailed and may be levied years after events, while fraud often occurs over many years before detection.

31. That is the quality of collateral and tougher margin rules, documented in previous OECD reports on Basel and FSB processes.

32. See Financial Stability Board (2015), (2017). The 2016 Shadow banking monitoring report will be published soon. The European Systemic Risk Board has similar products.

33. See for example the consultative document on resolution planning for central clearing counterparties: www.fsb.org/wp-content/uploads/Guidance-on-Central-Counterparty-Resolution-and-Resolution-Planning.pdf.

34. The DTD compares book value of liabilities to the market value of bank assets, which are not reported by banks (and indeed poor loans may well be hidden by banks). The market value of assets is therefore calculated using stock price levels and volatility measure via the Black-Scholes option formulas. See Blundell-Wignall and Roulet (2013) for a full description.

35. See page 14 of www.pbc.gov.cn/goutongjiaoliu/113456/113469/3254786/2017021719463365852.pdf.

36. A number of state-owned utilities in Europe have actually benefited from EU liberalisation to invest in neighbouring jurisdictions. However, they remain "domestic" in the sense that they operate only in the EU single market.

37. Classens et al. (2000) chooses above 10% as effective government control in complex Asian listing structures.

38. This sample excludes a sizeable unlisted SOE sector that still remains following the large privatisations between 1995 and 2005.

39. Measured at the company data level and a weighted average is calculated. This includes the effects of implicit subsidies that affect the COK.

40. Debt longer than one year; enterprise value is long term debt plus the value of common equity.

41. Maskin et al. (2000) identify China as an M-Form organisational structure. For a firm it would be one divided into autonomous divisions like GM's Chevrolet and Oldsmobile.

42. The Global Forum on Steel Excess Capacity, called for by G20 Leaders in September 2016 and co-Chaired by China, will foster international discussion on these issues through increased information sharing and co-operation among G20 and OECD members on ways to address steel excess capacity around the world. The outcomes from this work should be of value not only to the steel sector, but also more generally.

43. See *Chen* (2015) for an in-depth discussion of the solar photovoltaic industry.

44. Including some smaller European countries, which attract less attention due to their small size.

45. In competitive markets, the size of domestic firms may or may not rise. Where firms already produce at the minimum efficient scale, opening markets may allow them to introduce better technologies, improve products, reduce costs, but not to increase scale. In markets that are not initially competitive, globalisation may sufficiently increase the size of the market to allow

domestic companies to exhaust economies of scale and make the market competitive. In this latter case, domestic firms may become larger.

46. This is taken from the March 2016 edition of the Private International Cartels Database, the main private database source for cartels.

47. Total affected sales of cross-border cartels from 1990-2015 that were fined. This excludes the large Libor and London Gold Fix cartels.

48. See Connor (2016). The average overcharge for the cross-border fined cartels in the Private International Cartels Database, for which this data was available, was approximately 20.5%. Overcharge amounts were available for 84 of the 240 cartels.

49. See Boyer and Kotchoni (2015); Connor, (2014). Europe detects more cartels (due to the EU Commission's strong attitude on cartels). Overcharging in Europe is three to four times that of other jurisdictions. The United States is unique in having less fines, but makes this up with virtually all of the world's civil penalties located there.

50. Members of a cartel always have the temptation to raise margins in uncontested markets so 'impatient' existing 'partners' might deviate from the agreement and enter another's territory. If this would risk pushing down margins, the firms may agree to share each other's geographical markets—so that a form of 'equilibrium' with higher profits can still be sustained. See Baake and Norman (2002) and Bond and Syropulous (2008).

51. Sometimes the accusation of gouging (exploiting a monopoly position in the face of inelastic demand) in pharmaceuticals is played up unfairly by the press when, after decades of research without revenue, a drug comes onto the market and the company attempts to pay-back the costs with high prices. This issue of the cost of research and payback is not taken up in this *Outlook*.

52. For example, for a sample of 25 large banks, investment banking fees represented on average 11.82% of non-interest income in 2015. Source: OECD calculations based on balance sheets of 25 large investment banks.

53. OECD calculations based on gross premiums written to cover US companies as reported by Lloyd's (2016), and gross premiums written by US insurers as reported by the National Association of Insurance Commissioners.

54. Global Reinsurance Forum (2016). Transactions and transfers in connection with reinsurance and retrocession are included within the scope of the OECD Code of Liberalisation of Current Invisible Operations (OECD, 2016c).

55. It also depends on correlation and on exposure of the domestic equity market to overseas operations. For example, a fund from an OPEC country would not get much diversification benefit from investing in the United Kingdom or France if they are high weighting oil companies in local benchmarks. Similarly, a pension fund in the United Kingdom, investing in the United Kingdom, may be already exposed to companies that make all their profits in Asia, so it may not be in their best interest to buy into the Hong Kong, China market.

56. See Phillips et. al. (2012), of Vanguard and references therein.

57. These include currency risk; tax implications (repatriating dividends, coupons); intermediaries (local investors do not know the microstructure of foreign markets, which puts them at a disadvantage, so if they outsource investments to foreign experts/global equities it adds to costs); investors may need to grow teams and increase expertise, otherwise, if they do not internalise the benefits, they hardly internalise the costs (in other words, there are also potential agency problems); set up costs to operate and manage risks from a larger number of risk factors and due to short-termism in investment strategies, which could hinder the deployment of resources abroad; knowledge of the foreign country's legal system; political biased investment policies, etc.

58. However, there are restrictions on investing in certain regions. Some OECD countries (i.e. Denmark, Finland, Iceland, Israel, Luxembourg, Mexico, Norway, Poland, Portugal, Slovak Republic, Slovenia and Spain) and six reporting non-OECD jurisdictions (Albania, Bulgaria, FYR of Macedonia, Jamaica, Kosovo and Liechtenstein) allow investments abroad in selected geographical areas only while preventing investments elsewhere (or setting a lower ceiling). Foreign investments may not be restricted if they are made in OECD countries (e.g. Denmark) or EU countries (e.g. Bulgaria). Mexico and Jamaica set a list of eligible countries in which pension funds can invest. Israel does not allow investments in securities issued by countries rated below BBB- and which are not part of the OECD.

59. Governments may indeed encourage pension funds to invest domestically to lower the cost of capital for themselves or for local firms, which may be sub-optimal in terms of returns.

60. There are many reasons for investing domestically – liabilities are in your home currency so it makes sense for your assets to be denominated the same way (currency hedging is difficult and expensive); liabilities will grow in line with domestic inflation so assets should too (i.e. domestic equity is the best hedge).

61. An OECD gravity model study of FDI shows that these agglomerations are second only to GDP attractiveness as positive determinants of FDI flows. See Blundell-Wignall and Roulet (2017).

62. Although RBC is sometimes used interchangeably with corporate social responsibility (CSR), it is understood to be more comprehensive and integral to core business than what is traditionally considered CSR (mainly philanthropy). RBC focuses on integrating and considering environmental and social issues within core business activities.

63. The World Bank estimated a welfare price tag of USD 5.1 trillion in 2013. See: http://documents.worldbank.org/curated/en/781521473177013155/pdf/108141-REVISED-Cost-of-PollutionWebCORRECTEDfile.pdf

64. Ageron et.al, (2012) provide a survey of supply-chain managers in 178 French companies: 73 large, 96 medium and 9 small. 75% are manufacturing companies, and the rest are split evenly between: power generation; medical and pharmaceutical; logistics providers; and sales and distribution companies.

65. Friede et.al, (2015). The authors are from Deutsche Asset Management and the University of Hamburg. An earlier meta-study that looked at 127 studies published between 1972 and 2002 found that almost half of the studies pointed to a positive relationship between corporate social performance and financial performance. Only seven studies found a negative relationship; 28 studies reported non-significant relationships, while 20 reported a mixed set of findings. See Margolis and Walsh (2003).

66. See Blundell-Wignall and Roulet (2016) and references therein for a discussion of some of these indicators.

67. See OECD (2015). The main focus is that tantalum, tin, tungsten and gold in company products should not finance conflict in the Democratic Republic of Congo or an adjoining country—a high conflict zone region rich in minerals. Companies need to source responsibly from those regions, not just cut them out of their supply chains.

68. The Dodd-Frank Act defines "conflict minerals" as columbite-tantalite (coltan), cassiterite, gold, wolframite, or their derivatives, or any other mineral or its derivatives that are determined by the Secretary of State to be financing conflict in the Democratic Republic of Congo or an adjoining country. Columbite-tantalite, cassiterite, and wolframite are the ores from which tantalum, tin, and tungsten, respectively, are processed.

69. See New York City Bar Association (2011). The argument is that the United States taking the lead in global enforcement could invite strategic non-enforcement by other countries (as a kind of subsidy to their companies) and, via this effect, might actually make corruption worse. However,

the United States has an expansive concept of jurisdiction and many major foreign multinationals are subject to US jurisdiction under the FCPA. Indeed, many have been successfully prosecuted under the FCPA (7 of the 10 largest enforcement actions concerned foreign companies). The Bar Association paper correctly points out that this expansive definition of jurisdiction is an incentive for de-listing from US securities markets. This, of course, is a huge disincentive to corrupt behaviour—given the advantages of US listing. The argument about encouraging corruption could conceivably apply to foreign small and medium-sized enterprises not listed in the US, in cases where the crime is not committed on US territory. This small and medium-sized enterprise issue is less relevant to the global multinational enterprise issues discussed in this *Outlook.*

70. Larger numbers are found for around the same period currency demand approach (money laundering affects the usage of untraceable currency). Reuter and Truman (2004) quote estimates by others of around USD 3 trillion in 1999, i.e. double that of the micro survey based approach. The numbers include the informal economy; detected bribes brought before justice are much smaller, as the bulk of bribes and money laundering are not detected

71. The most up-to-date estimate suggests that to achieve sustainable development goals total public and private infrastructure spending between now and 2030 will have to run at an average rate of USD 3.4-4 trillion per annum for the global economy, and at around USD 1.5 trillion per annum for advanced economies. See Battacharia et al. (2016).

72. In some ways this turns conventional thinking on its head. While host countries can benefit from FDI, and some have, advanced-economy companies are major beneficiaries. See Box 4.

73. More corrupt countries invest more in each other, and their rent seeking behavior does not promote productivity growth. Less corrupt countries also invest more in each other and are larger and very much richer than the former.

References

Aceloglu, D, and D.H. Autor, (2011), "Skills, Tasks and Technologies: Implications for Employment and Earnings", *Handbook of Labor Economics*, Vol. 4b.

Ageron, B. and A. Spalanzani (2012), "Sustainable Supply Chain Management: An Empirical Study", *International Journal of Production Economics*, vol. 140.

Allen, F. J. Qian and M. Qian (2005), "Law, finance, and Economic Growth in China", *Journal of Financial Economics,* vol. 77.

Allianz, (2017), Allianz Risk Barometer Top Business Risk for 2017. www.agcs.allianz.com/assets/PDFs/Reports/Allianz_Risk_Barometer_2017_EN.pdf

Ames, T., T. Schuermann, H.S. Scott (2015), "Bank Capital for Operational Risk: A Tale of Fragility and Instability", Wharton http://fic.wharton.upenn.edu/fic/papers/14/14-02_feb2015update.pdf.

Atkeson, A. and A. Burstein (2008), "Pricing to Market, Trade Costs and International Relative Prices", *American Economic Review*, vol. 98:5.

Auerbach, A.J. and D. Holz-Eakin (2016), "The Role of Border Adjustments in International Taxation", *American Action Forum*, Washington.

Ayadi, R., De Groen, W. P., (2015), "Banking Business Model Monitor 2015 in Europe", International Research Center on Cooperative Finance, HEC Montreal.

Autor, D.H., D. Dorn and G.H. Henderson (2016), "The China Shock: Learning from Labour Market Adjustment to large Changes in Trade". *NBER Working Paper*, number 21906.

Baake, P and H.T. Normann (2002), "Collusive intra-industry trade in identical commodities," *Review of World Economics*, vol. 138.

Balsvik, R., S. Jensen and K. G. Salvanes (2015), "Made in China, Sold in Norway:

Local Labor Market Effects of an Import Shock, *Journal of Public Economics*, vol. 127: pp 137-144.

Bank of England (2015), "Building Real Markets for the Good of the People", Open Forum, June.

Bank for International Settlements (2013), "Regulatory Consistency Assessment Programme (RCAP) – Analysis of risk-weighted assets for market risk".

Bank for International Settlements (2016a), "Standardised Measurement Approach for Operational Risk-Consultative Document", March.

Bank for International Settlements (2016b), "Reducing Variation in Credit Risk-Weighted Assets", June.

Berka, M., M. B. Devereux and C. Engel, (2014), "Real Exchange Rates and Sectoral Productivity in the Eurozone," *NBER Working Paper No.* 20510, September.

Bhattacharya, A., J.P. Meltzer, J. Oppenheim, Z. Qureshi, and N. Stern (2016), "Delivering on Sustainable Infrastructure for Better Development and Better Climate", report for the *Global Economy and Development at Brookings*, December.

Bernanke, B. (2005), "The Global Saving Glut and the U.S. Current Account Deficit", Federal Reserve Board, *Homer Jones Lecture.*

Bernard, Andrew B., J. Bradford Jensen, Stephen J. Redding and Peter K. Schott (2007). "Firms in International Trade." *Journal of Economic Perspectives*, Vol. 21, No.3, pp. 105-130.

Benhamou, S. and M. Diaye (2016), "Corporate Social Responsibility and Competitiveness. Evaluation and Strategic Approach". www.strategie.gouv.fr/sites/strategie.gouv.fr/files/atoms/files/synthese-rse_en.pdf

BFC (2016), *Better Factories Cambodia: Garment Industry 33rd Compliance Synthesis Report*, June.

Borjas, G.J., R.B. Freeman and L.J. Katz (1997), "How Much Do Immigration and Trade Affect Labor Market Outcomes?", *Brookings Papers on Economic Activity*, vol. 1.

Boyer, M. and R. Kotchoni (2015), "How Much Do Cartels Overcharge?", *Journal of Industrial Organization*, vol. 47.

Blundell-Wignall, A. and Atkinson, P.E., (2008), "The Subprime Crisis: Causal Distortions and Regulatory Reform", in *Lessons from the Financial Turmoil of 2007 and 2008*, Kent and Bloxham (eds.), Reserve Bank of Australia.

Blundell-Wignall, A., Paul Atkinson and Se Hoon Lee (2009), "The current financial crisis: Causes and policy issues", *OECD Journal: Financial Market Trends*, Vol. 2008/2. http://dx.doi.org/10.1787/fmt-v2008-art10-en.

Blundell-Wignall, A., Gert Wehinger and Patrick Slovik (2010), "The elephant in the room: The need to deal with what banks do", *OECD Journal: Financial Market Trends*, Vol. 2009/2. http://dx.doi.org/10.1787/fmt-v2009-art11-en.

Blundell-Wignall, A.and Paul Atkinson (2012), "Deleveraging, Traditional versus Capital Markets Banking and the Urgent Need to Separate and Recapitalise G-SIFI Banks", *OECD Journal: Financial Market Trends*, Vol. 2012/1. http://dx.doi.org/10.1787/fmt-2012-5k91hbvgfq20.

Blundell-Wignall, A.and Paul Atkinson (2011), "Global SIFIs, Derivatives and Financial Stability", *OECD Journal: Financial Market Trends*, Vol. 2011/1. http://dx.doi.org/10.1787/fmt-2011-5kg55qw0qsbv.

Blundell-Wignall, A.and Paul Atkinson (2010), "Thinking beyond Basel III: Necessary Solutions for Capital and Liquidity", *OECD Journal: Financial Market Trends*, Vol. 2010/1. http://dx.doi.org/10.1787/fmt-2010-5km7k9tpcjmn.

Blundell-Wignall, A. and C. Roulet (2017), "Foreign direct investment, corruption and the OECD Anti-Bribery Convention", *OECD Working Papers on International Investment*, No. 2017/01, OECD Publishing, Paris. http://dx.doi.org/10.1787/9cb3690c-en.

Blundell-Wignall, Adrian and Caroline Roulet (2016), "Evaluating capital flow management measures used as macro-prudential tools", OECD Journal: Financial Market Trends, Vol. 2015/2. http://dx.doi.org/10.1787/fmt-2015-5jm0p44dlq6f.

Blundell-Wignall, A.and Caroline Roulet (2013), "Business models of banks, leverage and the distance-to-default", *OECD Journal: Financial Market Trends*, Vol. 2012/2. http://dx.doi.org/10.1787/fmt-2012-5k4bxlxbd646.

Blundell-Wignall, A., Paul Atkinson and Caroline Roulet (2014), "Bank business models and the Basel system: Complexity and interconnectedness", *OECD Journal: Financial Market Trends*, Vol. 2013/2. http://dx.doi.org/10.1787/fmt-2013-5jzb2rhkd65b.

Blundell-Wignall, A., P.E. Atkinson, C. Roulet (2013), "Integration versus Interdependence and Complexity in Global Trade and Finance in the Post-War Period", in Morten and Gnan (eds.) *50 Years of Money and Finance: Lessons and Challenges, SUERF 50th Anniversary Volume*, Larcier.

Blundell-Wignall, A., Atkinson, P.E. and Roulet, C., (2012), "The Business Models of Large Interconnected Banks and the Lessons of the Financial Crisis, *National Institute Economic Review,* No. 221.

Bond, E.W. and C. Syropoulos (2008), "Trade costs and Multimarket Collusion," *Rand Journal of Economics,* vol. 39:4.

Burstein, A. and J. Vogel (2016), "International Trade, Technology, and the Skill Premium", Columbia University, *mimeo.*

Cai, F, A Park and Z Yao (2008): "The Chinese labour market in the reform era", in L Brandt and T Rawski edit, *China's Great Economic Transformation*, Cambridge University Press, pp 167–214.

Case, K.E., J.M. Quigley and R.J. Shiller (2013), "Wealth Effects Revisited: 1975-2012", *NBER Working Paper, No. 18667.*

Carney, M. (2015), "Breaking the Tragedy of the Horizon – Climate Change and Financial Stability", *Speech to Lloyds of London*, Bank of England.

Chen, T-J. (2015), The Development of China's Solar Photovoltaic Industry: Why Industrial Policy Failed", *Cambridge Journal of Economics.*

Chinn, M. D., Ito, H. (2006). What matters for financial development? Capital controls, institutions, and interactions. Journal of Development Economics, 81 (1): 163-192.

Chinese Due Diligence Guidelines for Responsible Mineral Supply Chains, (2015), available at: www.globalwitness.org/documents/18138/201512_Chinese_Due_Diligence_Guidelines_for_Responsible_Mineral_Supply_Chains_-_En_K83fxzt.pdf Cimino and Hufbauer (2014), "Trade remedies targeting the renewable energy sector," *Green Economy and Trade. Ad hoc Expert Group 2: Trade Remedies in Green Sectors: the Case of Renewables*, UNCTAD, Geneva, http://unctad.org/meetings/en/SessionalDocuments/ditc_ted_03042014Petersen_Institute.pdf.

Classens, S., S. Djankov and L.H.P. Lang (2000), "The separation of ownership and control in East Asian Corporations", *Journal of Financial Economics*, vol. 58.

Clark, G. L. A. Feiner and M. Viehs (2015), From the Stockholder to the Stakeholder: How Sustainability Can Drive Financial Outperformance, University of Oxford.

Connor, J.M. (2016), "Cartel Overcharges", *Research in Law and Economics,* vol. 26.

Connor, J.M. (2016), "International Cartel Stats: A Look at The Last 26 Years", *Law 360*, New York.

Dauth, W., S. Findeisen and J. Suedekum (2014), "The Rise of the East and the Far East: German Labour Markets and Trade Integration", *Journal of the European Economic Association*, 12(6): pp 1643-1675.

Dombrovskis, V.P. (2016), "Embracing Disruption", *speech to the European Banking Federation*, 29 September.

Donoso, V., V. Martin and A. Minondo (2014), "Do differences in exposure to Chinese imports lead to differences in local labour market outcomes? An analysis for Spanish Provinces, *Regional Studies*, 1-19.

Eccles G.R., I. Ioannou I. and G. Serafeim (2011), "The Impact of a Corporate Culture of Sustainability on Corporate Behavior and Performance," *Harvard Business School, Working Paper* 12-035, November.

European Commission (2016), "Proposal for a Directive to the European Parliament and of the Council", COM (2016) 854 final.

Financial Stability Board (2017), *Global Shadow Banking Monitoring Report 2016.* http://www.fsb.org/wp-content/uploads/global-shadow-banking-monitoring-report-2016.pdf.

Financial Stability Board (2016), 2016 list of global systemically important banks (G-SIBs). www.fsb.org/wp-content/uploads/2016-list-of-global-systemically-important-banks-G-SIBs.pdf.

Financial Stability Board (2015), *Global Shadow Banking Monitoring Report 2015.* http://www.fsb.org/wp-content/uploads/global-shadow-banking-monitoring-report-2015.pdf.

Furman, J. and P. Orszag (2015), "A Firm-Level Perspective on the Role of Rents in the Rise in Inequality", Presentation at "A Just Society" Centennial Event in Honour of Joseph Stiglitz, Columbia University.

Friede, G., T. Buschi and A. Bassen (2015), "ESG and Financial Performance: Aggregated Evidence from More than 2000 Empirical Studies", *Journal of Sustainable Finance & Investment*, Vol. 5, Issue 4.

Freeman, R.B. (1995), "Are Your Wages Set in Beijing?", *Journal of Economic Perspectives*, vol. 9, 3.

Funke, M. and J. Rahn (2004), "Just How Undervalued is the Chinese Renmimbi?", *Bank of Finland Discussion Paper* , number 14/2004.

Global Environment Facility (2014), "Taking tropical deforestation out of global supply chains". www.thegef.org/sites/default/files/publications/GEF_Commodities-R3_0.pdf.

Global Reinsurance Forum (2014), "Global reinsurance: strengthening disaster risk resilience". www.grf.info/images/Publications/GRF2014-Global_reinsurance-strengthening_disaster_risk_resilience.pdf.

Goos, M., Manning A., Salomon A., (2009), "Job Polarization in Europe", *American Economic Review: Papers & Proceedings*, vol. 99:2.

Goos, M., Manning A., Salomon A., (2014), "Explaining Job Polarization: Routine-Biased Technological Change and Offshoring", *American Economic Review*, 104(8), 2509-2526.

Green, D.A. and B. Sand, (2011), Has the Canadian Labour Market Polarised?, University of British Columbia and Government of Canada, October. http://faculty.arts.ubc.ca/kmilligan/CanadianPolarization5.pdf.

Hoenig, T. (2016), "Strengthening Global Capital: An Opportunity Not To Be Lost" – Remarks by FDIC Vice Chairman Thomas M. Hoenig to the 22nd Annual Risk US Conference, New York, 9 November.

Helpman, Elhanan, Marc J. Melitz and Stephen Ross Yeaple (2004). "Export Versus FDI with Heterogeneous Firms." *American Economic Review,* Vol.94, No.1, pp.300-316.

Hellwig, M. and K. Hüschelrath (2016), "Cartel cases and the cartel enforcement process in the European Union 2001-2015: A quantitative assessment", *Centre for European Economic Research Discussion Paper* No. 16-063.

ILO (2015), *World Report on Child Labour 2015: Paving the way to decent work for young people*, Geneva. www.ilo.org/ipec/Informationresources/WCMS_358969/lang--en/index.htm.

ILO (2016), Forced labour, modern slavery and human trafficking website. www.ilo.org/global/topics/forced-labour/lang--en/index.htm; and Global Slavery Index Global Findings, www.globalslaveryindex.org/findings/.

KPMG (2016), "The return of the bank wealth management business to asset Management". Mainland China Banking Survey 2016. https://assets.kpmg.com/content/dam/kpmg/cn/pdf/en/2016/09/mainland-china-banking-survey-2016.pdf.

Kaufmann, Daniel (2005), "Myths and Realities of Governance and Corruption." *MPRA Paper* 8089, Munich. Subsequently published by the World Bank.

Kovak, B. (2013), "Regional Effects of Trade Reform: What is the Correct Measure of Liberalization?", *American Economic Review*, vol. 103(5): pp 1960-1976.

Krugman, P. (2000), "Trade, Technology, and Factor Prices", *Journal of International Economics*, 50(1).

Kwiatkowski, G., and P. Augustynowciz (2015), "State-owned enterprises in the global economy – analysis based on Fortune Global 500 list", *Management Knowledge and Learning Joint Conference*, Italy, 27-29 May.

Liu, Liying (March 2005) "Bidding farewell to this year's laid off workers", *China News Weekly*, vol. 220.

Levenstein, M., J. Sivadasan and S. Suslow (2015), "The Effect of Competition on Trade Patterns: Evidence from the Collapse of International Cartels*", Journal of Industrial Organization,* Forthcoming.

Ma, G. and Y. Wang (2010), "China's High Saving Rate: Myth and Reality", *BIS Working Papers*, No. 312, June.

Margolis, J.D. and J. P. Walsh (2003). "Misery Loves Companies: Rethinking Social Initiatives by Business", *Administrative Science Quarterly*, Vol. 48, No. 2, June.

Maskin, E., Y, Qian and C. Xu (2000), "Incentives, Information, and Organizational Form", *Review of Economic Studies*, vol. 67.

McLaren, J., and S. Hakobyan (2015), "Looking for Local Labour Market Effects of NAFTA, *Review of Economics and Statistics*. Melitz, Marc J. (2003). "The Impact of Trade on Intra-Industry Reallocations and Aggregate Industry Productivity", *Econometrica*, Vol.71, No.6, pp. 1695-1725.

Melitz, M.J. and S.J. Redding (2012), "Heterogeneous Firms and Trade", *NBER Working Paper*, No.18652.

Navarro, P. (2006), "The Economics of the China Price", *Varia (China Perspectives*), Number 68.

New York City Bar Association (2011), "The FCPA and its Impact on International Business Transactions – Should Anything Be Done to Minimize the Consequences of the U.S.'s Unique Position on Combating Offshore Corruption?", International Business Transactions Committee.

Qian, Y and Xu, C. (1993), *Why China's economic reforms differ: the m-form hierarchy and entry/expansion of the non-state sector.* CEP discussion paper, 154.

OECD (2016a), *OECD Business and Finance Outlook 2016*, OECD Publishing, Paris. http://dx.doi.org/10.1787/9789264257573-en.

OECD (2016b), *OECD Due Diligence Guidance for Responsible Supply Chains of Minerals from Conflict-Affected and High-Risk Areas*, 3rd edition, Paris. http://dx.doi.org/10.1787/9789264252479-en.

OECD (2016c), *OECD Code of Liberalisation of Capital Movements*, www.oecd.org/investment/codes.htm.

OECD (2016d), *Responsible Supply Chains in Artisanal and Small-Scale Gold Mining*, http://mneguidelines.oecd.org/FAQ_Sourcing-Gold-from-ASM-Miners.pdf.

OECD (2016e), *OECD Core Principles of Private Pension Regulation*, www.oecd.org/finance/principles-private-pension-regulation.htm.

OECD (2015a), Mineral Supply Chains and Conflict Links in Eastern Democratic Republic of Congo – Five years of Implementing Supply Chain Due Diligence http://mneguidelines.oecd.org/Mineral-Supply-Chains-DRC-Due-Diligence-Report.pdf.

OECD (2015b), *Overcoming Barriers to International Investment in Clean Energy,* OECD Publishing, Paris. http://dx.doi.org/10.1787/9789264227064-en.

OECD (2015c), *OECD Business and Finance Outlook 2015*, OECD Publishing, Paris. http://dx.doi.org/10.1787/9789264234291-en.

OECD (2015d), *OECD Employment Outlook*, Chapter 3, OECD Publishing, Paris. http://dx.doi.org/10.1787/empl_outlook-2015-7-en.

OECD (2013), *Annual Report on the OECD Guidelines for Multinational Enterprises: Responsible Business Conduct in Action*, Paris. http://dx.doi.org/10.1787/mne-2013-en.

OECD (2011a), *OECD Guidelines for Multinational Enterprises, 2011 Edition,* OECD Publishing, Paris. http://dx.doi.org/10.1787/9789264115415-en.

OECD (2011b), *Divided We Stand: Why Inequality Keeps Rising*, OECD Publishing, Paris. http://dx.doi.org/10.1787/9789264119536-en.

OECD (2009), The Financial Crisis: Reform and Exit Strategies, Paris (publication distributed to the London G20 summit). www.oecd.org/daf/fin/financial-education/43091457.pdf.

OECD, ILO, World Bank and WTO (2010), "Seizing the Benefits of Trade for Employment and Growth", Submitted to the Korea G20 Summit, November. www.oecd.org/trade/benefitlib/46353240.pdf.

Oxford Institute for Energy Studies (2016), *China's 13th Five-Year Plan: Implications for Oil Markets*, Oxford.

Phillips, C.B., F.M. Kinniri and S.J. Donaldson (2012), "The Role of Home Bias in Global Asset Allocation Decisions", Vanguard, June. https://personal.vanguard.com/pdf/icrrhb.pdf

Reinhart, C.M. and K. Rogoff (2011), *This Time is Different: Eight Centuries of Financial Folly*, Princeton.

Rodrik, D. (2008), "The Real Exchange Rate and Economic Growth", *Brookings Papers on Economic Activity*, Fall.

Rochlin, S., R. Bliss, S. Jordan, and C. Yaffe Kiser (2015), “Defining the Competitive and Financial Advantages of Corporate Responsibility and Sustainability, Babson College, available at: http://projectroi.com/wp-content/uploads/2015/07/Project-ROI-Report.pdf. The study was supported by Verizon and Campbell Soups.

Rose-Ackerman, S. (2004), “The Challenge of Poor Governance and Corruption”, in *Global Crises, Global Solutions*, edited by Bjørn Lomborg, Cambridge University Press.

S&P Global (2016), “The Climate Change Challenge from COP 21 to COP 22”, S&P Dow Jones Indices. http://eu.spindices.com/documents/research/research-the-climate-change-challenge-from-cop21-to-cop22.pdf.

Sarin, N., Summers, L. H. (2016), “Have Big Banks Gotten Safer?” Brookings Papers on Economic Activity (BPEA), Conference Draft. https://www.brookings.edu/wp-content/uploads/2016/09/2_sarinsummers.pdf.

Svensson, J. (2005), “Eight Questions About Corruption”, Journal of Economic Perspectives, vol. 19, Number 3.

Tica, J, and I. Druzic (2006), “The Harrod-Balassa-Samuelson Effect: A Survey of Empirical Evidence”, *University of Zagreb Working Paper Series*, No. 06-07.

Topalova, P. (2010), “Factor Immobility and Regional Impacts of Trade Liberalization: Evidence on Poverty from India”, *American Economic Journal: Applied Economics*, vol. 2, pp 1-41.

United Nations (2011), Guiding Principles for Business and Human Rights https://business-humanrights.org/en/un-guiding-principles.

UNEP (2009), “The Role of Supply Chains in Addressing the Global Seafood Crisis, http://unep.ch/etb/ publications/Fish%20Supply%20Chains/UNEP%20fish%20supply%20chains%20report.pdf.

United States Dept. of the Treasury (2016), “Foreign Exchange rate Policies of Major Trading Partners of the United States”, *Semi-annual Report to Congress*, October.

United States Energy Information Administration (2016), *Today in Energy*, 31 May. www.eia.gov/todayinenergy/detail.php?id=26452#.

Wang, Z. and J. Sarkis(2013), “Investigating the Relationship of Sustainable Supply Chain Management and Corporate Financial Performance”, *International Journal of Productivity and Performance Management*, vol. 62.

Leigh Wolfrom and (2016), "Financial instruments for managing disaster risks related to climate change", *OECD Journal: Financial Market Trends*, Vol. 2015/1, http://dx.doi.org/10.1787/fmt-2015-5jrqdkpxk5d5.

World Bank (2015), *Interwoven – How the Better Work Program Improves Job and Life Quality in the Apparel Sector*, https://openknowledge.worldbank.org/bitstream/handle/ 10986/22699/99729.pdf?sequence=1&isAllowed=y.

ANNEX 2.A1.

Company data and sample description

Company data are based on the Bloomberg World Equity Index (BWEI). The sample includes all companies which have been listed in the BWEI over the period 2002-2016. 10 098 listed companies in 76 countries were selected (i.e. 6 506 in advanced economies and 4 592 in emerging economies according to IMF country group classification) operating in 9 GICS industry sectors. See Annex 2.A2 for further details about the composition of each sector and industry group. Annual consolidated financial statements are collected on an annual basis, at the firm level and in current USD.[1] The current primary source of this information is Bloomberg and some data are extracted from Thomson Reuters. All variables are winsorised at the 1st and 99th percentile levels to reduce the effect of outliers. Table 2.A1.1 presents the number of companies by country and sector.

To examine the financial characteristics of firms that succeed, the several following financial variables are considered and are defined as follows:

- **Value added:** Sum of personnel expenses and EBITDA, i.e. income before interest, taxes, depreciation and amortisation. Personnel expenses include wages and salaries, social security, pension, profit-sharing expenses and other benefits related to personnel.
- **Number of employees:** Number of people employed by the company, based on the number of full time equivalents. If unavailable, then the number of full time employees is used, excluding part time employees.
- **Net sales:** Total operating revenues less various adjustments (i.e. returns, discounts, allowances, excise taxes, insurance charges, sales taxes, and value added taxes) to gross sales. It includes revenues from financial subsidiaries in industrial companies if the consolidation includes those subsidiaries throughout the report. It also includes subsidies from federal or local government in certain

1. The items on the balance sheet represent stock variables, and elements from the income statement as well as the cash flow statements represent a flow. Bloomberg provides the option to collect the information in current USD values. Bloomberg, for example, reports items on the balance sheet using the exchange rate set on the date of publishing; income statements and statements of cash flow items are reported using the average exchange rate for the period. Thomson Reuters on the other hand uses the WMR Spot Rate set on the date of publishing for items on the balance sheet, income statement and statement of cash flows.

industries (i.e. transportation or utilities). However, it excludes intra-company revenue and revenues from discontinued operations.

- **International sales:** Sales generated from operations in foreign countries. It excludes export sales, excise taxes, windfall profit taxes, value added taxes, general and services taxes.
- **Capital expenditure:** Amount the company spent on purchases of tangible fixed assets. It may include intangible assets when not disclosed separately.
- **R&D expenditure:** Operating expense related to the research and development of a company's products or services.
- **Leverage:** Total long-term borrowings divided by the sum of long-term borrowing and equity capital. Long-term borrowing includes all interest-bearing financial obligations that are not due within a year (i.e. convertible, redeemable, retractable debentures, bonds, loans, mortgage debts, sinking funds, and long-term bank overdrafts, subordinated capital notes, long-term hire purchase, finance lease obligations, long-term bills of exchange, bankers acceptances and other debt which is interest bearing). It may also include shares issued by subsidiaries if the group has an obligation to transfer economic benefits in connection with these shares. Long term borrowings are net with unamortised premium or discount on debt. Equity capital is share capital, plus retained earnings and minus treasury stock.
- **Profit margin:** Ratio of operating income to total revenues (which also corresponds to net sales).
- **Return on equity (ROE):** Ratio of net income to common equity. Net income is the profit after all expenses have been deducted. It includes the effects of all one-time, non-recurring, and extraordinary gains, losses, or charges. Common equity is the amount that all common shareholders have invested in a company.
- **Cost of capital (COK):** Weighted average (by the share of equity and debt in total assets, respectively) cost of equity and cost of debt.
- **Value of completed M&A deals:** Declared amount effectively paid by the acquirer for the target. "Acquisitions" include all deals with a 100% takeover of another entity (such as, acquisitions of business units, divisions, product lines or other operations of another entity, acquisitions of stakes, acquisition of pharmaceutical rights and brands). In "Mergers", the target is deemed to be the company for which the offer is being made, the owner of the smaller equity stake in the combined entity, or the one with smaller market capitalisation. If the merger is a 50/50 split of equals, and there is no clear indication of the larger firm, Dealogic will use its discretion in the selection of target. Joint ventures are eligible if two or more companies combine their existing assets or equity to form a new entity. Spin-offs and split-offs are eligible. Privatisations (but not government carve outs), government-awarded PCS/wireless licenses, real estate property transactions (excluding purchases consisting solely of land which fall outside the oil & gas and mining industries) and buy-back transactions structured as public tender offers are tracked and also eligible.

Table 2.A1.1. **Distribution of companies by country and sector**

Advanced economies	Number of companies	Emerging economies	Number of companies
Australia	457	Argentina	17
Austria	25	Bahrain	2
Belgium	38	Bosnia-Herzegovina	14
Canada	808	Brazil	144
Cyprus (1)	22	Bulgaria	25
Czech Republic	6	Chile	43
Denmark	43	China	1407
Estonia	4	Colombia	14
Finland	48	Croatia	51
France	205	Egypt	35
Germany	208	Gabon	1
Greece	79	Hungary	9
Hong Kong, China	129	India	971
Ireland	30	Indonesia	114
Israel (2)	46	Jordan	9
Italy	91	Kenya	3
Japan	1099	Korea	515
Latvia	7	Kuwait	20
Lithuania	9	Macedonia	4
Luxembourg	6	Malaysia	226
Malta	5	Mexico	55
Netherlands	58	Montenegro	1
New Zealand	18	Morocco	8
Norway	37	Oman	5
Portugal	19	Pakistan	21
Singapore	57	Peru	17
Slovakia	8	Philippines	29
Slovenia	13	Poland	190
Spain	65	Qatar	9
Sweden	149	Romania	138
Switzerland	81	Russia	120
Chinese Taipei	192	Saudi Arabia	53
United Kingdom	365	Senegal	1
United States	2079	Serbia	39
		South Africa	81
		Sudan	1
		Thailand	50
		Turkey	98
		Ukraine	21
		United Arab Emirates	15
		Venezuela	2
		Vietnam	14
TOTAL	6506		4592

Sector	Advanced economies	Emerging economies
Energy	607	220
Materials	838	870
Industrials	1366	1091
Consumer discretionary	1268	918
Consumer staples	402	447
Healthcare	653	308
Information technology	988	468
Telecommunication services	110	93
Utilities	228	223

1. Note by Turkey. The information in this document with reference to "Cyprus" relates to the southern part of the Island. There is no single authority representing both Turkish and Greek Cypriot people on the Island. Turkey recognises the Turkish Republic of Northern Cyprus (TRNC). Until a lasting and equitable solution is found within the context of the United Nations, Turkey shall preserve its position concerning the "Cyprus issue".

Note by all the European Union Member States of the OECD and the European Union. The Republic of Cyprus is recognised by all members of the United Nations with the exception of Turkey. The information in this document relates to the area under the effective control of the Government of the Republic of Cyprus.

Source: OECD compilation.

ANNEX 2.A2.

The structure of the Global Industry Classification Standard

In 1999, MSCI and Standard & Poor's developed the Global Industry Classification Standard (GICS), seeking to offer an efficient investment tool to capture the breadth, depth and evolution of industry sectors. GICS is a four-tiered, hierarchical industry classification system. Companies are classified quantitatively and qualitatively. Each company is assigned a single GICS classification at the sub-industry level according to its principal business activity. MSCI and Standard & Poor's use revenues as a key factor in determining a firm's principal business activity. Earnings and market perception, however, are also recognised as important and relevant information for classification purposes, and are taken into account during the annual review process. Excluding financial companies, GICS classification consists of nine sectors, 20 industry groups, 60 industries and 130 sub-industries. GICS structure is detailed in Table 2.A2.1.

Table 2.A2.1. **The Global Industry Classification Standard (GICS)**

Sector	Industry sector	Industry group	Sub-industry
Energy	**Energy**	**Energy equipment & services**	Oil & gas drilling
			Oil & gas equipment & services
		Oil, gas & consumable fuels	Integrated oil & gas
			Oil & gas exploration & production
			Oil & gas refining & marketing
			Oil & gas storage & transportation
			Coal & consumable fuels
Materials	**Materials**	**Chemicals**	Commodity chemicals
			Diversified chemicals
			Fertilisers & agricultural chemicals
			Industrial gases
			Specialty chemicals
		Construction materials	Construction materials
		Containers & packaging	Metal & glass containers
			Paper packaging
		Metals & mining	Aluminium

Sector	Industry sector	Industry group	Sub-industry
			Diversified metals & mining
			Gold
			Precious metals & minerals
			Steel
		Paper & forest products	Forest products
			Paper products
Industrials	**Capital goods**	**Aerospace & defence**	Aerospace & defence
		Building products	Building products
		Construction & engineering	Construction & engineering
		Electrical equipment	Electrical components & equipment
			Heavy electrical equipment
		Industrial conglomerates	Industrial conglomerates
		Machinery	Construction & farm machinery & heavy trucks
			Industrial machinery
		Trading companies & distributors	Trading companies & distributors
	Commercial & professional services	**Commercial services & supplies**	Commercial printing
			Data processing services
			Diversified commercial & professional services
			Human resource & employment services
			Environmental & facilities services
			Office services & supplies
			Diversified support services
			Security & alarm services
		Professional services	Human resource & employment services
			Research & consulting services
	Transportation	**Air freight & logistics**	Air freight & logistics
		Airlines	Airlines
		Marine	Marine
		Road & rail	Railroads
			Trucking
		Transportation infrastructure	Airport services
			Highways & rail tracks
			Marine ports & services
Consumer discretionary	**Automobiles & components**	**Automobile components**	Auto parts & equipment
			Tires & rubber
		Automobiles	Automobile manufacturers

Sector	Industry sector	Industry group	Sub-industry
			Motorcycle manufacturers
	Consumer durables & apparel	**Household durables**	Consumer electronics
			Home furnishings
			Homebuilding
			Household appliances
			Housewares & specialties
		Leisure equipment & products	Leisure products
			Photographic products
		Textiles, apparel & luxury goods	Apparel, accessories & luxury goods
			Footwear
			Textiles
	Consumer services	**Hotels, restaurants & leisure**	Casinos & gaming
			Hotels, resorts & cruise lines
			Leisure facilities
			Restaurants
		Diversified consumer services	Education services
			Specialised consumer services
	Media	**Media**	Advertising
			Broadcasting
			Cable & satellite
			Movies & entertainment
			Publishing
	Retailing	**Distributors**	Distributors
		Internet & catalogue retail	Catalogue retail
			Internet retail
		Multiline retail	Department stores
			General merchandise stores
		Specialty retail	Apparel retail
			Computer & electronics retail
			Home improvement retail
			Specialty stores
			Automotive retail
			Home furnishing retail
Consumer staples	**Food & staples retailing**	**Food & staples retailing**	Drug retail
			Food distributors
			Food retail
			Hypermarkets & super centres

Sector	Industry sector	Industry group	Sub-industry
	Food, beverage & tobacco	**Beverages**	Brewers
			Distillers & vintners
			Soft drinks
		Food products	Agricultural products
			Meat, poultry & fish
			Packaged foods & meats
		Tobacco	Tobacco
	Household & personal products	**Household products**	Household products
		Personal products	Personal products
Healthcare	**Healthcare equipment & services**	**Healthcare equipment & supplies**	Healthcare equipment
			Healthcare supplies
		Healthcare providers & services	Healthcare distributors
			Healthcare services
			Healthcare facilities
			Managed Healthcare
		Healthcare technology	Healthcare technology
	Pharmaceuticals & biotechnology	**Biotechnology**	Biotechnology
		Pharmaceuticals	Pharmaceuticals
		Life sciences tools & services	Life sciences tools & services
Information technology	**Software & services**	**Internet software & services**	Internet software & services
		IT services	IT consulting & other services
			Data processing & outsourced services
		Software	Application software
			Systems software
			Home entertainment software
	Technology hardware & equipment	**Communications equipment**	Communications equipment
			Networking equipment
			Telecommunications equipment
		Computers & peripherals	Computer hardware
			Computer storage & peripherals
		Electronic equipment & components	Electronic equipment & instruments
			Electronic components
			Electronic manufacturing services
			Technology distributors
		Office electronics	Office electronics

Sector	Industry sector	Industry group	Sub-industry
	Semiconductors & equipment	**Semiconductors & equipment**	Semiconductor equipment
			Semiconductors
Telecommunication services	**Telecommunication services**	**Diversified telecommunication services**	Alternative carriers
			Integrated telecommunication services
		Wireless telecommunication services	Wireless telecommunication services
Utilities	**Utilities**	**Electric utilities**	Electric utilities
		Gas utilities	Gas utilities
		Multi-utilities	Multi-utilities
		Water utilities	Water utilities
		Independent power producers & energy traders	Independent power producers & energy traders

Source: OECD compilation, MSCI.

Chapter 3

The internationalisation of state-owned enterprises

State-owned enterprises (SOEs) have become an important and, by some measures, growing part of the global corporate landscape. One reason for this is that the economic weight is shifting toward regions of the world where a large number of SOEs remain. The question is whether these SOEs operate in the global marketplace on the same terms as private enterprises, or whether their growing presence changes the competitive conditions in international trade and investment. Importantly, enterprises other than SOEs may be linked to the state, or considered to be "national champions", thereby benefitting from the support of their national authorities. This chapter reviews the changing trends and analyses the challenges that may arise from the renewed importance of SOEs. It concludes that SOEs, on average, have lower rates of return and higher leverage than private competitors and that, by continuing to produce amid falling profitability, they may have contributed to global overcapacity in some sectors. The chapter demonstrates how existing OECD instruments, including the OECD Guidelines on Corporate Governance of State-Owned Enterprises, can contribute to address these concerns.

3.1. Introduction

State-owned enterprises (SOEs) have become an important and, by some measures, growing part of the global corporate landscape. This is apparently interrelated with the changing geographic and sectoral patterns of the new global economy. The economic weight has been shifting toward regions of the world and at least some industrial sectors where a large number of SOEs remain. One question is whether these SOEs operate in the global marketplace in the same way as private enterprises in like circumstances, or whether their growing presence has changed competitive conditions in international trade and investment. Enterprises other than SOEs may, of course, also be linked to the state, or considered to be "national champions", and benefit from the support of their national authorities. This can give rise to similar issues as the globalisation of SOEs, but it is not the focus of this chapter.

This chapter reviews the changing trends and analyses the challenges that may arise from this modern-day "SOE renaissance". It takes stock of the concerns that have been voiced about possibly unfair international competition by SOEs and analyses evidence of SOE performance, international investment and signs that SOEs may recently have contributed to global overcapacity in some sectors. It demonstrates how existing OECD instruments, including the OECD Guidelines on Corporate Governance of State-Owned Enterprises, can contribute to address these concerns.

3.2. Cross-border mergers and acquisitions are increasing the global presence of state-owned enterprises

A large part of cross-border business investment consists of international mergers and acquisitions (M&A). These provide a clear indication of the emerging patterns of corporate globalisation. Their broader trends and geographic distribution over the last decade yield valuable insights into changing global value chains. Total cross-border M&A flows peaked in 2007, immediately prior to the onset of the financial crisis, at USD 1.7 trillion (current prices). By far the largest investing countries (and, to a lesser degree, also recipient countries) at the time were the United States and the United Kingdom – both of which have appeared close to the top of the league table in most years. The other large sources of outward M&A, prior to the crisis, were also mostly OECD countries, including France, Canada, Japan and Germany.

After 2008, an interesting inter-regional shift occurred (Figure 3.1). The EU countries as a group, who have traditionally been net outward investors, have in recent years become the world's largest net recipient of cross-border M&A, with net inflows exceeding USD 100 billion in 2015. Conversely, the Asian region, measured by M&A, has now become the world's main net provider of outward investors. The net outflows from Asia in 2016 reached USD 200 billion.

The change in Asia's position can be largely attributed to China. Outward M&A from the Chinese economy has been trending upward since before the financial crisis, reaching an unprecedented USD 145 billion in 2016. Since 2005, China's share of the world's inward M&A flows has fallen slightly, but generally hovered around 4% (Figure 3.2). Conversely, the Chinese share of M&A outflows has gone from barely significant at the beginning of the millennium to currently over 10% of totals.

Figure 3.1. **Net outward mergers and acquisitions flows by geographic regions (net of inward flows)**

(USD billion)

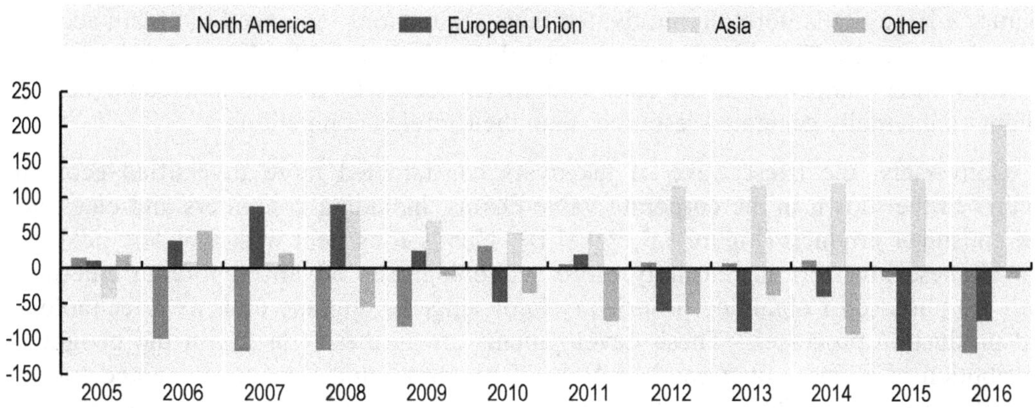

Source: Dealogic, OECD calculations

StatLink http://dx.doi.org/10.1787/888933476806

Figure 3.2. **Chinese inward and outward cross-border mergers and acquisitions flows**

(Share of world totals)

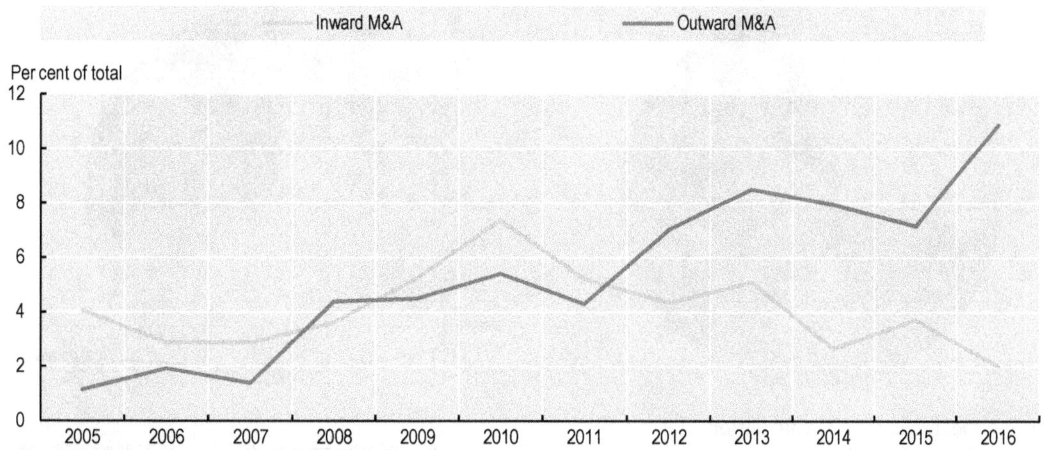

Source: Dealogic, OECD calculations

StatLink http://dx.doi.org/10.1787/888933476814

To some extent, the change in China's position was predictable: when an emerging economy approaches the mid-income level, it generally becomes less dependent on foreign direct investment (FDI) as opposed to domestic sources of capital. But the jump in outward M&A has been clearly influenced by government strategies, notably the "Go Out" policy announced in 1999, according to which enterprises were actively encouraged to invest abroad. However, by late 2016, the recent spike in outward M&A had apparently unsettled policy makers who, reportedly because of concerns about currency stability, imposed temporary restrictions on overseas acquisitions, clamping down in particular on large individual transactions, acquisitions outside the investors core business areas and real estate (Financial Times, 2016).

A sectorial and geographic analysis of China's evolving outward investments yields additional insights. Figure 3.3 compares the sectorial distribution, by target sectors, of

Chinese overseas M&A in the immediate aftermath of the recent financial crisis with that of today. In 2010, acquisitions mostly targeted the resource sectors, notably hydrocarbons and mining (Figure 3.3, Panel A). Chinese investors in 2010, who included several of the country's large SOEs, formally motivated their acquisitions by a need to obtain access to strategic resources. These investments seem also to have been facilitated by the fact that those Chinese companies at the time had easier access to finance and could be more reliant on internally generated resources than their foreign competitors.

Conversely, the latest wave of takeovers has targeted more diversified economic sectors further down in the corporate value chains, including computers and electronics and consumer products (Figure 3.3, Panel B). This is consistent with a widely held view that Chinese investors increasingly target technologically advanced foreign enterprises with the purpose of obtaining proprietary knowledge to upgrade their own technologies and production processes.[1] These developments are further reflected in the geographic distribution of Chinese overseas M&A. In 2010, Brazil and Canada accounted for over half of the totals. In 2016, the three main recipients of Chinese investment were the United States, Finland and the United Kingdom.

Figure 3.3. **Chinese outward mergers and acquisitions by target industries**

(Share of total value of deals)

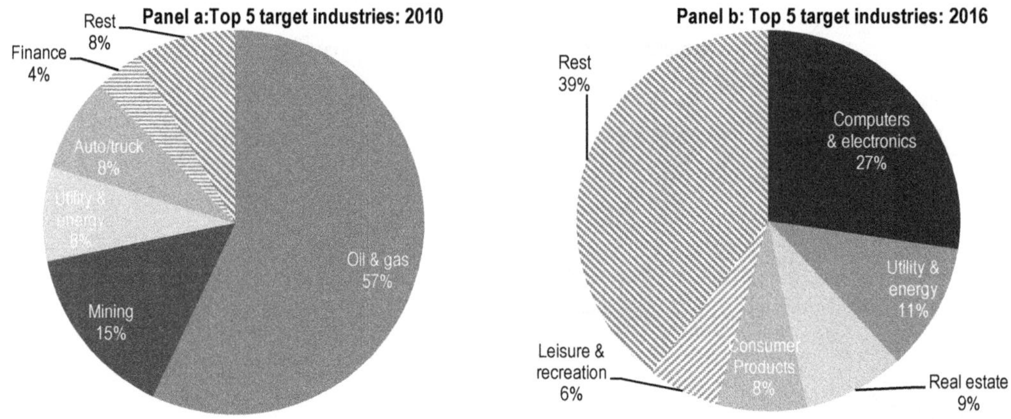

Source: Dealogic, OECD calculations

StatLink http://dx.doi.org/10.1787/888933476820

3.3. The evolving role of state-owned enterprises

One of the intriguing outcomes of the changing patterns of corporate globalisation is a recent resurgence of SOEs in global value chains. At first this seems to run counter to the fact that many governments remain engaged in processes of privatisation – including in emerging economies. However, those economies that have large SOE sectors are among the fastest-growing economies in the world and consequently their SOEs are increasingly felt in trade, investment and competition. Past OECD research indicates that the share of SOEs in total economic activity (e.g. GDP, employment or investment) is generally in the range of 10% to 30% in emerging economies. Within the OECD area the highest such shares (in certain Scandinavian and post-transition eastern European countries) are between 5% and 10%. The average of OECD countries is closer to 2%.

A forthcoming OECD study takes stock of the size of SOE sectors, as measured by employment and corporate equity value in selected economies – essentially covering the OECD economies plus Brazil, China and India (OECD, 2017a). The figures, which must be interpreted with caution as they are based largely on self-reporting and cover only SOEs whose shares are held at the central or federal levels of government, are summarised in Figure 3.4.[2] As would be expected, the SOE sectors of the world's largest countries, China and India, dwarf those of any other individual country, although the European Union as a whole accounts for comparable absolute numbers.

Similar numbers are not available as time series, but it would appear that while ongoing privatisation has shrunk the number of SOEs over the last decade, the value of remaining SOEs has increased. For instance, the proportion of the number of SOEs among the Fortune Global 500 (defined by Fortune as companies having 50% or more government ownership) grew from 10% to 23% from 2005 to 2014 (Kwiatkowski et al., 2015). The increase is accounted for by the emergence of SOEs based in emerging economies close to the top of the league table.

Figure 3.4. **Total employment and sectorial distribution of SOEs**

(As of 2015 or latest available)

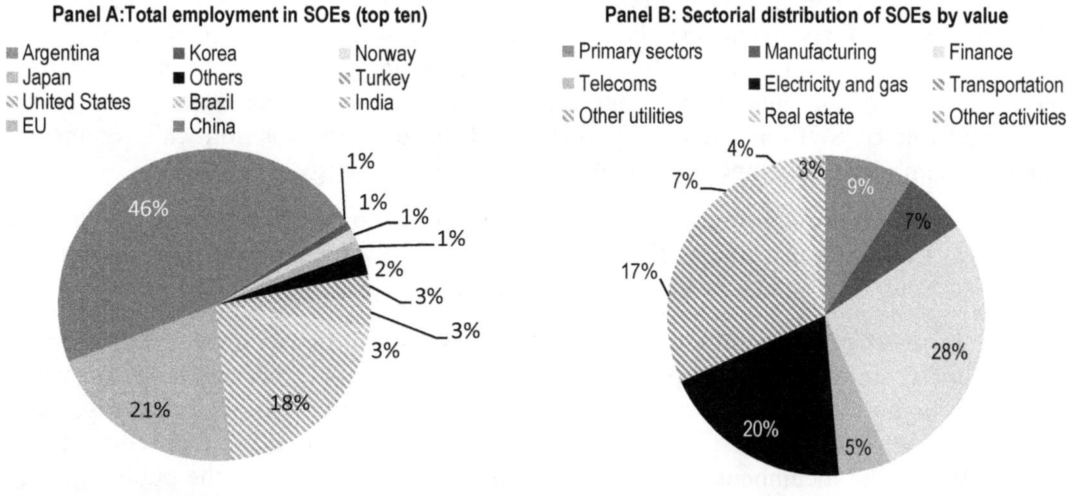

Source: OECD (2017a)

StatLink http://dx.doi.org/10.1787/888933476837

The relatively large absolute size of the EU countries' SOE sectors is mostly due to state ownership in public utilities and a few large financial institutions. This is important for a number of reasons, including the importance of these industries to the overall productivity and profitability of the rest of the economy. If SOEs are inefficient, the effect will be felt across a number of other industries – the effect of which, in the case of internationalisation of the SOEs, is felt across borders. A major difference between emerging and more mature economies arises from the fact that emerging economies still have relatively large portfolios of state-owned manufacturing companies. In OECD countries, SOEs in this sector were in most cases privatised in previous decades. A sectoral breakdown of the SOE (by company equity value) is provided in Figure 3.4 (Panel B).

3.4. Concerns about the internationalisation of state-owned enterprises

As mentioned in the previous section, the relative importance of state ownership appears to have changed in recent decades. The international economy is increasingly facing competition from economies operating at different levels and with varying models of economic development. Some of the largest economies give an active role to SOEs in carrying out industrial policies and stimulating growth.

The role attributed to SOEs may induce their government owners to grant them certain advantages, ranging from a privileged market position to soft loans and outright subsidies. Some such support may be justified by the cost of non-commercial objectives that the SOEs are charged with, but such costs are difficult to quantify and policy-makers' preference for their own enterprises may, in practice, go well beyond that.[3] Even where this is not the case, SOEs still typically benefit from preferential access to finance, because commercial lenders and investors perceive an implicit government guarantee to these enterprises. As the boundaries of markets extend well beyond geographic borders, domestic policy choices about the relationship between the state and enterprises are giving rise to extraterritorial effects. Compensation and special advantages granted by governments in return for public policy obligations at home may spill over to other jurisdictions – for instance, where continued "life support" to an ailing SOE keeps alive what, from an overseas perspective, may be an unwelcome competitor; or where subsidised over-production might lead to excessive capacity. This can, furthermore, have the effect of stifling innovation. Significant recent attention has been given to the continued role of SOEs in the energy sector and the potential for politically-connected market incumbents' to hamper the development of "green energy" (Box 3.1).

The effects can reverberate well beyond the domestic context and can have a negative impact on trade and investment flows, and more broadly on how the global economy allocates resources. The extraterritorial effects include:

- *Asymmetric contestability in the home market.* In the context of fostering cross-border competition, the presence of large incumbents in network sectors (which in both developed and emerging economies are often, but not necessarily, state-owned) has in some cases effectively impeded the entry of foreign competitors. Where the incumbents retain an element of legal monopoly in the public interest, this may be defended as an exercise of the national authorities' right to regulate. But if competition is, in principle, allowed and the incumbent is kept in place, mostly through preferential treatment, then this marks a serious departure from the principle of competitive neutrality.

- *Anti-competitive effects in partners' markets.* As economies with business sectors with a large share of SOEs (or state-based companies), grow and expand abroad, this can raise concerns as to whether advantages conferred upon SOEs in the home jurisdiction have not been carried over into the SOE's international operations, thus resulting in an anti-competitive effect in the partner's market. In the case of international investment, this may be a source of additional advantage because it enables the funding of individual transactions. Moreover, public policy objectives directly targeting foreign jurisdictions (e.g. information gathering, acquisition of sensitive technologies, establishing a strategic position in certain market segments) in the interest of the SOEs' home countries may be badly perceived by partner countries.

- *Competition in third markets*: The deepening of international commercial links and the geographical fragmentation of production often means that competition for inputs and supplies occurs in third markets between SOEs and other multinationals. Enforcement may be less stringent, or simply not carried out, when state enterprises compete in foreign markets. Disclosure and transparency, which take on a particular importance in state sector management, may also be more elusive in this context. Good practice calls for governments to disclose information about their SOEs' operations, objectives and corporate orientations on an ongoing basis, not just in the specific context of individual investment or trade projects.
- *Excess capacity and broader systemic risks:* The role of governments should be to let market mechanisms work properly and avoid measures that artificially contribute to global excess capacity. The concern with the growing role of SOEs in some sectors relates to the extent to which their investment decisions are market-based and how they are contributing to excess capacity. If investments are part of national development strategies, for example to attain self-sufficiency in a given sector and reduce a country's dependence on imports, this could encourage capacity expansions, but with broad extraterritorial impacts.

This can have an impact on the competitive landscape.[4] A business survey conducted by the OECD in 2014[5] shows that a majority of surveyed firms perceived that foreign-owned competitors benefited from government-granted preferential treatment, which they themselves had no access to. The economic effects of such intervention were reported to extend well beyond the markets they were intended to influence. This illustrates the greater difficulty of minimising the extraterritoriality of state intervention-related distortions. Ownership status of firms was also perceived to matter to some respondents, as the reported severity of the impact of preferential treatment by governments was higher for SOEs than for other types of firms (see Figure 3.5). The use of SOEs by governments to indirectly grant advantages to respondents' competitors, through lower prices or better accessibility of inputs, was also frequently reported.

Figure 3.5. **Business perceptions concerning preferential treatment granted to foreign competitors**

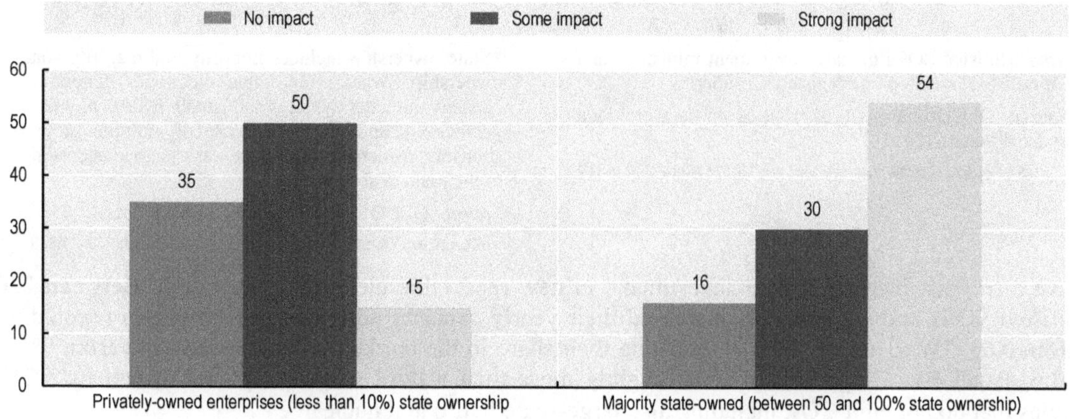

1. Preferential treatment is defined as government measures or actions, which affect costs or prices of commercial enterprises and which are extended only to certain specific enterprises or groups of enterprises.
2. Own government is defined as the government of respondent's country of headquarters.

Source: OECD Business Survey on State Influence on Competition in International Markets.

StatLink http://dx.doi.org/10.1787/888933476859

Box 3.1. **SOEs and the low-carbon transition**

SOEs are key actors in the fight against climate change as they remain dominant players in the global energy market. In the electricity sector, which (together with district heating) accounts for 42% of global CO_2 emissions from fossil fuel combustion, SOEs with full, majority, or minority state ownership accounted for 56% of total capacity installed in 2016, and for roughly 52 % of power plants that are currently in different stages of planning or construction.

Global pathways for a low-carbon future foresee a rapid shift away from coal-fired power generation towards zero-carbon electricity generation technologies including nuclear, hydro, and non-hydro renewables (OECD, 2017b forthcoming). A closer analysis of the coal power fleet reveals that fully SOEs own roughly 40% of total operating coal power capacity (see Figure 3.6, Panel A). If stock-market-listed companies with majority state-ownership and joint ventures involving SOEs are included in the analysis, the market share of state-invested companies increases to 53%. Looking to the pipeline of new projects, the same state-invested enterprises cover nearly the same proportion, with 51.5% of the coal power pipeline (projects that have been announced, permitted, or are under construction). On the other hand, companies identified as having no state ownership own 14% of operational coal power capacity while only accounting for 3% of the coal power pipeline. This would suggest that privately-owned firms are divesting faster from coal thanSOEs. However, it should be noted that the ownership of both 45% of coal power plants in the pipeline and of 30% of operational plants are not known in this dataset.

Figure 3.6. **Ownership of coal plant operators and yearly additions of renewable electricity generation**

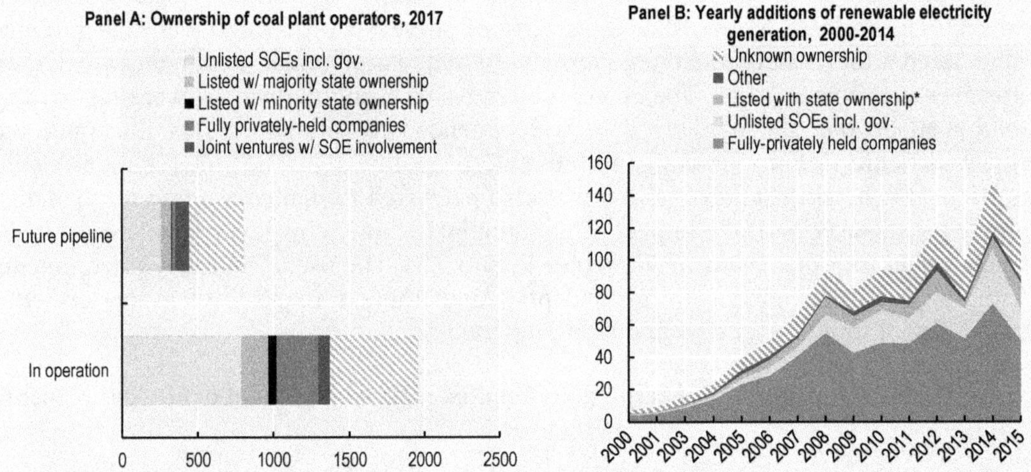

Note: Unlisted SOEs include government ministries and Chinese SOEs with partially listed subsidiaries.

Source: OECD analysis (2017) based on data provided by Coal Swarm (2017).

StatLink http://dx.doi.org/10.1787/888933476849

*State ownership includes minority and majority state ownership. *Notes:* Renewable electricity generation capacity includes wind, solar, small hydro, biomass, geothermal, and marine. In case of multiple project sponsors, ownership of project was assigned according to the main deal sponsor.

Source: OECD Analysis based on BNEF data.

StatLink http://dx.doi.org/10.1787/888933476849

SOEs have also been increasing their investments in new renewable electricity generation. Between 2000 and 2014, unlisted SOEs and governments increased their yearly capacity additions of renewables (excluding large hydro) from 0.63 GW to almost 34 GW, boosting their share in the market for new renewables from 9% to 23% (Figure 3.6, Panel B). Altogether, in 2016, slightly more than a third of power plants owned by SOEs used technologies that do not emit CO_2, including also large-scale hydro and nuclear.

Future research will be needed to better understand what drives SOE investment in low-carbon technologies. SOEs could be well suited to increase renewables investments, in part because their government owners' ability to apply low discount rates to investments match well with long-term investment horizons and the capital intensity of renewable electricity.

A second OECD policy survey (OECD, 2016a), corroborates the business view that there may be strong concerns regarding SOEs' position in the domestic marketplace and their ability to distort competition. The main areas of concern identified relate to preferential financing, outright subsidies, and regulatory exemptions. The forms of preferential treatment (granted to SOEs) with the "strongest" reported impact on foreign trade included: preferential treatment in public procurement; price support; grants/direct payments; and tax concessions. Finally, advantages granted by SOEs were also considered to impact the playing field.

3.5. Financial performance of state-owned enterprises

To address the question of whether SOEs operate at an advantage relative to private (or non-SOE) enterprises, some metrics of financial performance have been calculated. These are based on original data drawn from a database featuring company-level information about listed SOEs and other firms. The sample contains information on listed non-financial corporations incorporated in European and selected emerging markets.[6] The dataset contains 1 111 unique listed SOEs and 12 875 unique listed non-SOE corporations. Information about their ownership is taken from Factset and then merged with financial statement information from Thomson Reuters. For the remainder of this section, SOE is taken to indicate companies with a state ownership exceeding 20% of the shares.[7]

Since 2013, SOEs have generally been less profitable than other firms. As demonstrated in Figure 3.7, rates-of-return on equity (ROE)[8] in non-financial firms have fallen since (and even before) the onset of the financial crisis. However, they have been lower in SOEs than in the rest of the business sector, standing at slightly over half of the non-SOE level by 2015. This has taken place despite a cost of debt in SOEs that, according to the sample used, has generally been lower than in other firms.

Figure 3.7. **Rate of return on equity in SOEs and other companies**

(Per cent)

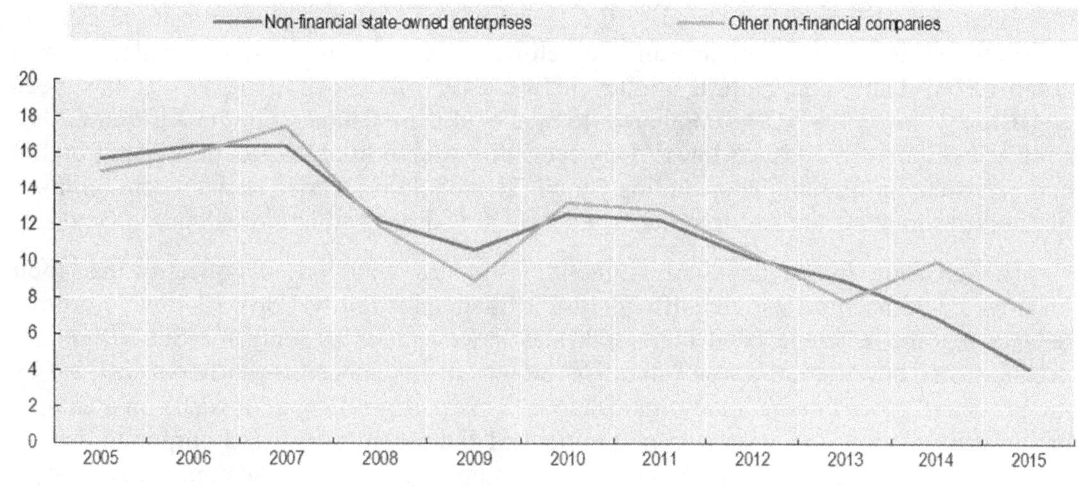

Source: Factset, Thomson Reuters and OECD calculations

StatLink http://dx.doi.org/10.1787/888933476868

At the same time, operational profits appear to have been squeezed in SOEs during the crisis. Figure 3.8 shows how operational income, relative to sales in SOEs one decade ago, was markedly above the levels in private firms, whereas in recent years they have shrunk to a similar – or lower – level than in the private sector. This may, to some extent, reflect a compositional effect since SOEs in some countries are concentrated in sectors that tend to be more cyclical than the rest of the economy. But it may also be indicative of over-capacity in many of the sectors where SOEs compete – a discussion further developed in the following section.

Figure 3.8. **Operating income in non-financial SOEs and other non-financial companies**

(As share of sales)

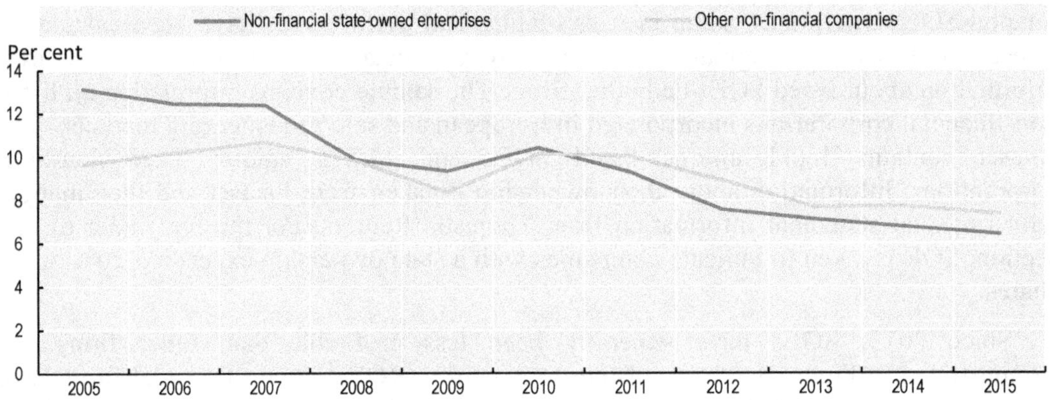

Source: Factset, Thomson Reuters and OECD calculations.

StatLink http://dx.doi.org/10.1787/888933476871

A question arises about the relative importance of China, given its very large portfolio of more than 800 listed SOEs, in the above observations. In fact, according to the database, the ROE of Chinese SOEs has developed largely in tandem with SOEs in other countries. The operating incomes relative to sales in Chinese SOEs tend to be lower than elsewhere, which could be related to the fact that non-Chinese SOEs are more heavily concentrated in utilities sectors and therefore, in some cases, more insulated from competition. The same pattern applies in the case of cost-of debt, which has been consistently lower in SOEs compared to non-SOEs in China, but the difference has vanished (Figure 3.9, dashed lines). However, this wedge in cost of debt is much higher and persistent in the sample, excluding China. This could be related to the recent build-up of liabilities in the Chinese corporate sector, which is discussed in more detail in Box 3.2.

The growing indebtedness of Chinese SOEs has also led to concerns that their leverage could become a source of widely-felt financial fragility.[9] Box 3.2 concludes that debt levels and leverage have increased, and indeed more strongly for SOEs than for private firms, but it paints a less "alarmist" picture than has been recently put forward by the press and other international organisations. This partly reflects our focus on a sample of listed enterprises, whereas a large segment of the recently incurred corporate debt is found in unlisted SOEs, mostly in railways and other heavy utilities sectors. Bonds issued by special-purpose vehicles, controlled by local levels of government, are moreover categorised as "corporate debt". Finally, given a continued accumulation of assets in most SOEs, leverage ratios have increased by significantly less than overall debt levels.

Figure 3.9. **Cost of debt for non-financial SOEs and other non-financial companies**

(Per cent)

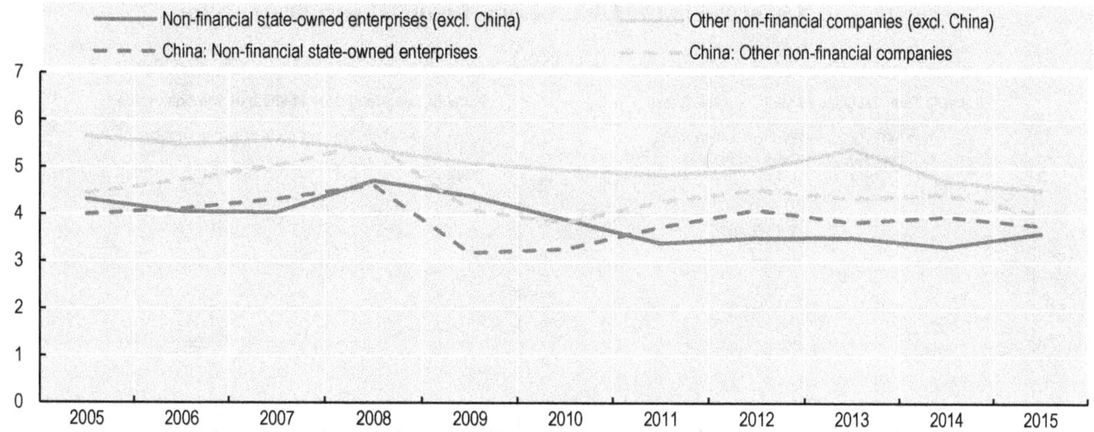

Source: Factset, Thomson Reuters and OECD calculations.

StatLink http://dx.doi.org/10.1787/888933476883

Box 3.2. Corporate debt in China

China's credit has been growing rapidly since the global financial crisis, reflecting government measures designed to boost domestic demand. Listed non-financial corporations have been accumulating larger amounts of debt on their balance sheet.[10] In 2015, total corporate liabilities accounted for 58% as share of total assets, whereas in 2000 total corporate liabilities only represented 44.7% of the total assets.

SOEs have frequently been invoked in discussions of growing corporate debt, inter alia because these firms are widely thought to have privileged access to financing due to implicit or explicit government guarantees and, in some cases, preferential treatment from state-owned banks. To understand the differences in the financial positions of SOEs, the sample of Chinese listed corporations is split into SOEs and non-SOEs (SOEs are defined in the sample as having higher than, or equal to, 25% state ownership).

Figure 3.10 shows the evolution of total liabilities (as a share of assets) and leverage (long-term debt over the enterprise value) for SOEs and non-SOEs since 2005. SOEs' liabilities have grown more rapidly than those of non-SOEs, reaching 60% as a share of total assets in 2015, whereas for non-SOEs, liabilities stayed almost unchanged at around 55%. Similarly, leverage has grown throughout the corporate sector, but for SOEs it has increased by almost 7 percentage points, compared to 3.3 percentage points for non-SOEs over the 2005 to 2015 period.

A breakdown of the liabilities by types reveals that a main factor behind the growth in SOE indebtedness has been a pick-up in short term liabilities in recent years – notably inter-firm credit (account payables). This type of credit represents an important short-term financing source in many countries. In the case of China, inter-firm credit does not yet represent as important a source of financing as elsewhere. On the other hand, if this is indicative of a build-up of intra-SOE arrears in recent years, then it could be a cause for concern.

Box 3.2. **Corporate debt in China** (cont.)

Figure 3.10. **Leverage in the Chinese non-financial corporate sector**

(Per cent)

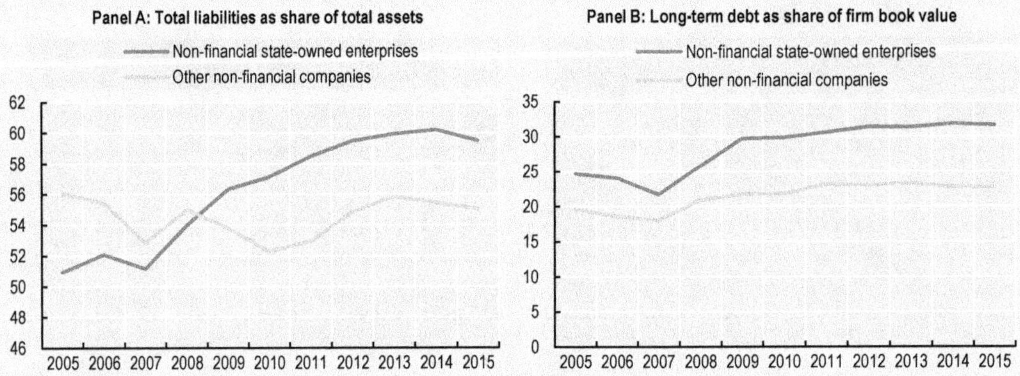

Note: Enterprise value is defined as long-term debt plus common equity.

Source: Thomson Reuters, Factset and OECD calculations.

StatLink http://dx.doi.org/10.1787/888933476899

Sectoral performance: state-owned enterprises versus other companies

The relative financial performance of SOEs is compared across a number of sectors[11] by subtracting private sector averages from SOE averages (Figures 3.11 and 3.12). When comparing on a sector-by-sector basis it appears that rates-of-return have been consistently, although not uniformly, lower in SOEs than in other firms during the period under review. This confirms a tendency, highlighted in earlier OECD publications, for governments to allow their SOEs to provide lower returns than what private investors demand in similar circumstances (OECD, 2014). The difference has, however, narrowed in the years following the financial crisis.

Conversely, profit margins (operating income relative to sales) have generally been higher for SOEs than for others, which can be taken to indicate that they operate in a less competitive environment than comparative private firms. The significant exception is the "materials" sector, which includes mining companies, as well as integrated metal producers. This could be quite significant since these are industries where overcapacity is currently widely perceived and SOEs have sometimes been considered as expanding in pursuit of objectives other than profit maximisation.

Figure 3.11. **Difference in returns on equity between non-financial SOEs and other non-financial companies**

(Percentage points)

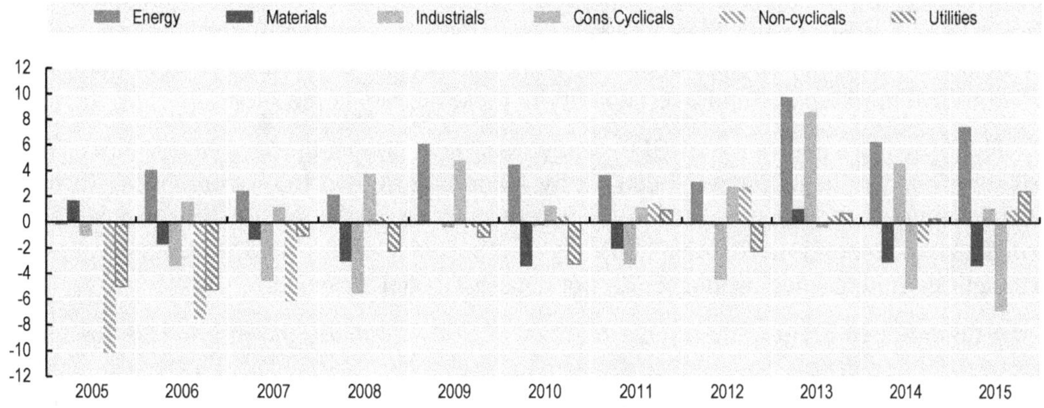

Source: Factset, Thomson Reuters and OECD calculations.

StatLink http://dx.doi.org/10.1787/888933476902

Figure 3.12. **Difference in profit margins between non-financial SOEs and other non-financial companies**

(Percentage points)

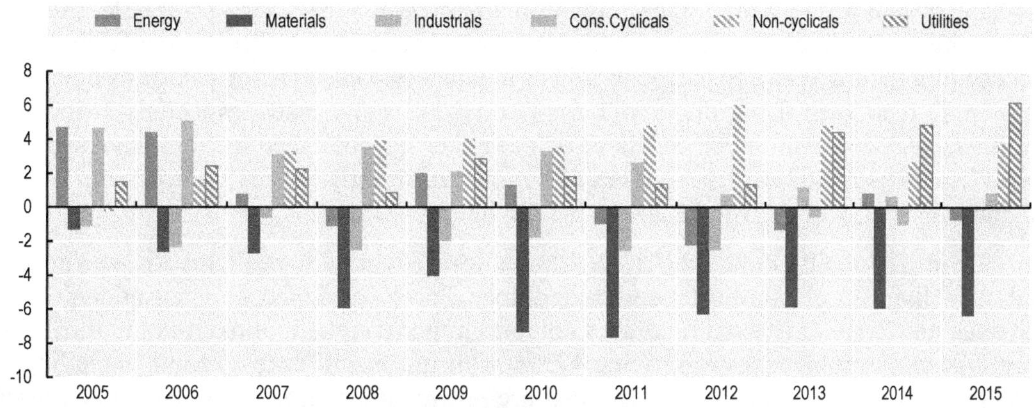

Source: Factset, Thomson Reuters and OECD calculations.

StatLink http://dx.doi.org/10.1787/888933476910

3.6. Overcapacity and crowding out

The advent of SOEs in the global economy may have aggravated an ongoing problem of overcapacity in a number of sectors. The sectors cited most frequently, in the economic literature and by their respective business associations, as having problems with overcapacity include aluminium, cement coal, iron and steel, oil refining, flat glass, paper and pulp and shipbuilding. Many of these activities take place relatively early in production value chains, and are particularly susceptible to cyclical fluctuations. These sectors have suffered from the worldwide demand slump that followed the 2008 to 2009 financial crisis. Moreover, most of them are characterised by large sunk costs, which effectively incentivise them to continue producing amid financial losses.

The sectors facing overcapacity are generally not characterised by a strong concentration of SOEs.[12] Also, the degree to which sustained overcapacity in any given sector is felt in the global economy depends on the degree of integration in global trade and investment. For instance, products such as flat glass, refined petroleum and cement are mostly sold within national markets, whereas coal, metals and ships are traded in the international marketplace and overcapacity in these sectors is felt globally.

The growing importance of SOEs may also have contributed to the problem. While private producers have, indeed, been hit by – and contributed to – overcapacity in recent years, private companies are generally assumed to be profit maximising and hence are expected to respond to overcapacity by halting investment and, eventually, cutting production. State-owned producers do not necessarily act likewise.

As mentioned earlier, the largest number of SOEs (outside the public utilities sector) are found in emerging economies. In general they play, or have in the past played, an integral role in national governments' development strategies and industrial policies, being generally found in sectors deemed "strategic" by their state owners.[13] In the interest of harnessing the outputs of these sectors to promote broader development objectives, these enterprises have, in some cases, at a minimum been shielded from the rate-of-return requirements applied by private investors in similar circumstances. They have also frequently enjoyed state support, such as concessionary credits, cheap inputs and land use and regulatory forbearance.[14]

This does not imply that SOEs have in the past been particularly profitable: in many cases, they are either relatively inefficient, or burdened by public policy obligations imposed by their owners, to the point where the concessionary treatment they enjoy does little more than keep them alive amid competition. In some cases, especially at the sub-national level of government, SOEs have moreover become seen as "employers of last resort" to the point where letting them close, or significantly reduce their activity, would have been socially controversial and politically impossible.

However, keeping alive inefficient companies obviously contributes to overcapacity and crowding out of more efficient competitors. Poorly designed compensation/subsidy schemes may also – by rewarding sales volumes rather than being linked to the fulfilment of public policy objectives – provide SOEs with an incentive to expand, including in foreign markets. Some of those SOEs that are profitable have, in a number of countries, moreover benefited from low dividend pay-out ratios compared with the private sector,[15] enabling them to continue expanding capacity, thus possibly aggravating the overcapacity challenge. SOEs held by sub-national levels of government may face particularly strong incentives to continue expanding amid overcapacity: local politicians tend to be rewarded (whether through the ballot box or political hierarchies) for growing employment in the local area.

Finally, the current overcapacity problems occur at a time when a period of particularly strong macroeconomic growth in emerging markets appears to be coming to a halt. Insofar as domestic demand in these economies now falls short of previous expectations, this has necessarily resulted in a mismatch between capacity and demand. An illustrative example is provided by the steel sector. Following years of rapid capacity expansion in some emerging economies, global demand was about 69% of global production capacity in 2015. Indeed, major steel-producing economies are engaging in international co-operation to address the excess capacity challenge currently facing the global steel sector.[16] The incidence of state-owned enterprises and the challenge of excess capacity in the steel sector are discussed in more detail in the following section.

State ownership and overcapacity in the steel sector: a case study

Many of these concerns have been felt in recent years in the steel sector, where SOEs (especially in emerging markets) are some of the main players and where issues of "undue advantages" related to state support have emerged. Concern with the growing role of SOEs in the global steel sector relates to the extent to which their investment decisions are market-based and how they might be contributing to excess capacity. SOEs play an important role in the steel industry, notably in several emerging economies. SOE production shares have been increasing in recent years. Data taken from the 40 largest steel producers in the world indicate that SOEs (defined as the state owning more than 20% of the company) accounted for around one-fourth of the sample's total production in recent years. Using the 50% ownership threshold suggests a production share of less than one-fifth, with steel SOEs being most prevalent in several emerging economies (OECD, 2012b).

Excess capacity (the difference between nominal steelmaking capacity and demand) is the biggest challenge facing the global steel industry today. According to the OECD's recent coverage of steel market developments (OECD, 2016b), the global steel industry's capacity to produce steel has more than doubled since the start of the current century, from a level of 1.05 billion tonnes in 2000 to more than 2.3 billion tonnes in 2015. Although global steel demand kept up with the pace of capacity growth until the first half of 2008, the eight years since the start of the global financial and economic crisis have been characterised by a sharp slowdown in world steel demand. The gap between growing capacity and stagnant consumption continues to increase, leading to lower capacity utilisation rates that may have important implications for the sustainability of the industry (Figure 3.13).

Figure 3.13. **World steelmaking capacity-demand imbalances**

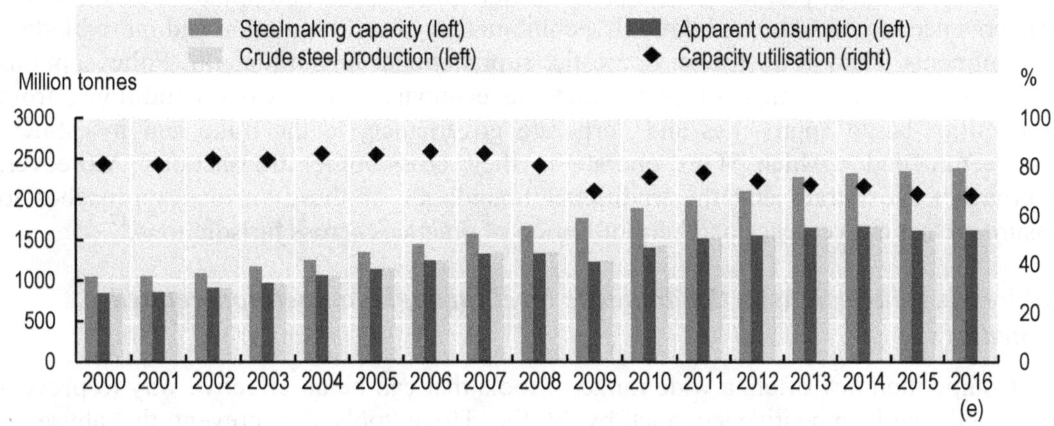

Note: Data refer to crude steel. Capacity is defined as nominal crude steelmaking capacity. Capacity utilisation is calculated as crude steel production divided by nominal crude steelmaking capacity.

Source: World Steel Association and OECD.

StatLink http://dx.doi.org/10.1787/888933476929

Despite this outlook, investment projects aimed at expanding steel production capacity continue to take place in many parts of the world, which has led to a significant increase in the level of global excess capacity. Excess capacity has surged from a level of around 205 million tonnes in 2006 to a level estimated at more than 700 million tonnes in 2015. Moreover, new capacity investment intentions, combined with a weaker outlook for steel demand, suggest that excess capacity might increase further in the near term. More specifically, new steelmaking capacity investment projects are being planned in some Asian economies and in the Middle East and North Africa region.

In the steel industry, periods of significant excess capacity are often associated with oversupply that results in trade disturbances and escalating trade frictions. Because of the important and strategic nature of the industry, high exit barriers and government interventions to preserve capacity during market downturns can often turn into steel "crises". For example, the downturn that followed the financial crisis led to an increase in the number of steel plant closures, a trend that is expected to intensify in the near future as a result of the weak demand outlook and challenging market conditions (resulting in social and human costs). Structural adjustment will be needed to ensure the economic viability of the global steel industry and help reduce trade frictions amongst trading partners.

In competitive economies, it is the responsibility of the steel companies themselves to identify ways to adapt to changing market conditions. That is, businesses are best placed to decide on when to invest in new capacity or when to scale back when market conditions change. The role of governments should be to let market mechanisms work properly and avoid measures that artificially contribute to global excess capacity. The concern with the growing role of SOEs in the global steel sector relates to the extent to which their investment decisions are market-based and how they are contributing to excess capacity.

3.7. How can the challenges be addressed?

As mentioned earlier, the concerns about "bad globalisation" can be exacerbated by the unique characteristics of SOEs, including widely perceived advantages received from the state and their proximity to the sovereign powers of individual nations. These concerns need to be addressed through a combination of self-regulation and more binding commitments taken at all levels: domestic, supranational or multilateral. Policy options must also address a range of issues and the economy's framework conditions, from competition-based approaches and corporate governance, to the trade and investment architecture under which SOEs operate in their cross-border transactions. Moreover, approaches must transcend the traditional boundaries of these various approaches to ensure greater convergence and harmonisation of practices across jurisdictions.[17]

Addressing distortions at the domestic level through competition-related remedies

Competition law offers a wide range of tools that can be an effective way to prevent or remedy anticompetitive conduct by SOEs. These tools can prevent the abuse of dominance (such as through predatory behaviour), they can block or remedy anti-competitive mergers, and can serve to break up cartels. However, not all aspects needed to ensure a level playing field on a global scale can be caught by competition enforcement. For this, comity and other reciprocal commitments may be necessary. In particular, increased harmonisation of competition policies across jurisdictions (including regulation, as well as advocacy) is one way to level the playing field. An overview of OECD guidance and legal instruments in the area of competition regulation is provided in Box 2.9 in Chapter 2.

Broader commitments to competitive neutrality (which are currently enshrined in the competition laws of a minority of OECD countries), more harmonized accountability and transparency requirements by SOEs, and more consistent application of rules concerning subsidies or state aid should be considered. These reciprocal commitments can help to ensure that policies in one jurisdiction do not advertently or inadvertently impact the competitive environment in others. In addition, regulatory and enforcement co-operation, as promoted in the OECD Recommendation concerning International Co-operation on Competition Investigations is key to ensuring that investigations, including those involving state-owned enterprises, can be effectively addressed by the competent authorities as the volume of cross-border transactions continue to rise.

Adjusting investment policy frameworks toward preserving a level playing field

Traditionally, international investment agreements have identified foreign governments as a class of investors like any other, and granted them equal market access and/or national treatment protections. International investment instruments (including those hosted by the OECD – such as the Codes of Liberalisation referenced in Chapter 2, Box 2.6) allow governments to close specific sectors to foreign investment and, more generally, to take necessary steps to prevent investment infringing on their national security. In practice, governments have given themselves a relatively wide berth in deciding what elements of the national interest can be considered as covered by the latter carve-out.

Governments have only relatively recently begun to address demands, in bilateral and regional investment agreements, regarding the operating conditions, information disclosure and governance of foreign SOEs entering their jurisdictions. Going forward, policy makers should consider addressing the sources of undue advantage of SOEs in such agreements to preserve a level playing field in international investment and adequately equipping investment policy frameworks with tools to address a level playing field. Failure to do so could lead to a bout of investment protectionism, which would leave participants in international trade and investment in a lose-lose situation. It should be a priority for all involved to maintain an open, transparent and rules-based environment for international investment.

Converging trade and investment approaches to remedy gaps in the coverage of multilateral rules

Trade regulation is equipped to deal with the "undue advantages" market participants in the global trading system (at least where trade in goods is concerned). These are enshrined in World Trade Organization rules, notably the Subsidies and Countervailing Measures Agreement, discipline subsidisation – including of SOEs – and the dispute settlement rulings on the question of "public body" which provide guidance regarding the importance of ownership when determining cases of possible subsidisation by state-owned or otherwise state-linked enterprises.

However, the continued high level of concern about trade-distorting subsidies indicates a need for strengthened disciplines on subsidies and other advantages. For example, in the context of international trade agreements, rules on subsidies granted to and by state enterprises might be a priority for further deliberations. Recent developments in international treaty practice indicate that more focused rule-making on SOEs may warrant special attention and reciprocal commitments between parties of such agreements. Such a focus may also help to ensure that trade and investment approaches are convergent in their dealings with SOEs.

Implementing the OECD Guidelines on Corporate Governance of State-Owned Enterprises

Many, if not indeed all, of the challenges for the investment, trade and competition communities that arise from the internationalisation of SOEs could be solved by a consistent implementation of the recommendations laid down in the OECD Guidelines on Corporate Governance of State-Owned Enterprises (See Chapter 2, Box 2.8). In providing guidance and best practices on the implementation of adequate ownership, corporate governance and transparency practices, the Guidelines have stood the test of time. The 2015 revised version of the instrument takes important additional steps to cover issues related to maintaining a level playing field where SOEs operate in the marketplace.

The Guidelines offer specific recommendations for how to maintain a level playing field (nationally, as well as in the global economy), identifying non-commercial objectives pursued by SOEs, avoiding ad-hoc political interference in state-controlled companies, and ensuring adequate disclosure by SOEs and their government owners. The revised Guidelines further added a section recommending that the state develops and communicates a rationale for state ownership of enterprises, in both general and specific cases. A review of these rationales can provide a useful indication of whether the internationalisation of a given SOE is appropriate and in accordance with its mandate.

The Guidelines can consequently be useful in addressing shortcomings in the coverage of existent trade and investment approaches to dealing with the context of the cross-border operations of SOEs. Implementing the Guidelines is conformant with operating at internationally high standards of transparency and disclosure, which is of great timely relevance since most newly-negotiated trade and investment treaties include provisions about SOE transparency and information sharing. The OECD could further take the lead in establishing standards that would, in turn, inform the development of more integrated disciplines in future trade and investment agreements.

Notes

1. Conversely, the recent policy action could indicate concerns that the overseas investment in property (real estate and leisure and recreation) may have been used to circumvent Chinese capital accounts restrictions.
2. Also, the data collection exercise applied a relatively restrictive definition of SOEs, including only enterprises where the state owns more than 50% of the voting shares.
3. OECD (2012a) discusses how, regardless of whether SOEs operate nationally or abroad, a level playing field with the private sector can be maintained.
4. A recent study concluded that, on the whole, the growing role of emerging economies in global markets has tended to reduce concentration. However, this finding is reversed in a few sectors where the dominant players are SOEs (Freund and Sidhu, 2017).
5. The OECD Business Survey on State Influence on Competition in International Markets was conducted in 2014 and covered 157 firms. The survey solicited information from the business community on the cross-border activity of SOEs with a view to determining the extent to which the various trade or investment-distorting advantages that may be granted by governments are inherent to SOEs. The survey included questions on both private and state-owned entities.

6. The sample contains information on 13 959 unique listed non-financial corporations incorporated in the following economies: Austria; Belgium; Brazil; Bulgaria; China; Croatia; Cyprus; Czech Republic; Denmark; Estonia; Finland; France; Germany; Greece; Hong Kong, China; Hungary; India; Ireland; Italy; Latvia; Lithuania; Luxembourg; Malta; Mexico; Netherlands; Poland; Portugal; Romania; Russia; Slovenia; Spain; Sweden; Turkey; and United Kingdom. The sample contains information on 1 111 unique listed non-financial SOEs and on 12 848 unique listed non-financial other corporations. The sectorial composition of the sample is the following: Energy (SOE: 62; Non-SOE: 424); Materials (SOE: 222; Non-SOE: 1 894); Industrials (SOE: 294; Non-SOE: 2 697); Consumer cyclicals (SOE: 174; Non-SOE: 3 586); Consumer non-cyclicals (SOE: 76; Non-SOE: 1 163); Healthcare (SOE: 57; Non-SOE: 993); Technology (SOE: 73; Non-SOE: 1 566); Telecommunications (SOE: 13; Non-SOE: 185); Utilities (SOE: 140; Non-SOE: 340).

7. The OECD Guidelines on Corporate Governance of State-Owned Enterprises recommend that an enterprise should be considered as an SOE if "the state [is] the ultimate beneficiary owner of the majority of voting shares or otherwise exercises an equivalent degree of control". The definition of equivalent degree of control should be determined on a case-by-case basis; the Guidelines posit that it could, in principle, be any stake above 10% of the shares.

8. Defined as net income divided by common equity.

9. See, for example, IMF (2016).

10. The risks emanating from China's debt build-up were highlighted by the previously cited IMF paper. It is also addressed by the OECD's most recent Economic Survey of China.

11. The sectoral classification follows Thomson Reuters Business Classification. The "Energy" sector is integrated by oil and gas, renewable energy and uranium as the major categories. The "Basic materials" sector contains all metal and mining companies, chemicals, and construction materials among others. The "Industrials" sector is comprised by aerospace and defence, machinery, equipment and components, construction and engineering, industrial and commercial services, industrial conglomerates, and transportation. The "Consumer cyclicals" sector is comprised by cyclical consumer products and services and retailers. The "Consumer non-cyclical" sector is integrated by food and beverages, personal household, product services, and food and drug retailing. The "Telecommunication Services" sector contains companies in the integrated telecommunications services and wireless telecommunications services. The "Utilities" sector contains companies in the electrical utilities and independent power producers, natural gas utilities, water utilities, and multiline utilities.

12. And, in some other sectors, such as agriculture, one could argue that there are cases of structural worldwide overcapacity triggered by private producers responding to politically-determined incentives.

13. For an overview, see OECD (2015).

14. For an early overview of the competitive challenges arising from this, see OECD (2012a).

15. The U.S.-China Economic and Security Review Commission, in its annual 2016 report to Congress, noted that, until recently, Chinese SOEs paid no dividends to their owner, and cited this as an important source of these enterprises' rapid expansion.

16. For example, the recently established Global Forum on Steel Excess Capacity, called for by G20 Leaders in September 2016, will lead to increased information sharing and cooperation among G20 and OECD members on ways to address excess capacity in the steel sector.

17. For a detailed discussion, see OECD (2016a).

References

European Chamber of Commerce in China (2016), *Overcapacity in China: An Impediment to the Party's Reform Agenda,* www.europeanchamber.com.cn/en.

Financial Times (2016), "China weighs outbound deal curbs to buoy renminbi", 30 November 2016.

Freund and Sidhu (2017), "Global Competition and the Rise of China", Working Paper 17-3, Peterson Institute for International Economics).

IMF (2016), "Resolving China's Corporate Debt Problem", Working Paper, WP/16/203.

Kwiatkowski, G., Augustynowciz, P., 2015, "State-owned enterprises in the global economy – analysis based on Fortune Global 500 list", Management Knowledge and Learning Joint Conference, Italy, 27-29 May.

OECD (2017a, forthcoming), *The Size and Sectoral Distribution of SOEs in OECD and Partner Countries*, Volume 2, OECD Publishing, Paris.

OECD (2017b, forthcoming), *Investing in Climate, Investing in Growth,* A report for the 2017 G20 Presidency. See OECD project on Growth, Investment and the Low-Carbon Transition, www.oecd.org/economy/g20-climate.htm.

OECD (2016a), *State-Owned Enterprises as Global Competitors: A Challenge or an Opportunity?*, OECD Publishing, Paris. http://dx.doi.org/10.1787/9789264262096-en.

OECD (2016b), "Steel Market Developments", www.oecd.org/sti/ind/steel-market-developments.htm.

OECD (2015), *State-Owned Enterprises in the Development Process*, OECD Publishing, Paris. http://dx.doi.org/10.1787/9789264229617-en.

OECD (2014), *Financing State-Owned Enterprises: An Overview of National Practices*, OECD Publishing, Paris. http://dx.doi.org/10.1787/9789264209091-en.

OECD (2012a), *Competitive Neutrality: Maintaining a Level Playing Field between Public and Private Business*, OECD Publishing, Paris. http://dx.doi.org/10.1787/9789264178953-en.

OECD (2012b), "State Ownership in the Steel Industry: Issues for Consideration", unpublished working document, Directorate for Science, Technology and Industry.

Chapter 4

Protecting and promoting competition in a global marketplace

The globalisation of business activity is generally associated with an increase in competition, as businesses reach beyond their borders to offer goods and services to new markets, encouraging cost reductions and innovation. However, while multinational firms operate on a global scale, the competition rules that protect consumers, and economic efficiency, do not. Thus, competition policy and law enforcement requires international co-operation to match the scope of potential competition problems. This chapter describes four areas in which market distortions can be addressed with a common commitment to the promotion of competition: investigation co-operation for cross-border cartels, addressing taxation and SOE policies that interfere with competition, careful design of public interest review mechanisms for mergers, and the consideration of the impact of export cartels. The OECD instruments on international cooperation in competition law enforcement, hard-core cartels and procurement bid-rigging, can help achieve these outcomes.

4.1 Introduction

The globalisation of business activity is generally associated with an increase in competition, as businesses reach beyond their borders to offer goods and services to new markets. This is broadly beneficial for consumers and market efficiency, since widening a market to include new firms will set in motion competitive processes by which firms will be forced to improve efficiency and innovate, or disappear. At the same time, firms will enjoy access to bigger markets that allow them to take advantage of economies of scale. While sometimes cast as a threat to domestic businesses, openness to foreign competition has been observed in many cases to impose productivity discipline on domestic firms in traded goods sectors. In Japan, for example, Sakakibara and Porter (2001) found that industries facing foreign competition exhibited greater productivity growth than those insulated from overseas competitors.

On the individual level, however, competition can produce short-run winners and losers. The latter include employees and owners of any domestic firms charging supra-competitive prices, and any beneficiaries of inefficiencies that disappear after the entry of new firms. But these challenges will be more easily addressed with the resulting economic vitality that competition brings: for every "loser", there are many "winning" consumers and firms (as well as employees and shareholders), provided price competition occurs in a manner consistent with economic efficiency. Openness to foreign competition alone will not ensure this. The same market problems that have been the focus of competition law since its inception, such as firms taking advantage of barriers to entry to form a cartel or using a dominant position to suppress competitors, can manifest themselves across national borders. Thus globalised markets can only work if rules are set to ensure that they operate in a competitive way, and the primary tool for this is competition law and policy.

As it currently stands, the scope of globalisation has been asymmetric. While multinational firms operate on a global scale, the competition rules that protect consumers and economic efficiency, do not. Thus, while the competition issues that exist in international markets are, in many respects, the same as those that occur in domestic markets, competition law enforcement must be enhanced with international co-operation to match the scope of potential anticompetitive conduct.

To reach its potential, globalisation therefore requires competition enforcement co-operation that avoids hampering productive business activity and effectively detects cross-border misconduct. At the same time, a common commitment to competition on a level playing field may need to be reemphasised. Without action on these issues, there are risks that anticompetitive reactions to globalisation may dampen its positive aspects. For example, in an effort to assist domestic export industries, governments can permit, or even lead, the establishment of export cartels (although such measures provide no protection against prosecution of cartels in the importing jurisdiction). These cartels may produce gains for the owners of export firms at the expense of foreign consumers – the wrong sort of globalised business activity, which can create distortive economic rents, dampen competition and lead to calls for further anticompetitive retaliatory measures.

Similarly, governments seeking to promote particular domestic firms, including state-owned enterprises (SOEs) or industries, can grant a range of advantages to them which distort competition and the productive efficiency it brings. In particular, these measures may insulate the advantaged firms from pressures to reduce costs or innovate, meaning that globalised business activity may not bring its expected benefits in terms of productivity (and may, in some cases, create inefficient dislocations). Several countries have responded to these measures by instituting an additional layer of review for mergers involving foreign firms. These reviews can include applying "public interest considerations" to the approval of mergers. While they can be perceived as a reasonable response to state-sponsored firms pursuing distortionary acquisitions of domestic firms (thus interfering with normal competitive mechanisms), these measures can also carry risks when they are not associated with clear criteria and specific conditions. Broad, ill-defined measures can expose mergers to uncertainty, as well as political pressures that may prevent or alter their procompetitive and productivity-enhancing effects.

In order to prevent the continuous escalation of measures, such as politicised transaction review mechanisms and anticompetitive advantages for domestic firms and export cartels, strengthened international co-operation is necessary. Limiting the use of these measures would represent a commitment to harnessing the positive forces of openness, and would leave governments equipped with a more productive, competitive economy to better respond to the challenges of globalisation. Failing to achieve this coordination may skew the patterns of globalisation, prevent governments from responding to negative aspects of globalisation, or lead to policy reactions that limit the economic benefits of globalisation.

The analysis in this chapter deals with four issues that require the type of co-operation described above:

- Cross-border cartels
- Addressing taxation and state-owned enterprise policies that distort competition
- Public interest review mechanisms in merger control
- Export cartels

4.2 Cross-border cartels

The national scope of competition authority jurisdiction does not match the increasingly international nature of cartel and other anticompetitive activity. Consequently, the detection and punishment of cartel conduct will require effective co-operation among competition law enforcement authorities and policy makers.

As noted in Chapter 2, cartels cause obvious harm to the consumers of cartelised products, who pay substantially higher prices. Box 4.1 describes the OECD instruments aimed at fighting cartels.

Globalisation and openness to trade are pro-competitive forces that have made cartel formation more difficult. In particular, openness can undermine two enablers of cartel conduct, via the removal of barriers to entry (due, for example, to government policies that limit competition), and downward pressure on industry concentration (since the higher the number of required cartel members, the less stable a cartel is – see, for instance, Levenstein and Suslow, 2006).

However, while globalisation can encourage new competition that undermines cartels, it can also create challenges for the enforcement of antitrust laws. For instance, a substantial share of cartelised commerce occurs in markets for intermediate industrial outputs which, due to global value chains, leads to consumer impacts that expand across industries and borders. Price increases for these inputs are often passed on to the ultimate consumer of a product, even if the cartel is several steps (and countries) removed from the final product. This creates competition law enforcement challenges in terms of establishing jurisdiction and accessing evidence. OECD (2015d) explores some of the practical considerations for competition authorities on this issue. Another challenge occurs in oligopolistic industries where firms compete in several markets (in terms of both geography and product or service). Here there might be less incentive to compete, and it may also become easier to find ways to avoid competing (see, for instance, Eftychidou and Maiorano, 2016). In particular, market sharing or extending a cartel agreement to include new geographies or products, may be more practical for firms in such industries. There can be a jurisdictional element to these challenges as well – when tacit collusion involves oligopolistic firms sharing markets on a national basis, it may elude competition authority jurisdiction. One such example relates to the African beer market, where major beer producers effectively shared national markets amongst themselves but did not face competition authority scrutiny since the market sharing did not occur within a single jurisdiction (OECD, 2014a). In addition, colluding firms can more easily justify national market sharing (i.e. apportioning out different countries as exclusive territories for a firm) on the grounds of cultural or other barriers between countries.

Box 4.1. **Fighting hard core cartels and bid rigging**

The detection and enforcement of laws against collusive behaviour (including cartels and bid-rigging in public procurement) has been a priority of competition authorities since the inception of competition law and policy. As described in Chapter 2 of this *Outlook*, the OECD has developed several instruments that evidence the commitment of OECD countries to fight collusion, and provide practical assistance for doing so. The Recommendation of the OECD Council concerning Effective Action against Hard Core Cartels sets out a common approach to cartels, calling for adherents to ensure their competition laws effectively halt and deter hard core cartels by providing for effective sanctions, and ensuring enforcement procedures and institutions are adequate to detect and remedy hard core cartels (including powers to obtain information and impose penalties for non-compliance).

To combat bid rigging, the Recommendation of the OECD Council on Fighting Bid Rigging in Public Procurement and the accompanying Guidelines are effective tools for procurement officials. They highlight the importance of having a thorough understanding of an industry before preparing a bid (including factors that raise the risks of collusion), designing tenders to maximise bidder participation, defining clear requirements, avoiding tender predictability and minimising vendor communication (which facilitates collusion), and ensuring staff awareness, as well as training to identify potential bid rigging.

The detection of cartels that reach beyond national borders has increased in recent years. In the European Union, for example, the average number of countries with firms participating in a given cartel from 2001 to 2015 ranged from a low of approximately three (in 2002) to a high of eight (in 2010) (Hellwig and Hüschelrath, 2016). Despite the significant growth in the number of countries prohibiting cartels, there remain gaps between the geographic scope of cartels and the number of jurisdictions imposing fines on them. Our analysis indicates that more than half of the cross-border cartels in the Private International Cartels dataset that have been discovered since 1983 have been fined in only one jurisdiction (Figure 4.1).

Figure 4.1. **Cumulative cross-border cartel detection and fines**

(Number of cases)

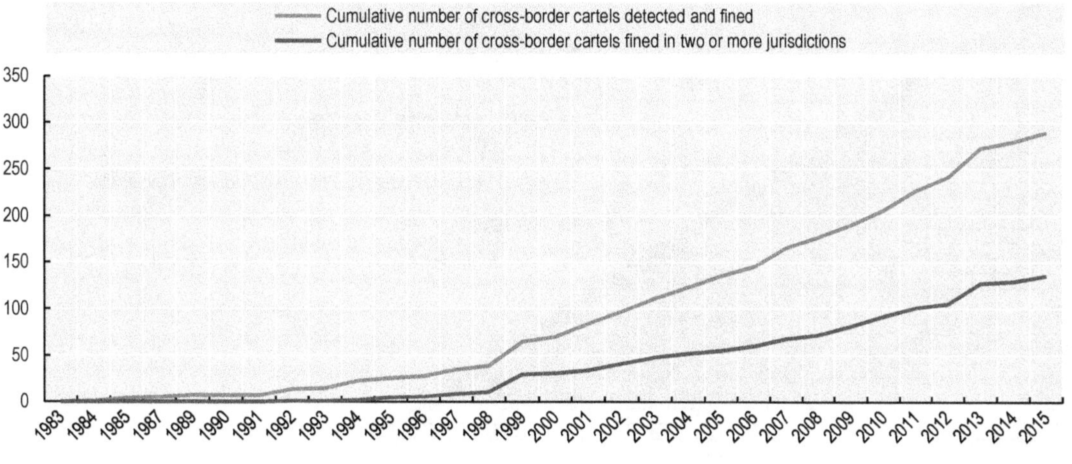

Note: The European Union is counted as a single jurisdiction for the purposes of classifying cartels as "cross-border" (so a cartel involving European Union countries only would not be considered "cross-border").

Source: OECD analysis of the cartels contained within the Private International Cartels dataset.

StatLink http://dx.doi.org/10.1787/888933476937

The gap between cartel detection and fines could be due to several factors, including: differing enforcement intensity; variations in local market realities (and the impact of the conduct in question); challenges in small jurisdictions to enforcement of antitrust law vis-à-vis large multinational firms; differing competition laws; limits to competition authority powers; and limitations to the use of information from other jurisdictions in cartel prosecutions. On the latter point, it is clear that the scope of international cartels may not always be matched by the investigative and sanctioning powers of cartel law enforcers. This may affect the incentives of firms to form cartels if they observe that partial enforcement is likely.

The number of bilateral co-operation agreements between competition authorities has grown in recent years: 62 such agreements have been signed since 2011,[1] although these agreements vary in their content and strength. Agreements that permit the systematic sharing of confidential information for investigatory purposes are, in particular, relatively rare (Figure 4.2). In the absence of broad agreements, informal, piecemeal methods have developed, namely waivers provided by companies that allow information sharing, such as for merger cases, or applications for leniency from prosecution for anticompetitive conduct. Regardless of the reason for this lack of systematic, confidential information sharing (including legislative limitations or differing procedural safeguards), it may be hampering efforts to prevent, detect and punish cross-border cartels.

Figure 4.2. **Prevalence of agreements permitting confidential information sharing for anticompetitive conduct law enforcement among selected countries**

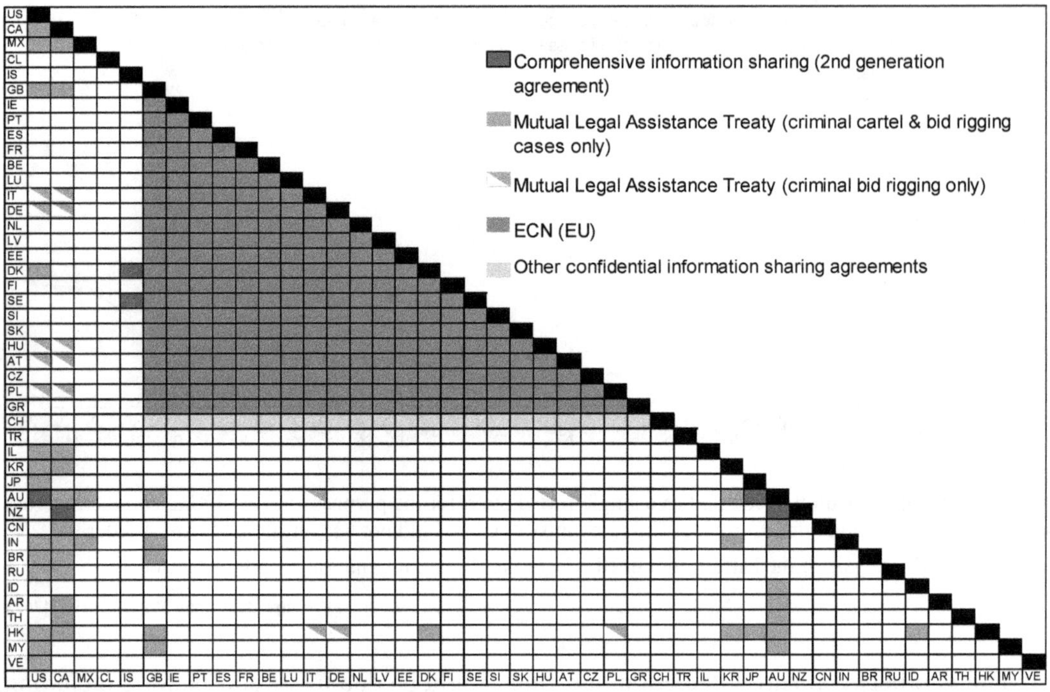

Source: OECD analysis based on information gathered from OECD (2016a), MLAT.info and the European Competition Network

Box 4.2. **International co-operation in competition investigations**

Recognising the importance of information-sharing for fighting cartels, the Recommendation of the OECD Council concerning Effective Action against Hard Core Cartels calls for adherents to seek ways to improve such co-operation. In 2005, the OECD Competition Committee also published "Best Practices for the Formal Exchange of Information between Competition Authorities in Hard Core Cartel Investigations", which contains practical guidance for competition authorities seeking to share information with their counterparts. It focuses on safeguards for information sharing, including ensuring the required authority to share information and protecting confidentiality as well as legal privilege.

The Recommendation of the OECD Council concerning International Co-operation on Competition Investigations and Proceedings evidences the commitment of OECD members to this issue. The Recommendation notes that such co-operation can range from information sharing, to voluntarily supporting investigations in other jurisdictions, to proactively sharing input regarding investigations that affect their domestic interests.

In addition to information-sharing, the mutual recognition of cartel decisions by competition authorities has been identified as an opportunity to reduce the burden on investigators and enhance consistency (see OECD, 2014b). Possible approaches include: promoting positive comity in competition enforcement actions (e.g. competition authorities considering requests by other countries to open an investigation with respect to potential anticompetitive conduct); relying on a finding of guilt in other jurisdictions while calculating local damages; and the organisation of multi-authority investigations with a single authority designated as "lead authority." This concept could, in particular, assist smaller, less well-resourced competition authorities in enforcing their competition laws, but involves significant practical and legal feasibility challenges. The benefits of ensuring that no jurisdiction is a "safe haven" for cartel conduct may well justify the effort required to tackle the associated challenges in operationalising enhanced enforcement co-operation.

In the event these challenges cannot be surmounted, competition authorities can pursue practical alternatives that could also promote internationally consistent, effective competition law enforcement. For instance, there remain substantial opportunities to promote improved informal investigation coordination and a common approach to emerging issues. One example of the latter is the subject of tacit collusion in oligopolistic markets in the digital era, for which there is not yet a consensus among competition authorities (see OECD, 2015e). There are many markets where potential concerns have been raised in a range of sectors across the economy, and while explicit agreements among firms in oligopolistic markets are captured by competition law, tacit collusion is more difficult to detect and prosecute. Kovacic et al (2011) describes these challenges as follows:

> *"In highly concentrated markets, the recognition of interdependence can lead firms to coordinate their conduct simply by observing and reacting to their competitors' moves. In some instances, such oligopolistic coordination yields parallel behavior (e.g., parallel price movements) that approaches the results that one might associate with a traditional agreement to set prices, output levels, or other conditions of trade. The line that distinguishes tacit agreements (which are subject to [US antitrust laws]) from mere tacit coordination stemming from oligopolistic interdependence (which eludes [the reach of US antitrust laws]) is indistinct."*

Competition authorities have taken varying approaches to potential tacit collusion, and the precise legal approach requires careful consideration to avoid chilling procompetitive conduct. International fora, including the International Competition Network and OECD Competition Committee, should be leveraged in crafting such an approach.

Box 4.3 describes another emerging area of antitrust research and an opportunity for international co-operation: the advent of "free" online services.

When dealing with emerging competition issues with an international dimension, or differing interpretations of competition principles, competition authorities require fora to share experiences and interact outside of formal investigation proceedings. The International Co-operation Network and OECD Competition Committee provide such opportunities, which have substantial value in terms of encouraging a common approach to competition principles, and solutions to challenges requiring multijurisdictional co-operation. In fact, while many additional opportunities remain, international co-operation in competition enforcement has been a success: OECD research indicates that there are 128 jurisdictions in the world with competition laws, and 121 competition authorities. In many respects, there is broad agreement about the core concepts and design of competition legislation. Further co-operation is necessary, however, in terms of the application of concepts, addressing legislative barriers to co-operation, and dealing with emerging issues in markets.

Box 4.3. **Globalisation, digitalisation and the "zero price economy"**

The global proliferation of "free" online platforms is reshaping an increasing number of industries, whether through entirely new services or through offerings that displace incumbent firms. These platforms are characterised by network effects and often low (or zero) marginal costs. As a result, firms can expand the global reach of their services with greater ease than ever before. While the provision of new services into a region is, in general, beneficial for consumers, anticompetitive conduct can be introduced into markets along with those services, particularly given the "winner takes all" nature of competition in digital markets. For instance, dominance in a market for "free" services can be leveraged to improve a firm's position in related markets, and even determining whether a firm is dominant can be challenging. Notwithstanding this, in the zero-price economy, costs of entry may also be lower and the potential for new entry as well as "leap frog" innovation provides dynamism – including a competitive threat to current leaders. Potential competition concerns may differ across markets depending on whether customers can readily multi-home for free services.

Data collected from consumers of "free" online services can be used to improve the services offered. For example, companies may offer free services with the objective of collecting consumer data to improve advertisement targeting, and therefore revenues as well as other related services (see, for example, Stucke and Ezrachi, 2016). It can be challenging, however, for competition authorities to assess market participant conduct and mergers in these types of digital markets. In particular, free goods, the importance of big data, and the increasingly global nature of online platforms are raising questions in several areas. Relatively few competition cases have been concluded so the case law in this area is likely to evolve in the future.

- **Consumer protection**: when consumers use a free service, they are often unaware of what they give up in exchange, in terms of their personal data as well as their exposure to targeted advertisements. Without understanding the extent and conditions on reuse of the data they are implicitly providing, they are not in a position to make a rational decision about whether or not to use an online service. This uncertainty is compounded by the fact that the full range of data use is often not even apparent to the firms that collect it at the time. Some have proposed granting consumers property rights over the data that firms collect, ensuring portability and greater transparency (see, for instance, Hoofnagle and Whittington, 2014).
- **The application of traditional analytical competition tools built around the assessment of prices in markets for "free" goods:** competition authorities assess mergers and the dominance of firms which typically involves the analysis of the likely impact of pricing changes in a market. In markets with "free" services, which have been considered in the past but are becoming increasingly common in digital markets, careful analysis will be required to identify instances of firm dominance or competitive concerns from mergers. Such analysis may require the consideration of subjective factors, such as innovation and quality. For example, some have proposed considering the impact of a decrease in quality in place of price increases for free goods. Consideration could also be given to non-monetary "prices" (e.g. payment by consumers with their personal data). These adjustments could prove challenging for competition authorities in terms of implementation, obtaining the required data and ensuring transparency in their reviews.
- **The use of data to abuse or maintain a dominant position**, or to expand one into new markets: it is likely that competition authorities will be called on in the future to determine whether data in a given market can lead to anticompetitive effects. Assessing these issues can be difficult in fast-changing markets where the lines between different types of services can be blurred in unexpected ways (a platform can be adapted to offer dramatically different services from its original purpose). However, these challenges do not mean that a wholesale reassessment of competition economics is necessary.

Box 4.3. **Globalisation, digitalisation and the "zero price economy"** (cont.)

- **The use of data and algorithms to facilitate cartel formation:** data may facilitate the formation and administration of cartels, and pricing algorithms may lead to collusion regardless of whether that was an intention of their design. However, there may also be opportunities to use big data analytics to detect cartel behaviour.
- **Geographic market scope:** as the geographic scope of online platforms expands, the nature of dominance and the scope of remedies to abusive behaviour will extend beyond the jurisdiction of a single competition authority, underlining the importance of co-operation. For example, a small country may be faced with the threat of withdrawal by a large firm when considering appropriate remedies.

Policy challenges from free platforms are not limited to competition issues. More broadly, free, borderless services may escape the reach of a variety of regulatory mechanisms without a global concerted effort and new thinking, including competition enforcement, taxation, consumer protection, privacy issues, legal dispute settlement and product regulation.

4.3 Addressing taxation and policies toward state-owned enterprises that distort competition

Government policies with asymmetric impacts across businesses or national borders can have significant consequences, particularly in the case of SOEs that benefit from advantages granted by governments, and tax policies. Specifically, there is a risk that policy responses to these distortions may worsen competition in markets, with corresponding effects on domestic and global welfare. Alternative policies that address the globalisation of competition distortions are therefore essential. Box 4.4 describes recent efforts to address distortionary tax policies – which highlights the need for coordination to prevent such distortions from having broader negative impacts.

A common concern in globalised markets are measures by governments to promote a given national company or industry by granting it distortionary advantages and "national champion" status. These types of measures can, in particular, favour SOEs over private or foreign firms. The OECD has looked extensively at this matter, and identified a number of ways through which governments may undermine the existence of a level playing field between SOEs and private businesses (in other words, policies that undermine the principle of competitive neutrality).

Table 4.1. **Competitive neutrality – policy frameworks**

Distortive Measures	Corrective measures
Subsidisation	Anti-subsidy and state aid control
Discriminatory selection of an entrusted player (special rights, public services)	Public procurement rules (open competitive process), public service comparator mechanism
Excessive or insufficient compensation for a public service	Public service compensation standards
Distortive regulation	Regulatory impact assessment framework, including competition and competitive neutrality factors
Cross-subsidisation and hybrid companies	Good governance rules
Conflicts of interests	Good public and governance rules
Abuse of state power	Public laws against abuse of administrative powers
Discrimination and unfair treatment	Rules on equality, non-discrimination and fair treatment

Source: OECD (2015b), p.17.

Box 4.4. **Distortionary taxation and competition**

An example of asymmetric treatment on the part of governments that may distort competition is in the area of tax policy. In particular, a lack of coordination in the design of tax policies may give rise to base erosion and profit shifting (BEPS) – "tax planning by multinational enterprises that makes use of gaps in the interaction of different tax systems to artificially reduce taxable income or shift profits to low-tax jurisdictions in which little or no economic activity is performed" (OECD, 2015c). BEPS can result in significant asymmetries in effective tax rates within a given jurisdiction. This includes disparities in tax treatment among multinational enterprises, and disparities between domestic and multinational firms, creating an unlevel playing field.

In considering competition issues related to taxation, the European Commission investigated and issued a decision on the subject of Apple's tax agreement with Ireland, requiring payment by Apple of up to EUR 13 billion, plus interest. The decision made specific reference to selective treatment, stating that it gave "Apple a significant advantage over other businesses that are subject to the same national taxation rules" (European Commission, 2016). Apple and the Government of Ireland are appealing the decision.

Broader measures to permit national tax authorities to identify the global tax treatment of companies have been identified and adopted as part of an OECD/G20 initiative on BEPS. As part of implementing the BEPS minimum standard on country-by-country reporting, the US Treasury Department and Internal Revenue Service, issued regulations in June 2016 that require multinational enterprises with annual revenue of over USD 850 million to report the amount of taxes they pay in each country in which they operate, in addition to other information. This measure, commonly referred to as "country-by-country" reporting, could permit tax authorities to identify potential risks of multinational enterprises having taken advantage of base erosion and profit shifting. This BEPS minimum standard is also being implemented by all members of the Inclusive Framework on BEPS.

As efforts to address BEPS recognise, competition on a level playing field requires fair taxation treatment. Preventing asymmetric tax rates within a given jurisdiction that advantage certain firms over others will ensure that all firms pay their fair share of tax, and therefore that the distribution of the benefits of globalisation will reflect market performance rather than inequitable distortions.

SOEs often benefit from advantages conferred upon them by existing legislative and administrative frameworks, such as financial support, tax preferences, regulatory privileges, and immunities not generally available to their privately-owned competitors. As a consequence, competition between favoured enterprises and those that are not may be distorted with consequences at both the domestic and international level (McCarthy, 2012). These types of advantages, and their impacts on competition, are described in greater depth in Chapter 3.

The domestic regulation of favoured firms under a variety of domestic rules – including not only antitrust but also rules on state action, subsidies and other types of competitive neutrality – is not usually concerned with cross-border effects and does not protect against the export of anticompetitive effects or of market power (Fox and Healey, 2014). At the international level, the advantages from which favoured firms benefit are not subject to control, with the exception of rules on state subsidies and state aid (such as those in place in economic unions such as the European Union) as well as additional provisions specific to SOEs in bilateral investment treaties and regional trade agreements.

While countries may be able to enforce their own competition rules with respect to favoured firms, such rules may not fully address competition distortions when competitive neutrality is not applied. This may confer on favoured firms undue advantages over competitors in a number of scenarios. For example when economies of scale and scope are at play, SOEs may be made more efficient than they otherwise would have been relative to their competitors, and thus be able to exclude competition without infringing competition law.

Unless a level playing field is ensured through the application of principles such as competitive neutrality, state-granted advantages to particular firms may compel governments to institute additional foreign direct investment reviews. One example of such a measure is the US-China Economic and Security Review Commission's recommendation to Congress to change the mandate of the Committee on Foreign Investment in the United States to "to bar Chinese SOEs from acquiring or otherwise gaining effective control of U.S. companies" (USCC, 2016, p.26). Concerns about foreign SOE activity could also lead domestic competitors to advocate for protectionist measures that extend beyond the scope of competitive neutrality concerns, and which may further worsen competitive conditions in markets. These include the adoption of regulations that unreasonably advantage domestic industry under the banner of "fair" competition or the protection of "national interests".

4.4 Public interest review mechanisms in merger control

Public interest clauses (with significant variations in terms of scope and depth of review) exist in all OECD jurisdictions except Chile, Denmark, Luxembourg, Norway and Turkey, and are most often applied to a narrow set of industries (Figure 4.3, Panel A) outside of competition authority merger review processes (Figure 4.3, Panel B). Box 4.5 describes one such example in Canada, where the Minister of Innovation, Science and Economic Development takes into account a range of criteria when reviewing significant foreign investments made by SOEs to determine if they are likely to be of net benefit to Canada. However, concerns about the "wrong sort of globalisation" could lead to calls for greater usage of public interest review provisions for protectionist purposes. Concentrating broad public interest reviews (i.e. those that are not limited to a specific set of sectors or circumstances) within competition authorities raises significant risks, namely diluting the focus of competition authorities and reducing business certainty as well as policy transparency. This would be contrary to the current practice in many jurisdictions of applying public interest considerations through other public bodies, such as sector regulators.

Figure 4.3. **Public interest clauses in OECD jurisdictions**

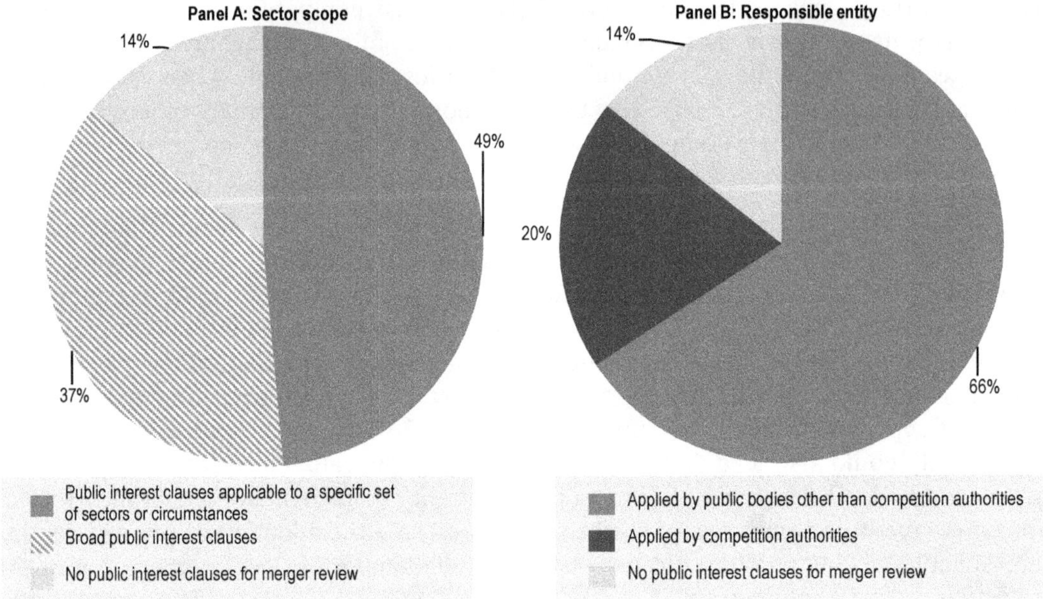

Source: Reader (2016) and, for information on sector application, Davies (2016).

StatLink http://dx.doi.org/10.1787/888933476940

Box 4.5. The application of public interest considerations under foreign investment review of acquisitions by SOEs in Canada

Acquisitions by foreign SOEs pose a challenge for competition policy to the extent that SOEs do not operate as fully commercial entities. One approach to address such concerns is illustrated by Canada's SOE Guidelines regarding acquisitions of Canadian companies (issued in 2007 and updated in 2012). Direct acquisitions of control of Canadian businesses above prescribed monetary thresholds by foreign investors can be reviewed based on whether they would likely be of "net benefit" as defined by the Investment Canada Act.[2] For reviewable acquisitions by foreign SOEs, the SOE Guidelines outline some key considerations the Minister examines, as part of this assessment:

- whether the SOE adheres to Canadian standards of corporate governance (e.g., commitment to transparency and disclosure, independent members of the board, independent audit committees and equitable treatment of shareholders);
- the extent to which the SOE is owned, controlled or influenced by a foreign state;
- whether the Canadian business will continue to operate on a commercial basis post-acquisition, including with regard to:
- where it will export;
- where it will process;
- the participation of Canadians in its operations in Canada and elsewhere;
- the impact of the investment on productivity and industrial efficiency in Canada;
- its support of ongoing innovation, research and development in Canada; and
- the appropriate level of capital expenditures to maintain the Canadian business in a globally competitive position.

Source: Innovation, Science and Economic Development Canada, Investment Canada Act Guidelines.

4.5 Export cartels

While the harm from cartels operating within a country is universally acknowledged, export cartels are permitted to operate freely in several markets. Some countries allow the formation of export cartels by exempting domestic firms from local competition laws when firm production is entirely exported. In other jurisdictions, export cartels are implicitly exempted due to competition laws that are confined in scope to domestic markets. This situation is not limited to countries that have recently adopted a competition law or that lack an antitrust culture, but is also common among traditionally strong antitrust law-enforcing countries (Levenstein and Suslow, 2005).

Figure 4.4. **Forecast impact of competition on Saskatchewan potash production and prices**

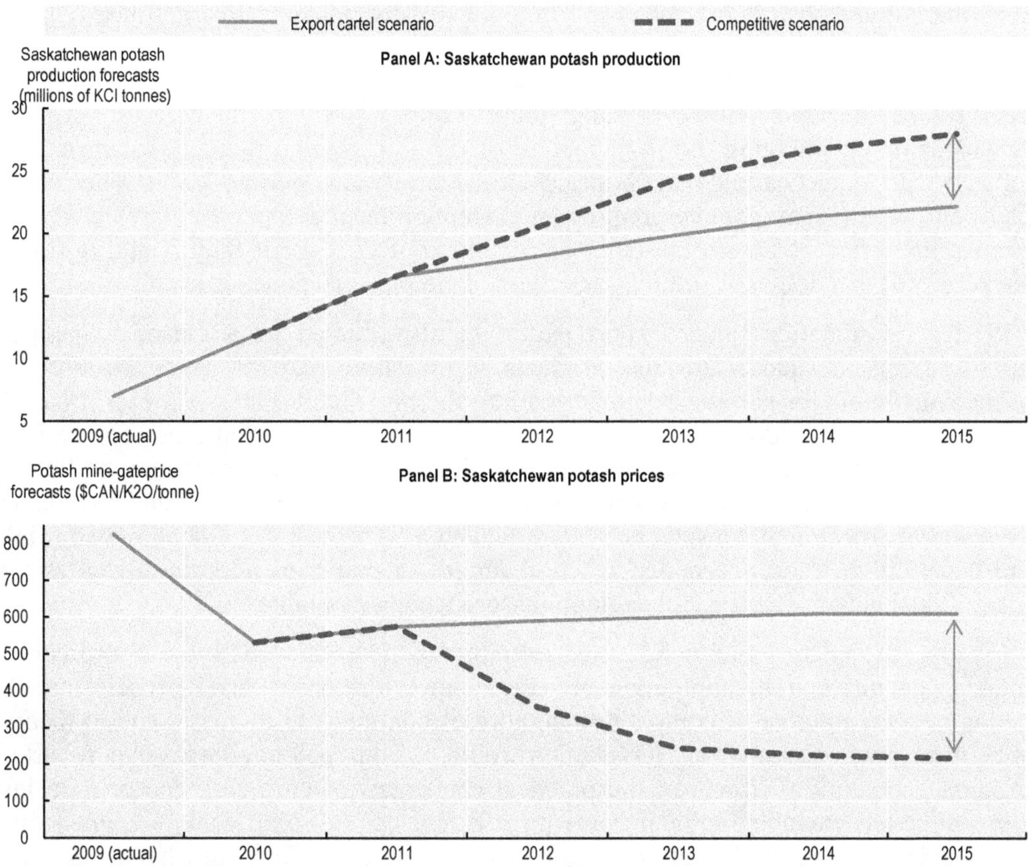

Source: Conference Board of Canada (2010)

StatLink http://dx.doi.org/10.1787/888933476953

Firm co-operation that dampens price competition will harm consumers while allowing a few firms to benefit from economic rents, supressing competitive pressures to reduce costs and innovate. Export cartels that fix prices or share markets are akin in objective and effect to any other cartel agreement, with the notable exception being that export cartels directly harm only foreign consumers. If this type of co-operation were among firms operating in a domestic market, it would generally be considered a per se violation of competition law (a practice that is automatically considered a violation of the law regardless of its effects).

Figure 4.5 illustrates the significant impact export cartels can have for some of the world's poorest populations: Jenny (2012) reviewed forecasts of potash production in Saskatchewan and prices under a status quo export cartel scenario and a competitive full production scenario (prepared by the Conference Board of Canada). The full production scenario envisioned a price drop of approximately 65% (Figure 4.5, Panel B) and an increase in Saskatchewan production of approximately 25% in 2015 (Figure 4.5, Panel A), a total impact of approximately CAD 6 billion. Notably, these forecasts were prepared with respect to a potential acquisition that could have undermined the integrity of the export cartel. However, for domestic economic policy reasons, the transaction was blocked under a public interest review mechanism.

Export cartel exemptions are sometimes defended on efficiency grounds: proponents of export cartels argue that they permit small producers to cooperate in order to develop the marketing and distribution network required to participate in international markets (see, for instance, Sokol, 2009). In other words, export cartels are characterised by their advocates as mechanisms to promote competition by enabling exports that would not otherwise be feasible. However, the joint-venture-type agreements that produce efficiencies by encouraging the participation of firms in foreign markets should not be conflated with export cartels that fix prices or share markets (Jenny, 2012). The former type of agreements may not even require an exemption from competition law given their objective and effect, whereas the latter are a source of concern if they would not have been permitted in a domestic setting, regardless of claimed efficiency effects.

Pricing coordination under export cartels is also framed as a means to support domestic terms of trade. But the products in question may at times be used as intermediate inputs for goods later imported into the jurisdiction, meaning export cartels can indirectly harm domestic consumers as well. Further, domestic competition authorities' ability to advocate in favour of fighting international cartels may be limited when export cartels are permitted because they help domestic producers and the impact on the welfare of foreign consumers is not articulated.[3] The case for a level playing field more generally is also undermined when examples of countries adopting distortionary policies, like blanket export cartel exemptions, are readily available.[4]

Finally, defenders of export cartel exemptions note that they do not preclude importing countries from applying competition laws to export cartel participants. As noted above, the number of competition authorities continues to increase, and in theory, competition law in an importing jurisdiction would be equipped to address export cartels that harm competition. However, the practical challenges of enforcing competition law for export cartels exempted in their home jurisdictions can be significant. A country may lack a viable substitute to the cartelised good, suggesting cartel fines may have a minimal effect on firm conduct or could be passed on to consumers. Export cartel prosecution may also be avoided by a country for fear of repercussions for its own export cartels (see Jenny, 2012, p. 121). Further, it can be challenging for competition authorities to obtain the information they need to investigate firms based outside their jurisdiction – particularly when competition authorities in the exporting jurisdiction would be unable to assist with prosecutions for actions that are not illegal in their jurisdiction (due to the export cartel exemptions). Authorities with substantially limited resources in emerging economies, which can be most affected by export cartels, may in particular find these information gaps difficult to overcome.

The elimination of explicit export cartel exemptions in competition laws will not be sufficient to address these challenges. Competition authorities in the exporting jurisdiction may for example face jurisdictional hurdles in prosecuting cartel behaviour that harms only foreign consumers. However, removing exemptions will facilitate greater sharing of information and investigation co-operation across jurisdictions. Thus, a new cooperative approach will require both (1) policy makers reducing export cartel exemptions when they are likely to be harmful, and (2) competition authorities sharing information and collaborating in investigations. This collaboration can include the measures described in the cross-border cartel section above, including positive comity (e.g. exporting country competition authorities alerting importing country authorities about potential harmful export cartel conduct), and joint investigations.

4.6 Conclusions

In a globalised world, competition law and policy should be placed in the wider context of international commerce and economic regulation. Globalisation has outpaced efforts toward regulatory co-operation in many areas, including competition law enforcement as well as the application of competitive neutrality to ensure a level playing field between SOEs and private sector firms.

Competition promotion can be an effective measure to harness the benefits of globalisation and respond to distortionary market behaviour that extends beyond borders. This will require tangible steps toward intensifying competition enforcement co-operation and removing policy-induced distortions in competition – even if preserving them would benefit some domestic interests in the short term. While these measures cannot alone ensure the benefits of globalisation reach all segments of a society, it is clear that a failure to defend competition can produce widespread harm, often with outsize consequences for the most economically vulnerable in a globalised world.

Notes

1. These include 58 memoranda of understanding, three second-generation co-operation agreements and one special co-operation agreement dedicated to positive comity. Source: OECD (2015a) and OECD (2016a).

2. In determining whether an investment is of "likely net benefit", the Minister of Innovation, Science and Economic Development considers the factors enumerated in section 20 of the Investment Canada Act.

3. See, for example, Fox (2000), p. 1795-1797; Guzman (2001), p. 1152-1154; and Sokol, (2007), p.57.

4. Another example of competition law being set aside to achieve alternative policy goals is that of crisis cartels: cartels that are permitted to function with the justification that they are required to protect an industry from the impacts of a market crisis (see OECD, 2011).

References

Boyer, M. and R. Kotchoni (2011), "How Much do Cartel[s] Overcharge", *CIRANO Scientific Publication* No. 2011s-35.

Conference Board of Canada (2010), "Saskatchewan in the Spotlight: Acquisition of Potash Corporation of Saskatchewan Inc. – Risks and Opportunities", www.gov.sk.ca/adx/aspx/adxGetMedia.aspx?mediaId=1245&PN=Shared

Connor, J. (2014), "Price-Fixing Overcharges: Revised 3rd Edition", Purdue University.

Connor, J. and C. Helmers (2006), "Statistics on Modern Private International Cartels, 1990-2005", Working Paper #06-11, Purdue University, http://ageconsearch.umn.edu/bitstream/28650/1/wp060011a.pdf.

John Creedy & Robert Dixon (1998), "The Relative Burden of Monopoly on Households with Different Incomes," *Economica,* 65(285).

Davies, J. (2016), "Getting the Deal Through: Merger Control", *Law Business Research Ltd.,* London, https://gettingthedealthrough.com/area/20/merger-control/

Eftychidou, T. and F. Maiorano (2016), "Once Burned Twice Shy: What Does Economics Say About Repeated Cartel Offences?", *Journal of European Competition Law & Practice*, 7 (9): 622-627, https://academic.oup.com/jeclap/article/7/9/622/2647005/Once-Burned-Twice-Shy-What-Does-Economics-Say.

European Commission (2016), "Press release: State aid: Ireland gave illegal tax benefits to Apple worth up to €13 billion", http://europa.eu/rapid/press-release_IP-16-2923_en.htm.

Fox, E. and D. Healey (2014), "When the State Harms Competition", Antitrust Law Journal (2014)79, 769, p. 787-788.

Hellwig, M. and K. Hüschelrath (2016), "Cartel cases and the cartel enforcement process in the European Union 2001-2015: A quantitative assessment", Centre for European Economic Research Discussion Paper No. 16-063.

Hoofnagle, C. and J. Whittington (2014), "Free: Accounting for the Costs of the Internet's Most Popular Price", *UCLA Law Review*, Vol. 61, pp. 606-670, http://papers.ssrn.com/sol3/papers.cfm?abstract_id=2235962

Jenny, F. (2012), "Export Cartels in Primary Products: The Potash Case in Perspective" in *Trade, Competition, and the Pricing Of Commodities*, p. 99, Simon J. Evenett and Frédéric Jenny, eds.

Kovacic, W., Marshall, R., Marx, L. and H. White (2011), 'Plus Factors and Agreement in Antitrust Law', Michigan Law Review 110(3), 393–436.

Levenstein, M. and V. Suslow (2005), "The Changing International Status of Export Cartel Exemptions", *American University International Law Review,* Vol. 20(4), pp. 785-825, http://digitalcommons.wcl.american.edu/cgi/viewcontent.cgi?article=1144&context=auilr

Levenstein, M. and V. Suslow (2006), "What Determines Cartel Success?", *Journal of Economic Literature,* Vol. XLIV(1), pp. 43-95, http://pubs.aeaweb.org/doi/pdfplus/10.1257/002205106776162681

McCarthy, D. (2012), "State Capitalism and Competitive Neutrality", available at www.state.gov/e/eb/rls/rm/2012/181520.htm.

Mena-Labarthe, C. (2012), "Mexican Experience in Screens for Bid Rigging", *CPI Antitrust Chronicle,* March 2012 (1), www.cofece.mx/cofece/images/Estudios/Externos/Mexican_Experience_in_Screens_for_Bid_Rigging.pdf.

OECD (2016a), "Note by the Secretariat and Inventory of Provisions in Inter-agency Co-operation Agreements", *OECD Competition Committee Working Party No. 3 on Co-operation and Enforcement,* https://one.oecd.org/document/DAF/COMP/WP3(2015)12/REV1/en/pdf.

OECD (2016b), *Roundtable on public interest considerations in merger control,* Background Note by the Secretariat and Summary of Contributions, www.oecd.org/daf/competition/public-interest-considerations-in-merger-control.htm .

OECD (2015a), "Note by the Secretariat and Inventory of Co-operation Agreements", *OECD Competition Committee Working Party No. 3 on Co-operation and Enforcement,* https://one.oecd.org/document/DAF/COMP/WP3(2016)1/REV2/en/pdf.

OECD (2015b), "Issues paper by the Secretariat for the Roundtable on Competitive Neutrality", *OECD Competition Committee,* https://one.oecd.org/document/DAF/COMP(2015)5/en/pdf.

OECD (2015c), "Addressing the Tax Challenges of the Digital Economy – Action 1 Final Report", *OECD Publishing,* http://dx.doi.org/10.1787/9789264241046-en.

OECD (2015d), "Background Paper by the Secretariat for the Roundtable on Cartels Involving Intermediate Goods", *OECD Competition Committee Working Party No. 3 on Co-operation and Enforcement,* https://one.oecd.org/document/DAF/COMP/WP3(2015)18/en/pdf.

OECD (2015e), "Summary of Discussion of the Hearing on Competition Enforcement in Oligopolistic Markets", *OECD Competition Committee,* https://one.oecd.org/document/DAF/COMP/M(2015)1/ANN4/FINAL/en/pdf.

OECD (2014a), Challenges of International Co-operation in Competition Law Enforcement, www.oecd.org/daf/competition/Challenges-Competition-Internat-Coop-2014.pdf.

OECD (2014b), "Summary of Discussion of the Hearing on Enhanced Enforcement Co-operation", *OECD Competition Committee Working Party No. 3 on Co-operation and Enforcement,* https://one.oecd.org/document/DAF/COMP/WP3/M(2014)2/ANN2/FINAL/en/pdf.

OECD (2013), *Roundtable on competition and poverty reduction,* Summary of discussion of the OECD Global Forum on Competition, https://one.oecd.org/document/DAF/COMP/GF(2013)11/FINAL/en/pdf.

OECD (2011), "Policy Roundtables: Crisis Cartels", *Global Forum on Competition,* https://one.oecd.org/document/DAF/COMP/GF(2011)11/en/pdf.

OECD (2010), State Owned Enterprises and the Principle of Competitive Neutrality, www.oecd.org/daf/competition/46734249.pdf.

Reader, D. (2016), "Accommodating Public Interest Considerations in Domestic Merger Control: Empirical Insights", *CCP Working Paper* 16-3, http://ssrn.com/abstract=2736917

Sokol, D. (2007), "Monopolists Without Borders: The Institutional Challenge of International Antitrust in a Global Gilded Age", *Berkeley Business Law Journal,* 4, 37, p. 62.

Sokol, D. (2009), "What Do We Really Know About Export Cartels And What Is The Appropriate Solution?", *University of Florida Legal Studies Research Paper,* No. 2009-05, https://papers.ssrn.com/sol3/papers.cfm?abstract_id=1144003.

Stucke, M.E. and A. Ezrachi (2016, forthcoming), Virtual Competition, Harvard University Press, United States, www.hup.harvard.edu/catalog.php?isbn=9780674545472.

US-China Economic and Security Review Commission (USCC, 2016), "2016 Report to Congress: Executive Summary and Recommendations", http://origin.www.uscc.gov/sites/default/files/annual_reports/Executive%20Summary%202016.pdf.

Chapter 5

Moving towards more responsible globalisation

There has been much progress with respect to the promotion and uptake of responsible business conduct (RBC) practices in recent years and a considerable body of evidence showing that RBC is good for businesses. While gaps remain in the implementation of RBC principles and standards, governments, companies, and other stakeholders have been developing innovative initiatives aimed at filling them. In the context of the current backlash against globalisation, this is an important element for rebuilding trust in an open, rules-based global economy.

5.1. Introduction

A challenge related to RBC often cited by business concerns the divergence of both coverage and stringency of such standards across countries and sectors. This can give rise to heightened uncertainties and risks for companies, as well as lead to competitive disadvantage.

In addition, opponents of globalisation have often used examples of harmful effects of irresponsible business conduct to argue against regimes that favour trade and investment without sufficiently safeguarding labour and human rights and the environment. Yet, globalisation is the wrong enemy. Indeed, many of the gains in promoting and broadening the uptake of RBC have been precisely thanks to globalisation, since it is often through the international production networks and global value chains that coverage of RBC standards has broadened.

This chapter will show that there has been much progress with respect to the promotion and uptake of RBC standards in recent years. There is also a considerable body of evidence showing that RBC is good for business, as highlighted in Chapter 2. At the same time, gaps in approaches and coverage across countries and sectors persist. These represent a challenge for businesses and societies.

The first section in this chapter examines recent trends in RBC. The second outlines recommended practices for companies under OECD frameworks for RBC and the extent to which these frameworks are addressing identified gaps. The third section examines the role of business. The concluding section identifies gaps in the international RBC framework and proposes actions that governments and business might take to address these.

5.2. Trends in responsible business conduct

The implementation of the OECD Guidelines for Multinational Enterprises (Guidelines) provides insight into the nature of RBC issues that have arisen in global supply chains. All adherents to the Guidelines, currently 47 countries, are required to establish a National Contact Point (NCP), to promote the Guidelines and serve as a grievance and mediation mechanism in cases (referred to as "specific instances") of alleged non-observance of the Guidelines.

In terms of geographic distribution of specific instances, Table 5.1 highlights a key feature of the Guidelines, namely their global coverage. Of the 354 specific instances that have been closed since the NCP system was established in 2000,[1] almost half (169) concern operations in countries that are not adherents to the Guidelines.[2] The geographic distribution of the specific instances also shows that issues related to non-observance of the Guidelines have arisen in countries in all regions of the world and at all levels of economic development.

With regards to the thematic coverage of closed specific instances since 2000, over half address employment issues (193), and a fifth address environmental issues. Since the 2011 update of the Guidelines, and the introduction of a new human rights chapter, this area has generated the majority of specific instances in recent years (Figure 5.1), with more than half of closed specific instances addressing human rights filed after 2011.

Table 5.1. **Geographic and thematic coverage of closed specific instances under the OECD Guidelines for Multinational Enterprises**

Specific instances:	Employment	Human rights	Environment	Other*
Notified to NCP in same country	87	28	25	118
Notified to NCP in different country	106	64	43	191
of which:				
Issues arose in adherent country	28	13	6	24
Issues arose in non-adherent country	78	51	37	167

* Other themes include Concepts and Principles, General Policies, Disclosure, Combating Bribery, Bribe Solicitation and Extortion, Consumer Interests, Science and Technology, Competition and Taxation.

Source: OECD calculations based on the OECD Guidelines for Multinational Enterprises Database of Specific Instances, http://mneguidelines.oecd.org/database.

Figure 5.1. **Number of closed specific instances and the share dealing with human rights by year of submission**

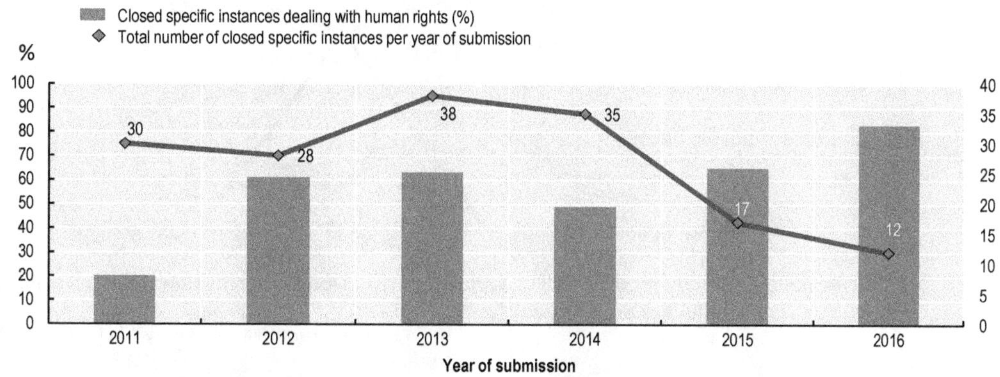

Source: OECD calculations based on the OECD Guidelines for Multinational Enterprises Database of Specific Instances, http://mneguidelines.oecd.org/database.

StatLink http://dx.doi.org/10.1787/888933476965

The number of specific instances and the issues they raise, reflect how NCPs have been used to address societal concerns about the consequences of business conduct in specific areas covered by the Guidelines. Other aspects of RBC covered in the Guidelines are also covered in many countries by legislation and regulations with their own dispute resolution procedures, thus providing other options to handle disputes. One example is cross-border bribery, which is covered by the Guidelines and also by the OECD Anti-Bribery Convention and by legislation in many countries, and is primarily dealt with by national courts.

One of the key challenges concerns big differences with respect to the enabling environments countries put in place to support RBC. These gaps can be seen across well-established indicators and indices that cover issues such as environment, human rights, employment and industrial relations, rule of law, and perception of corruption.[3]

While business responsibility to respect rights does not depend on the existence of government regulation or its enforcement, closing governance gaps and levelling the playing field for responsible businesses is a shared and complementary responsibility between governments, enterprises, workers, and other stakeholders. Figure 5.2 illustrates how the enabling environment in some areas can be uneven across different countries at different levels of development. This asymmetry raises important questions about the environments in which multinational enterprises operate. First, large gaps undoubtedly reflect uneven playing fields, with different firms operating and competing across very different enabling environments. Second, given that companies from adherents to the Guidelines collectively account for around half of cross-border investments going to non-adherents,[4] this suggests that FDI has had limited impact in terms of closing the gap shown in Figure 5.2.

Figure 5.2. **Enabling environment for RBC differs for countries at different levels of development**

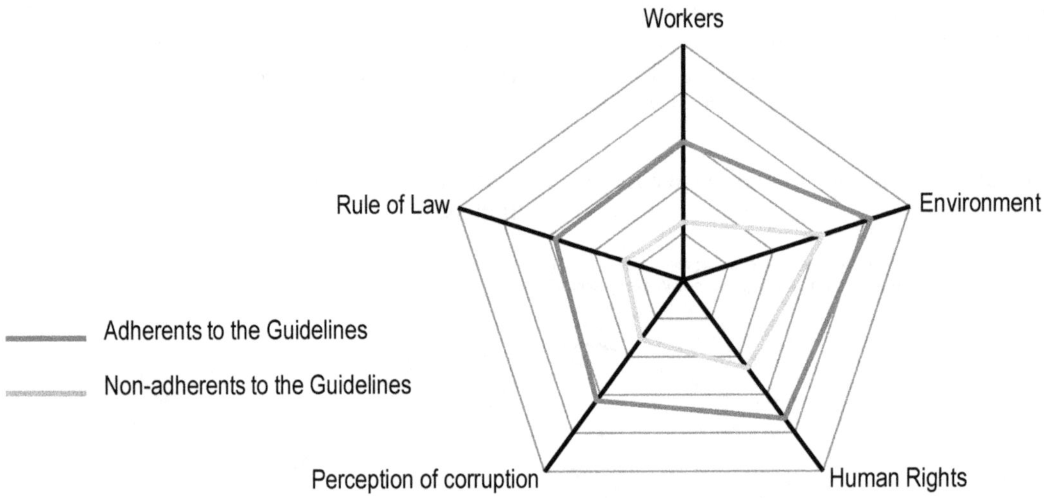

Source: OECD calculations based on the OECD Guidelines for Multinational Enterprises Database of Specific Instances, http://mneguidelines.oecd.org/database.

StatLink http://dx.doi.org/10.1787/888933476977

5.3. The role of OECD frameworks in supporting responsible business conduct

This section examines how OECD instruments contribute to enabling environments for RBC.

The OECD Guidelines for Multinational Enterprises

The Guidelines are the core OECD instrument for promoting RBC and form part of a broader OECD investment instrument, the Declaration on International Investment and Multinational Enterprises. Adherence to the Declaration (and by extension the Guidelines) is not limited to OECD members.

The Guidelines express the shared views of adhering governments. They are "recommendations jointly addressed by governments to multinational enterprises" that provide "principles and standards of good practice consistent with applicable laws and internationally recognized standards". The Guidelines seek to encourage the positive contributions firms can make to economic, environmental and social progress.

They comprise a set of recommendations in all major areas of corporate citizenship, including employment and industrial relations, human rights, environment, information disclosure, combating bribery, consumer interests, science and technology, competition, and taxation. From a business perspective, the key operational link to these recommendations is the expectation that multinational enterprises (MNEs) put due diligence processes in place to ensure that they respect international norms and standards throughout their international operations.

While the Guidelines are primarily addressed to MNEs, they are not aimed at introducing differences of treatment between multinational and domestic enterprises. Accordingly, multinational and domestic enterprises are subject to the same expectations with respect to their conduct, at least in the case of firms based in countries that are adherents to the Guidelines. In addition, while small and medium-sized enterprises may not have the same capacities as larger enterprises, they are also expected to observe the Guidelines "to the fullest extent possible".

The Guidelines provide specific guidance for how MNEs should ensure they act responsibly in their value chains. This was a key result of the 2011 review of the Guidelines, which resulted in a stronger emphasis on due diligence and on RBC throughout the supply chain. This approach of supply chain responsibility underpinned discussions on the new Human Rights chapter that was added to the Guidelines during the 2011 review, and reflects the expectation embedded in the UN Guiding Principles on Business and Human Rights, adopted in 2011.

The updated Guidelines recommend that enterprises should carry out risk-based due diligence to identify, prevent, or mitigate actual and potential adverse impacts and account for how these impacts are addressed. In addition, they should seek to prevent or mitigate adverse impacts, even where they have not contributed to those impacts, when the impacts are nevertheless directly linked to their operations, products or services through a business relationship.

OECD supply chain due diligence tools that promote RBC

Specific challenges arise when implementing the Guidelines in various contexts and sectors. Accordingly, the OECD engaged in collaborative, demand-driven work with governments from OECD and non-OECD countries, business, workers and civil society to provide implementation guidance for the Guidelines in specific sectors and geographies. This work now entails projects on responsible mineral supply chains, stakeholder engagement in the extractive sector, responsible agricultural supply chains, responsible garment and footwear supply chains, and RBC in the financial sector.

This work across sectors marks a shift away from traditional commercial risk management to a more holistic approach that addresses risks of business impacts on society and the environment, with a view to promoting inclusiveness and growth. The most advanced of these projects, in terms of implementation and global uptake from business, is the project on due diligence in responsible mineral supply chains from conflict-affected and high-risk areas.

The Guidance, adopted by the OECD in 2011 by the then 34 OECD members and 9 non-OECD adherents to the Guidelines, was endorsed by the countries of the African Great Lakes region – where the extraction of natural resources, such as tin, tungsten, tantalum and gold, finances conflict and human rights abuse. Its objective is to help companies respect human rights and avoid contributing to conflict through their mineral production and sourcing practices. Given the focus of the Due Diligence Guidance on Minerals on value chains, as opposed to individual firms, it covers business activities from mining to production of final products.

In very practical terms, the Due Diligence Guidance proposes a five-step due diligence framework for companies in those mineral supply chains.

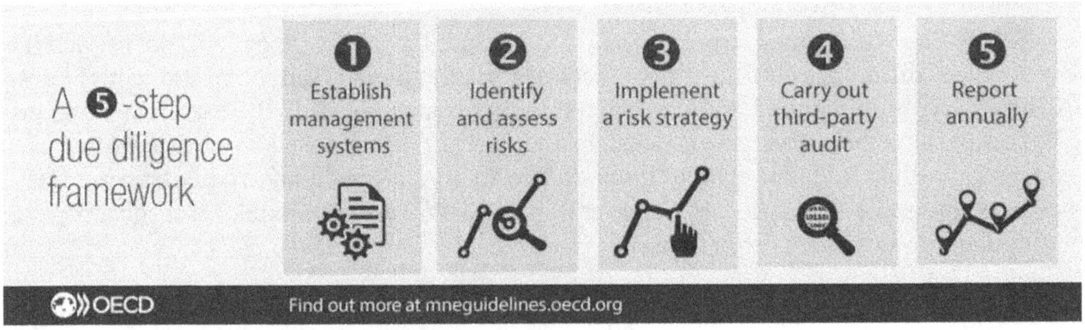

The Guidance provides companies with detailed recommendations for these five steps as well as a "model supply chain policy" which companies throughout the supply chain are encouraged to incorporate into their existing policies on RBC. Finally, the Guidance suggests measures for risk mitigation as well as indicators for measuring improvement.

Given the success of the supply chain due diligence approach for responsible mineral supply chains in tin, tantalum, tungsten and gold, work is now expanding to other minerals (such as cobalt, copper and coal, among others) and sectors, as well as new geographies (such as new producer regions in West Africa and Latin America, but also refining economies like Dubai, Turkey and India and consumer economies, such as China).

Other OECD instruments and policy tools also address RBC issues or, at least, reference the Guidelines for Multinational Enterprises or the Due Diligence Guidance for Minerals. For example, the Policy Framework for Investment (PFI), a policy tool to help governments improve business climates, and the OECD Principles for Private Sector Participation in Infrastructure, both have their own RBC chapters, and the Anti-Bribery Convention deals directly with an important RBC issue.

How have these instruments supported responsible business conduct in practice?

Sector-specific work in recent years has supported collaborative approaches and a more holistic view of the challenges associated with the promotion of RBC. With a stronger focus on whole value chains, upstream production that was previously "invisible" from an RBC perspective is increasingly getting coverage.

For example, despite sometimes extremely low levels of capacity and resources, many upstream mining operators in the African Great Lakes region (most of them small and medium-sized enterprises that work with artisanal and small-scale miners) have taken steps to implement the Due Diligence Guidance for Minerals. Of the 110 companies involved in the pilot implementation of the Guidance in 2011, 80% had adopted a policy commitment setting forth due diligence principles by 2012. A programme set up by the tin industry – the ITRI Tin Supply Chain Initiative (iTSCi) – supports responsible sourcing of tin, tantalum, tungsten (3T) minerals from the region through the development of a traceability and on-the-ground due diligence system that tracks and monitors minerals from mine to smelter. In very practical terms, it uses tags and logbooks to ensure traceability of minerals and a due diligence system that includes independent audits of its members and mine site and transportation route assessments.

A range of initiatives has also been created to facilitate the implementation of responsible sourcing by smelters and refiners. For example, the Conflict-Free Sourcing Initiative (CFSI) developed a white paper on how to implement Due Diligence Guidance for US Dodd Frank Act compliance and issued a "conflict minerals reporting template" that facilitates the transfer of information through the supply chain regarding mineral country of origin and smelters and refiners.

Such initiatives are not limited to advanced economies. A programme of work between the OECD and China is the framework for implementation of the OECD Due Diligence Guidance for Minerals in China; this work focuses on company implementation of due diligence, risk assessment, mitigation, audit and public reporting and has seen significant uptake with Chinese companies through its promotion by the China Chamber of Commerce of Metals, Minerals and Chemicals Importers & Exporters (CCCMC),[5] which adopted a Chinese version of the OECD Guidance in 2015.[6] The General Administration of Quality Supervision, Inspection and Quarantine (AQSIQ) in China is, furthermore, developing a standard on responsible mineral supply chains that is expected to come into force in 2017.

Governments are increasingly putting in place legislation on due diligence in supply chains which refer to OECD RBC instruments and tools, such as the new EU legislation making due diligence checks mandatory for importers of tin, tungsten, tantalum, gold, and ores originating from conflict and high-risk areas. Non-binding due diligence guidance is also being developed for other sectors, such as the new OECD Due Diligence Guidance for Responsible Supply Chains in the Garment and Footwear Sector issued in February 2017.

The concrete and operational nature of recent RBC initiatives at the OECD and elsewhere has arguably played an important role in promoting RBC, as well as in efforts to improve enabling policy frameworks for RBC. This is reflected, for example, in the 2015 update of the Policy Framework for Investment, which now includes a strengthened chapter on RBC, with recommendations on how to enable responsible investment.

5.4. The role of business

Recently, more evidence is emerging that RBC can improve financial performance. For example, a cross-sector study on the performance of companies over a period of 18 years, found that "high sustainability" companies, those with strong environmental, social and governance systems and practices in place, outperformed "low sustainability" companies, as measured by stock performance and in real accounting terms (Eccles, Ioannou, Serafeim, 2012). In another study, covering 8 500 French enterprises, there was a 13% difference in economic performance between enterprises that implemented RBC and those that did not (Benhamou, Diaye, 2016). According to these (and many other) studies,[7] businesses that work towards sustainable supply chains and put responsible practices in place are able to reconcile RBC and financial performance.

One possible explanation for varying implementation of RBC is that, although pursuing responsibility has been shown to yield positive results in terms of financial performance, it nonetheless requires significant time and effort. This view is consistent with the experience of the sector-focused due diligence work. Only through the development of RBC frameworks tailored for specific value chains can results be achieved; to enable companies to apply the supply chain due diligence approach across sectors and operations spanning the globe, the OECD is developing a broader Due Diligence Guidance for RBC that enables companies to carry out due diligence for all the aspects covered in the Guidelines, and across all sectors.[8]

Approaches to support RBC through due diligence in value chains have, to date, been effective precisely because they have been based upon in-depth understanding of how specific supply chains function and are structured, allowing for the identification of critical points in the value chains (such as choke points). This has been achieved through engagement with all stakeholders.

5.5. Addressing responsible business conduct gaps

This chapter has highlighted the significant progress that has been made with respect to the promotion and uptake of RBC practices in recent years, and a considerable body of evidence showing that RBC is good for businesses. While gaps remain, governments, companies, and other stakeholders have been developing innovative policy initiatives aimed at filling these. Two options to help further progress include the following:

- Increase engagement through international instruments on RBC with the aim of improving the enabling policy environment for RBC. Adherence to the OECD's Investment Declaration, which includes the OECD Guidelines for Multinational Enterprises, is a sign by a country of its commitment to promote RBC among companies operating in or from its territories. The OECD Policy Framework for Investment also provides useful guidance to governments on how to create an enabling environment for RBC.
- Promote the implementation of due diligence in all sectors, with a focus on those where the highest risks of adverse impacts can be found, for example child slavery or irreversible environmental damage.

Notes

1. See OECD (2016), "Implementing the OECD Guidelines for Multinational Enterprises: The National Contact Points from 2000 to 2015". Since 2000, a total of 407 specific instances have been notified to NCPs, of which 53 remain open.

2. It should be emphasised that specific instances should not be interpreted as an indicator of a country's enabling environment for RBC.

3. OECD/Inter-American Development Bank Indicators of Employment Protection; World Economic Forum Global Competitiveness Indicator on Labour Market Efficiency (Pillar 7); International Trade Union Confederation Global Rights Index; World Bank Doing Business – Building Quality Control index; Yale Environmental Performance Index; Freedom House Freedom of the Press Index; Reporters Without Borders World Press Freedom Index; Global Slavery Index; Transparency International Corruption Perception Index; and World Justice Project Rule of Law Indicators.

4. Adherents to the Guidelines account for three quarters of global foreign direct investment flows and 48% of cross-border mergers and acquisitions creating investment in non-adherents.

5. CCCMC public consultation for draft Chinese Due Diligence Guidelines for Responsible Mineral Supply Chains, available in English at: http://en.cccmc.org.cn/news/cccmcinformation/41161.htm

6. Chinese Due Diligence Guidelines for Responsible Mineral Supply Chains, launched in December 2015, available in English at: www.globalwitness.org/documents/18138/201512_Chinese_Due_Diligence_Guidelines_for_Responsible_Mineral_Supply_Chains_-_En_K83fxzt.pdf.

7. For a short review of the literature, see Chapter 2.

8. http://mneguidelines.oecd.org/due-diligence-guidance-for-responsible-business-conduct.htm.

ORGANISATION FOR ECONOMIC CO-OPERATION AND DEVELOPMENT

The OECD is a unique forum where governments work together to address the economic, social and environmental challenges of globalisation. The OECD is also at the forefront of efforts to understand and to help governments respond to new developments and concerns, such as corporate governance, the information economy and the challenges of an ageing population. The Organisation provides a setting where governments can compare policy experiences, seek answers to common problems, identify good practice and work to co-ordinate domestic and international policies.

The OECD member countries are: Australia, Austria, Belgium, Canada, Chile, the Czech Republic, Denmark, Estonia, Finland, France, Germany, Greece, Hungary, Iceland, Ireland, Israel, Italy, Japan, Korea, Latvia, Luxembourg, Mexico, the Netherlands, New Zealand, Norway, Poland, Portugal, the Slovak Republic, Slovenia, Spain, Sweden, Switzerland, Turkey, the United Kingdom and the United States. The European Union takes part in the work of the OECD.

OECD Publishing disseminates widely the results of the Organisation's statistics gathering and research on economic, social and environmental issues, as well as the conventions, guidelines and standards agreed by its members.

OECD PUBLISHING, 2, rue André-Pascal, 75775 PARIS CEDEX 16
(21 2017 04 1 P) ISBN 978-92-64-27488-4 – 2017

www.ingramcontent.com/pod-product-compliance
Lightning Source LLC
Chambersburg PA
CBHW061215240926
51846CB00006B/1229
9789264274884